International Series of Monographs in
Library and Information Science, Volume 4

THE PROVISION AND USE OF LIBRARY AND DOCUMENTATION SERVICES

Some Contributions from the University of
Sheffield Postgraduate School of
Librarianship

Edited by W.L. Saunders
Director, University of Sheffield
Postgraduate School of Librarianship

The studies contained in this volume reflect
on the one hand the increasing attention
being paid to specialized library provision
for particular groups of the community, and
on the other, the need felt by present-day
librarians and information workers to
measure and evaluate the services they are
providing and using. Of the seven studies
which comprise the symposium two are
concerned with problems of Academic
Librarianship, three with Scientific
Information work and Special Library
matters, and two with Public
Librarianship.

Practising librarians and documentalists
will find the book extremely valuable; it is
written in a manner which also makes it
very suitable for students taking courses in
professional librarianship or information
and documentary work.

INTERNATIONAL SERIES OF MONOGRAPHS IN
LIBRARY AND INFORMATION SCIENCE
GENERAL EDITOR: G. CHANDLER

VOLUME 4

THE PROVISION AND USE OF
LIBRARY AND DOCUMENTATION SERVICES

*Some Contributions from the University of Sheffield
Postgraduate School of Librarianship*

INTERNATIONAL SERIES OF MONOGRAPHS IN
LIBRARY AND INFORMATION SCIENCE

Vol. 1. WHITE—*Bases of Modern Librarianship*
Vol. 2. ANTHONY—*Sources of Information on Atomic Energy*
Vol. 3. BLAUG—*Economics of Education*

THE PROVISION AND USE OF
LIBRARY AND DOCUMENTATION
SERVICES

*Some Contributions from the University of Sheffield
Postgraduate School of Librarianship*

EDITED BY

W. L. SAUNDERS

*Director, University of Sheffield,
Postgraduate School of Librarianship*

PERGAMON PRESS

OXFORD · LONDON · EDINBURGH · NEW YORK
TORONTO · SYDNEY · PARIS · BRAUNSCHWEIG

Pergamon Press Ltd., Headington Hill Hall, Oxford
4 & 5 Fitzroy Square, London W.1

Pergamon Press (Scotland) Ltd., 2 & 3 Teviot Place, Edinburgh 1

Pergamon Press Inc., 44–01 21st Street, Long Island City, New York 11101

Pergamon of Canada, Ltd., 6 Adelaide Street East, Toronto, Ontario

Pergamon Press (Aust.) Pty. Ltd., 20–22 Margaret Street, Sydney, N.S.W.

Pergamon Press S.A.R.L., 24 rue des Écoles, Paris 5ᵉ

Vieweg & Sohn GmbH, Burgplatz 1, Braunschweig

CONTENTS

FOREWORD   vii

1. J. P. Lamb, MA, FLA   1
    By ELIZABETH A. MELROSE

2. Trade literature: its value, organization and exploitation   29
    By ELIZABETH B. SMITH

3. A survey of the provision and use of library services in certain London prisons   55
    By PENELOPE A. ROWLINSON

4. Library service for undergraduates   85
    By M. W. MOSS

5. Survey of borrowing from the University of Sheffield Library during one
    academic year   115
    By W. L. SAUNDERS,
        E. W. ROBERTS, and
        LISBETH J. WICKISON

6. A critical review of the surveys of scientists' use of libraries   145
    By A. STEPHANIE BARBER

7. Documentation and information science abstracts: the *Referativnyi zhurnal:
    nauchnaya i tekhnicheskaya informatsiya*   181
    By H. SCHUR

INDEX   189

FOREWORD

This volume originated from a suggestion by Dr. G. Chandler, an External Examiner to the University of Sheffield Postgraduate School of Librarianship. He felt that some of the special studies prepared as part of the requirement for the University's Postgraduate Diploma in Librarianship would be of interest to a wider audience of librarians and documentalists, and the contributions which follow represent the work of seven diplomates supplemented by contributions from two members of staff.

Deciding which studies were to be included was not easy. The idea of the special study is that it should enable each student to study in some depth an aspect of librarianship or information work which is of particular interest to him, and even with the modest total of twenty-three students which comprised the first, 1964–5, course at Sheffield, the result was an extremely wide range of subjects. Clearly certain contributions, such as one or two excellent bibliographies, were not suitable for inclusion in a symposium of this sort, and other studies, though rating high for the purpose of the course, were of largely domestic or otherwise restricted interest.

The contributions which follow, then, cannot be taken to represent the full range of interests of the course of 1964–5. They are, however, linked by a theme which is in many ways the heart of the matter so far as the School is concerned: the interdependent considerations of use and service.

It is particularly appropriate that the subject of the first study in this volume should be Mr. J. P. Lamb, a man whose work raised the Sheffield Public Library system to a position of national and, indeed, international leadership during the years leading up to his retirement in 1956. His departure from active work is too recent for him to be described as a "giant of yesterday" and it is too early to see his work in full historical perspective, but Mrs. Melrose's "interim" assessment is a timely reminder of what this one man contributed to a British library scene which is still very fresh for many of us. Many of Lamb's former colleagues helped Mrs. Melrose with personal recollections, which she acknowledges in her study, but it is a particular pleasure to record the interest and assistance of Mr. Lamb's successor as City Librarian of Sheffield, Mr. J. Bebbington. Mr. Bebbington has been kind enough to read through Mrs. Melrose's study and has made many valuable suggestions, which are gratefully acknowledged.

The contribution of Miss E. B. Smith is on a subject which is closely linked with Mr. Lamb's pioneering interest in commercial libraries: *Trade Literature.* The success of the short courses on this subject which Aslib offers from time to time is evidence of the importance of trade literature to industry, commerce and many other communities of library users, but in general this is an area which is curiously neglected by librarians and information officers. Miss Smith's study has stimulated at least one major library to bring trade literature within the scope of its acquisitions programme; there may well be others. She acknowledges with gratitude the information provided by the librarians and information officers mentioned in her bibliography.

The next two studies provide further evidence of the range of needs for which present-day librarianship is providing and of the way in which libraries are responding to the requirements of two very different sections of the community.

First of all, Mrs. P. A. Rowlinson surveys the provision and use of library services in four London prisons. Few people today would question the value of such services, but progress has not always been as rapid as might have been hoped. It is therefore particularly encouraging to read of the great improvements which can be brought about in a comparatively short space of time when enlightened public library authorities bring their resources and professional skills to bear on this important branch of library activity. The literature on prison library services is not very plentiful and Mrs. Rowlinson's study should be of interest not only to librarians but to all concerned with the administration of our prisons and with penological developments in general.

A very different kind of library user is then considered by Mr. M. W. Moss, who has traced the emergence of specialized service to undergraduate users of university libraries. His study is inevitably concerned in the main with conditions in the United States, for it is that country which has pioneered the development of reader service in the university library and, in more recent years, the provision of special services, in special buildings, for the undergraduate members of their universities. Mr. Moss's study of the American scene has particular relevance in the post-Robbins years of rapid expansion which most British universities are now facing, for present library provision is rarely likely to be adequate for the campuses of up to 10,000 students for which many of our universities are now planning. In considering the extra library provision which such populations will require, the possibility of special arrangements for undergraduate members is likely to be considered by many university librarians, and it is not without significance that the first undergraduate library in this country is at present being built for one of the most progressive of our university libraries, the Brotherton Library at Leeds.

It was from the University of Leeds, too, that the first large-scale survey of borrowing from a British university library appeared, and the report by Mr. B. S. Page and Mr. P. E. Tucker on the Nuffield Pilot Survey prompted me to plan the similar survey for Sheffield which forms the next section of this symposium. Soon after the raw material was collected I went to Uganda for a year on an unexpected UNESCO secondment, and shortly after my return from Africa, a term in the USA occasioned a further delay in the analysis and interpretation of the survey material. I was therefore particularly pleased when Mr. E. W. Roberts and Miss L. J. Wickison undertook as their special studies two distinct sections of the survey, the borrowing of higher degree students in the case of Mr. Roberts and that of undergraduates in the Faculty of Pure Science in the case of Miss Wickison. Mr. Roberts subsequently carried out further work on the postgraduate part of the survey and Miss Wickison extended her work to cover the whole of the undergraduate population. The postgraduate part of the survey, then, is largely the work of Mr. Roberts, the undergraduate section of Miss Wickison. Mr. J. E. Tolson, the Sheffield University Librarian, has been kind enough to read through the survey and thanks are due to him for many valuable suggestions.

The surveying art is not new, of course, and it has perhaps been directed with special force to the problems arising from the proliferation of scientific and technological literature with which the present generation of librarians and information officers is depressingly familiar. The use which scientists themselves make of libraries and literature has attracted particular attention, so much so that we are at the stage where a "survey of the surveys" is called for, and the contribution of Mrs. A. S. Barber to this symposium is a revealing and informative review of the surveys of scientists' use of libraries. Her occasional astringent observations about surveys and surveyors provide a salutary check for those who incline to think that a survey is the remedy for all ills.

The Sheffield School has a particular interest in scientific and industrial information work, a field in which it offers a specialized course for science graduates and in which it is developing a substantial research programme. The effectiveness of research in this field, as in any of the branches of science and technology which it serves, is dependent to a considerable extent on support from efficient bibliographical services. Amongst the largest and most interesting of such services is *Referativnyi zhurnal*, published for the benefit of Soviet science and technology, and the product of a massive, centralized and systematic effort to abstract all the relevant literature on a world basis. For the last few years a special section of the journal has been devoted to scientific and technical information, and Mr. H. Schur, one of the School's lecturers in scientific and industrial information work, has contributed as the final study in this symposium a critical assessment of this section. Though it is too early for effective assessment of its value for retrospective searching, Mr. Schur has some revealing information to report about its value for current awareness, and its coverage, particularly in comparison with the principal abstracting services produced in the West.

Most of the studies in this symposium include an acknowledgement of assistance and advice from various quarters. In concluding this foreword it should be mentioned that Mrs. Melrose, Miss Smith, Mrs. Rowlinson, Mr. Moss, Mr. Roberts, Miss Wickison and Mrs. Barber all wish to acknowledge assistance received from members of staff who supervised their respective studies. As editor I wish to make my own acknowledgement of criticism and advice received from colleagues and others, too numerous to mention individually.

W. L. SAUNDERS

1. J. P. LAMB, MA, FLA

ELIZABETH A. MELROSE

University Library, Sheffield

"He is indeed out of the ordinary and what he has done for libraries in Sheffield and, by extension, throughout the country, is beyond the achievement of most."[1]

These words were written in 1956 on the retirement of Mr. J. P. Lamb, MA, FLA, City Librarian of Sheffield. They seem to sum up the work and personality of that forceful man and to give a hint of his many-sided character which enabled him to attempt so many things with success—from short-story writing and a taste for amateur dramatics to a full study of librarianship.

Lamb was Chief Librarian of the Sheffield public libraries for 29 years. He had come to the city as deputy chief at a time when public libraries throughout the country were at a low ebb. Library service had existed for many years on the penny rate and was in a sad state of decay. It has been suggested that the badge of the Library Association should have been Cruikshank's drawing of Oliver Twist asking for more. Lamb himself said that "It took thirty years to bring down a good system to the level of Sheffield in 1920; and precisely that time has been needed to re-build it".[2] Lamb's own achievement can be seen in the library service of Sheffield today, for he was instrumental in its creation. And this was only one result of the tremendous energy which the man possessed.

Joseph Percy Lamb was born at St. Helens, Lancashire, on 19 June 1891. Much to his own surprise, he succeeded in gaining a place by scholarship at Cowley Grammar School. There were only twelve scholarships for the whole town. His school reports, in extreme contradiction to his later years, reported that he was "a good boy but lacking in energy".[3] Like all schoolboys, Joe and his friends took great pride in dodging work of any kind. As a result of this, perhaps, he found in later life that although German conversation was incomprehensible to him, he could never be cheated over the price of his German beer. He had had to recite the German multiplication tables too often for this.

Although he was too young at this stage to be thinking of his future life, Lamb used the experience of his early youth to draw up some of his own principles of librarianship. He was a member of a large family and one of his

1

brothers and one of his sisters had encouraged him to read by their own example. From fairy stories which many a time made the small boy scamper up the dark stairs to bed Joe graduated to the *Boy's Friend* and the *Boy's Herald*. He and his brother were such enthralled readers of some of the serials in these papers that they were quite content on the evenings before publication to walk the two miles from their home to the shop of an obliging newsagent who would let them have advance copies. Joe became an enthusiastic reader. In contrast to the dislike in which he held Shakespearian drama because of his forced study at school—he only recovered from this in middle age—Joe developed a life-long interest in palaeontology from his reading of a certain story in one of the "Boy's papers". He always considered that it seemed to matter very little what a child read so long as it did read. This he surmised from his own experience. Because of it, he planned and directed those junior libraries under his care in the way he did. His policy was not to direct the child's reading by forcing it to read those books that adults thought might be good for it. Jast's statement of "Freedom of choice in an atmosphere of beauty"[4] was one that most appealed to Lamb and, in this tradition, he preferred to entice children to read in pleasant surroundings without attempting to give an air of formal education or to classify books into age groupings—this to Lamb was an obnoxious habit common in many American libraries.

Unfortunately for Joe, his appreciation of literature came just as he was obliged to leave school. Before this, he tells us, he had seen "no use in poetry", although, in comparison with his other classes, he had enjoyed the English lessons. When he was 14 years old, he suddenly realized the joys of literature taught by Mr. Hanley, and for his last months at school he eagerly looked forward to this teaching.

But on 4 December 1905 Lamb's schooldays ended. He began work at the public libraries of St. Helens, his home town. Each week he took his earnings of 4s. to his family at 16 Cowley Hill Lane. It may have been this early start in life that gave him the belief that suitably qualified non-graduates should have equal chances with graduates in obtaining posts in public libraries. He, himself, came up the strict, hard way. His father had died the very week that Lamb received his scholarship news. The family was left in poor circumstances and Lamb's inability to raise the fee for the Oxford "locals" meant that he never obtained the language qualifications required for the L.A. examinations. The ease of further education in later years may have contrasted with his own struggle. At the time, however, the Public Library of St. Helens was in his eyes

> a dull, dreary place with great stacks of dirty books, screened from the profane public gaze by a long Chivers Indicator. After consulting out-of-date printed catalogues, the hopeful reader found the number on the indicator and if it was underlined by the end of the white ivorine tab, he claimed the book at one of the three openings in the indicator wall, behind which the staff lurked, reluctant dragons, who, to the disheartened

reader seemed to delight in saying "Sorry, a mistake" . . . mistakes were more common than "found" books. (5)

Lamb wrote this description within a few months of retirement after he had seen the delights of a cheerful open access system which was also efficient. In 1905, however, the work would have been new and exciting to a 14-year-old boy and Lamb would not have been so critical.

The hours at the library were extremely long, 9.30 a.m. to 9.0 p.m. every weekday except one, when staff would be permitted to leave at 1.0 p.m. Every third Sunday the assistants took a rota turn from 2.0 p.m. to 9.0 p.m. without overtime pay or extra time off in its place. But there were compensations—there was time for reading on duty. On Sundays, staff were not expected to work, but merely to superintend the reading rooms. Also, no clerical work had to be done in the evenings. Lamb took advantage of this when he was on one of the three open counters. He read all the articles in the monthly reviews and from these developed a strong interest in international politics and foreign affairs which lasted throughout his career.

He became one of a circle of acquaintances who discussed their problems and interests together. With Tom, a special friend, Lamb sharpened his mind by practising literary writing and by inventing epigrams "full of brilliant wit". One of their amusements was to pretend to be connected in a far-off manner to some man of letters. Lamb decided to invent a relationship with Charles and Mary Lamb until Tom crushed the idea with heavy humour by saying that he had not believed the story until he had found out that there was insanity in the author's family!

During Sunday spells of duty in the Reference Library, Lamb began to read the works of many writers such as Ruskin and Rousseau. When he was about 16 he became a keen admirer of Boswell through the latter's *Life of Johnson*. This led to what Lamb considered the most outstanding book that he ever read. It took him 6 months of Sunday reading and half-days to journey through Gibbon's *Decline and fall of the Roman Empire* in "a shady nook in the town cemetery" (6)—his favourite spot for outdoor reading, as he later tells. Every minute spent this way seemed worth while, and if Gibbon bequeathed to him an unlucky taste for lengthy sentences in his own writing, he found great pleasure in the majestic phrases and the magnificent irony of the *Decline and fall*.

Before attempting the works of Gibbon, Lamb had been told of the Library Association examinations as the way to promotion in librarianship. He had obtained the syllabus and had chosen to study classification. It is interesting to note that although Lamb, on his own evidence, began to examine the prescribed texts for the classification examination in 1907, he did not pass until 1911, in the same year that he passed library history but *after* he had gained the certificate in cataloguing and library routine in 1910. He passed library routine with merit. The recommended material for classification had not inspired him with much enthusiasm. Even then he wondered what connection there was between classification, as then studied, and librarianship. Yet although he advocated the simplification of classified schemes in libraries, he never went as far as a Mr. Wellard of the Graduate Library School, Chicago, believed he had. "Mr. Wellard", Lamb wrote, "informs a wondering world that I am the unclaimed leader of the rebels who seek to abolish classification in public libraries; indeed I am astonished to learn that it has been partially put into effect in the Sheffield libraries."[7] Lamb's idea was not to make classification an end in itself but to concentrate rather on attractive display of books to tempt people into the library.

In 1913 when he was 22 years old, Lamb was promoted from St. Helens to the staff of the Birmingham free libraries. He began his duties in the Central Lending Department on 15 September at a salary of £70 per annum plus a yearly increment of £2 for each of the four Library Association certificates that he possessed. He shared lodgings with two other library assistants whom he describes as being "devoid of any interest in books or music. . . . They thought me a peculiar fellow for preferring the symphony concerts in the Town Hall to the delights of the Music Hall". Lamb adds with wry humour —"they may have been right".[8]

The change from the small library at St. Helens to the Birmingham public libraries had a profound influence on Lamb and completely altered his amateur views of librarianship. He describes the Central Lending library as

> a murderous place in which only those with sound bodies and hardened minds could survive. Most of its large stock was shelved in three tiers of iron galleries reaching to the ceiling. In a closed library with an average issue of 900, the amount of leg work demanded of the staff was enough to qualify them as Everest climbers. Card changing with double date stamping of book label and book card was used, and a reversible indicator showed whether books wanted were "in". At 8.30 a.m. every morning the duty assistant, armed with a ruled book in which he entered in table order the hundreds of newspapers and periodicals in the Reading Room, dashed round checking that the current number of each was in its appropriate cover in a box. Each was initialled in the book, so that, before the public came in, a sweating assistant had certified that all was in order for his lords and masters.[9]

At first Lamb laughed at these rigid procedures. There were the daily, weekly and other series of routine books which the staff had to sign continually to show their responsibility for various tasks. However, it was not long before he realized that, at St. Helens, he had merely been on the fringes of library discipline. He saw the need to set his own standards much higher— later he was to draft out a routine book for his staff at Sheffield on similar lines to the one at Birmingham. Before he came to Birmingham, Lamb was slow and unobservant. He went through a trying period ridding himself of his old bad habits, but the experience stood him in good stead, especially in his later career. His mind had been sharpened by his interchanges with his friends in St. Helens, and he began to question the routines that he had formerly scorned. Although much of the library technique in Birmingham public libraries was old fashioned, Lamb discovered that it had a basis of sound reasoning. From this time it was characteristic of Lamb to examine any new proposition on procedure and to judge it on its own merits rather than to accept it blindfold. Later he realized that because of his searchings during his very short stay in Birmingham, he must have built up a volume of experience in the organization of a city library that he would not have done had he remained at St. Helens.

At one period Lamb was sent for a brief spell to act as relief at the Constitution Hill branch library in Birmingham. This branch seemed a dreadful place to him. Compared by modern standards, the 48 duty hours per week was very heavy. During the long-duty days, it was hardly worth while leaving the library. Juniors ate in a basement staff room that reminded Lamb of the Dickens' novels he had read. It is all the more interesting that Lamb, at this point in his career, should be notable for his skill in writing short stories for boys' adventure papers, the very kind of stories that he had read with such eagerness when he had been younger. Stories written by J. Percy Lamb were also accepted for boys' annuals. "Holroyd's luck. The story of an escapade and its consequences" was published in *Young England*, 1912–13. One of his close friends at this time, Mr. Arthur J. Avery, recalls that Lamb was once asked to submit a story based on an illustration sent to him by the publisher. The illustration showed a boy rescuing a small animal at the bottom of a railway embankment from the path of an oncoming train. The tale that Lamb wrote was later accepted.[10]

Lamb left his mark in Birmingham as a man of forceful character, though Mr. H. M. Cashmore, then Deputy Chief Librarian at Birmingham, states that he cannot say that Lamb showed many signs of the valuable work he afterwards did.[11] This is very likely, as Lamb was too busy acquiring new impressions of library work that were to be of great use to him in his work at Sheffield. He himself remembers with particular gratitude the influence of Harry Grindle, the cultured Central Lending Librarian, and the daily contact with a magnificent book stock.

In July 1914 Lamb passed the bibliography examination of the Library Association. He now had five out of a possible six certificates. Soon afterwards he was promoted again, this time as Senior Assistant in the Rochdale public libraries, Lancashire. A new phase of his career had begun. Lamb relates that he was about to begin his duties there one December morning, when he was warmly greeted by Mr. R. J. Gordon, the Chief Librarian.[12] Mr. Gordon was to have a deep influence on Lamb's work. A most inspiring partnership sprang up between these men, both in Rochdale and later in Sheffield, where they worked together during the period of reconstruction. Lamb, in his first years as Chief Librarian, expanded and elaborated the system that had been laid down by himself and Gordon from 1921 to 1926.[13] Both men look back on their partnership with great affection. Lamb recalls Gordon having a mystifying sense of the politics of librarianship. He tells how his former chief could talk and persuade a committee to his side by the sincerity of his own beliefs even though his accompanying argument might be illogical. Gordon seems to have had the gift of bringing out the best in his staff and those working with him. "When he was in charge, libraries became marvellously alive."[14]

On the other hand, Gordon remembers a man of spare build, neatly dressed but reserved in manner. His work seemed to imply great ability. "His independent mind", said Gordon, "and advanced views often lead [sic] him into many arguments in which he more than held his own, for few could vanquish him when warmed up."[15] Lamb was obviously continuing to question as he had begun to do at Birmingham. But at the same time he found time to laugh. Gordon recalls that he mixed well with his colleagues and that the staff room was a cheerful place when Lamb was there.

The library at Rochdale served a population of 90,000 at that time, with the main central library and one branch library. Even for a system of 1914 it was out of date—closed access with book issues recorded in an awkward heavy ledger. Funds were difficult to obtain, as usual, and this hampered any alterations that were needed to convert the system to open access. Gordon had hoped that this could be achieved, but little could be done under the circumstances. Unfortunately, the outbreak of the First World War intervened. Lamb joined up in 1915. The *Library Association Record* for 1916 reports that he was serving in the Royal Navy. He had spells of duty at the Royal Navy Barracks in Portsmouth and also, when he was later serving in the Royal Air Force, he was sent to France.

After the war years, Lamb returned to Rochdale. He and the other male assistants retold many stories of their war experiences "some true and some, no doubt, not so true".[16]

Mr. Gordon reopened the question of open access throughout the system. The lending stock was classified and several delivery stations were opened. The staff began to think that Rochdale was at last becoming really "modern". Meanwhile Lamb studied off duty for the certificate of literary history of the Library Association and he passed the examination with merit in December 1920.

That winter the staff at Rochdale were surprised by a deputation of Libraries Committee members from Sheffield who had come to inspect the organization of the system. Gordon had heard that the post of Chief Librarian at Sheffield had fallen vacant through the death of Mr. Samuel Smith. Greatly daring, as he says, Gordon had applied for the position and, much to his own satisfaction, was appointed. Thus the happy partnership between

Gordon and Lamb was broken. Neither realized that it was to be for only a short time.

In Sheffield, Gordon began a policy of cautious revival which had been sadly overdue. He recalls that he missed having a deputy beside him who could check his ideas and schemes for the reconstruction of the library service. He felt that his own deputy was not accustomed to the type of work he was now being given, and was thus unwilling to discuss future plans with Gordon or to see further than the system as it had been before 1920. There was no rapport. Fortunately, both for the internal administration of Sheffield libraries and for Mr. Gordon's plans, this situation was to change. The deputy asked to be transferred to a branch library as the post fell vacant. From many suitable candidates for the position who came in answer to the advertisement, J. P. Lamb was selected by the Libraries Committee as being the best fitted. Both Lamb and Gordon were extremely pleased.

For most of his library career, Lamb seems to have been connected with old-type libraries such as Rochdale and Sheffield which needed drastic overhauling. At the present time, such systems, as they were then, are criticized only too strongly. However, when he was reviewing his life's work, Lamb looked back wistfully at this type of library. He wondered if the change from closed access to modern libraries with eye appeal had been entirely for the better. In explaining his reasons for this point of view, Lamb stated that there had been in the closed access systems a personal contact between the staff and the reader, which had been lost to a great extent. He remembers, from his own experience in the early days, that those who came to the libraries were those who really wanted to read—only these people would be persistent enough to brave the frustrations of the obsolete printed catalogues and the inaccurate indicator system. These substantial drawbacks had to be overcome by the personal service of the assistants, who usually found out the tastes of the particular readers and made small selections of titles for them from which they could choose. At this point Lamb even shows his irritation against the numerous calls on the time of a modern librarian "attending ceaseless conferences and committees, arguing over library techniques, studying the nonsense taught by the library schools and reading the stream of professional literature".[17] He looked back to a time when assistants could devote all their energies, if they wished, to providing a service without the distractions that modern librarianship seems to offer.

Be that as it may, Lamb in 1921 was fully in accord with the school of thought in librarianship that considered that the public library system required instant revision. Later, he may have looked back on the earlier systems with a mellower outlook, when his work in Sheffield was coming to an end. It was in Sheffield that Gordon and Lamb were to show how much they believed that library service should be overhauled. After 1927, Lamb was to continue this work. Lamb's achievement is in the city library system in Sheffield as it stands today.

Those who had dealings with the Sheffield public library system in 1921 considered it to be as bad as a library system could be. Sheffield had been the eleventh town in Britain and the first in Yorkshire to bring about public library provision. A library had been established in 1855 only 5 years after the first Public Libraries Act. But since 1904 Sheffield had become "a devastated area in the library sense".[18] The old buildings were unsatisfactory and the service was managed by an elderly staff to whom changes in library thought were unknown. Large areas of Sheffield had no library facilities whatever. The situation was completely the reverse on Lamb's retirement, so a description of Sheffield Public Library in 1920 might be appropriate at this point.

On the appointment of Gordon as Chief Librarian in Sheffield, the Libraries Committee asked the Chief Librarian of Leeds, Mr. Hand, to make an independent report on the Sheffield library service as an outsider to the city. His unbiased survey shows many faults within the fragmented library services. Library development seemed to have stopped 20 years before. As a result of this, library branches were clustered in groups that might have borne some relation to population areas when the branches were built, but were long out of date. The library buildings themselves were unsuited to modern usage. There were uneconomic and wasteful habits in the internal administration, too, which could not lead to an efficient service. Each branch library functioned individually. There were several methods of book issue, each of which seemed more useless than the last. The registration of stock was highly inaccurate, while the bookbinding department had to depend on the goodwill of the bookbinders. The books were bound not when they required it so much as when the local binders wanted some trade.

The stocks of the lending library were out of date. Many of the titles still on the shelves clearly showed that little serious book selection had been carried on since the turn of the century. The very idea of discarding a book had seemed monstrous. As a result, the number of titles on record (even if this number had been correct) was misleading—books had been kept that should have been "weeded out" years before. Modern technical literature, on the other hand, was unknown in the lending libraries. There was a small reference collection of technical books in the Central Library, but the complaints of readers indicate that this so-called Commercial and Technical Library was totally inadequate. Classification of books was by main classes and by shelf sizes, but this again could not be relied upon, as it differed in each library. The catalogues were archaic and "had a disconcerting originality".[19] Morale must have been low among the staff, as there was evidently no concerted effort from within to improve this dreadful state of affairs until 1920.

Mr. T. E. Osborn, who retired in 1956 after almost 50 years of service with the public libraries in Sheffield, wondered how present-day staff would have stood up to the conditions that prevailed in the library before the advent of Lamb. There was no staff room and the assistants ate their meals in the basement of the old library building. The tables possessed newspaper table-cloths and there was a gas-ring on which to boil the rusty iron kettle. Dishes could be washed at a stone sink. The staff always shared these quarters with plenty of mice, cockroaches and crickets which helped to enliven mealtimes. Also in the basement were the filing rooms, similarly lit with bare gas-jets. Any member of staff who had to search these rooms for a book or a patent specification had to carry a yard-long taper. Mr. Osborn was surprised that there was never a fire as a result of this rather dangerous practice.[20]

Staff at the public libraries were exclusively recruited from Sheffield, so it was rarely that new ideas were circulated. There was no staff library in the building nor any opportunities for study. The authorities discouraged assistants from sitting the Library Association examinations and those who were strongwilled enough to disregard this had to work for the certificates at their own expense without any guidance whatsoever. Members of staff had to sit these examinations during their holidays. Naturally in these circumstances, very few took the trouble to look ahead, and the failure rate among the more daring was extremely high.

At the branches the same conditions prevailed. There were some rough times at the Attercliffe branch just before the First World War, when it was quite usual for the assistant to be forced to call in the police to restore order, especially on a Sunday in the Reading Room. It was also not uncommon for staff to be chased by gangs of young toughs into the police station after closing time. Thus it was not surprising that the service provided by these libraries was of the scantiest, while the respect shown in turn to the libraries was practically nil. There were, however, some cheering discoveries. The historical manuscripts in the Central Reference Library had been completely classified in 1912 by an enthusiastic member of the Libraries Committee, Mr. T. Walter Hall. This gentleman had also borne the cost of publication of this catalogue. The Reference Library had been classified, catalogued and arranged for open access, while in Walkley branch library the librarian had conceived a more logical system of issue and converted his stock to open access, not without the disapproval of his superiors. But it was certainly evident that new direction and interest was required from the top.

The recommendations of the Chief Librarian of Leeds echoed the plans of an up-to-date library of the 1920's. He advocated recataloguing on cards, links between the branches by telephone, abolition of the ladies' reading rooms and many other improvements. Now in charge of Sheffield were an active chief and deputy who had already put some of these ideas into practice. Both Lamb and Gordon were full of schemes for the improvement of the system and each was prepared to argue the case for his own point of view. They discussed library problems endlessly with each other during working hours and at weekends as well. Sometimes Lamb's opinions would prevail and sometimes those of his chief, but when they agreed to differ, they always did so cheerfully, knowing that on most issues they were in perfect accord.

Gordon had created a Central Cataloguing Department in the Sheffield public libraries on his appointment there. Already the reorganization had begun. This central department superseded the cataloguing of books, often inconsistently, in the branches, and it greatly aided the task of recataloguing the book stocks at the branches. These years were those of bad trade depression, and extra money that was urgently needed for the reconstruction of the system was not forthcoming. Money had to be saved from wasteful procedures so that it could be diverted into more necessary channels. Gordon closed down eight delivery stations. A storm of criticism arose immediately but Gordon had saved almost £1000 per year. Without this extra grant he could not even have begun to realize his aim to have "a supply of good books at every point of service maintained from the best of current literature".[21]

With co-operation established between Gordon and Lamb, the work of reconstruction could be pushed forward with as much speed as possible. The majority of the library staff were themselves amazed at the improvements which followed. They had been accustomed too long to regarding themselves as the "Cinderella service" in the city and to enduring public criticism for which they had no answer. So they entered with eagerness into the scheme of remoulding the library. Under difficult and often exacting conditions, nearly 20,000 volumes were prepared for the shelves in less than one year by a staff that had increased by only five persons in that period. Both Gordon and Lamb had the ability to infuse some of their own enthusiasm into their colleagues.

While the new stock was being assembled, other innovations were established. The Board of Education approved new by-laws and regulations which allowed the Chief Librarian to replace archaic forms of library government by more modern methods. It was seen that any changes in procedure would have to be so drastic that they would virtually amount to a complete re-creation of library service. Under these circumstances all the previous administrative methods were ruthlessly scrapped. Card-changing was introduced in all the libraries in place of the indicators. At least a selection of the book stock was placed on open shelves on the counters so that the public could examine the titles and a semblance of open access provided. All the administration was greatly simplified in order that costly errors should be avoided—within the financial department, for example, the clerical work was reduced to a minimum, thus making an expensive system of ledgers unnecessary. When any new item of stationery was required, the process involved was carefully examined and if necessary it was modernized. A curious "forfeit system" for overdue books was abolished in favour of a reasonable scale of fines.

These may seem small points, but they do demonstrate the aim of the chief and his deputy to improve the whole standard of library service in Sheffield. It was encouraging to find that the overhaul of the system had not gone unnoticed by the general public. Even before open access in the libraries could be accomplished, the number of book issues showed a sharp rise. From April 1921 to January 1922 the issues had risen at the average rate of 10,000 to 15,000 a month.

The Central Lending Library was the first to be reconstructed in a massive plan to convert one library per year to open access. The books in stock were examined, and it was astounding to discover that from a supposed number of 40,000 recorded books, only 8000 were thought fit for the shelves. A list of basic books was compiled and each year a careful selection of current titles was ordered so that the pitiful book fund could be eked out to best advantage. In June 1922 Central Lending was reopened, complete with modern open access shelves and oak fittings. The book stock had been augmented by 8000 books, catalogued and registered by the new methods in a more systematic way. The conversion was proved to be worth while despite the great difficulties that beset the library administration, including the unsatisfactory state of the building itself. Whereas in 1920–1 the book issue was 91,000 volumes, in the same period 1925–6 the issue had jumped to 373,000.

This upsurge of interest in the library had been accomplished by making the service more attractive to the average reader. Gordon and his staff sought to overcome the indifference of the Sheffield public by a programme of publicity. This was an innovation in Sheffield—publicity had more usually been given to complaints against the library in former times and, indeed, the public libraries could have hardly been expected then to boast about their virtues. But under Gordon and Lamb the idea that people could be attracted to the library by publicity came into force. Here Lamb carried on the tradition of his friend. He was always a great admirer of the strength of publicity, and when he was in control of the libraries he was known to have very close contact with the local Sheffield newspapers. Lists of books were made in 1921 to be distributed at public lectures. With the beginning of open access in the Central Lending, a 10-page booklet was prepared which explained the workings of the system to the uninitiated reader. Later, a pamphlet was issued showing the services which the Commercial and Technical Library could offer. Articles appeared in the local press and exhibitions were staged in the Reference Library. Nothing seemed to have been neglected which would catch the eye of the public and especially that section of the population who believed that an efficient Library was rather an unnecessary luxury in those days.

The Chief Librarian and his deputy were in all instances backed by the willing aid of their committee. In the Commercial and Technical Library the books had been, in the main, rather useless in serving its function—the main industry of Sheffield, steel, was represented by a meagre collection of out-of-date books, while literature on American and German practice was almost unrepresented. The publicity given by the staff to this library department brought its existence to the notice of the Chamber of Commerce. Collections of directories, codes and trade catalogues were obtained, while a sadly needed information index was set up. This in itself brought certain research staffs of the city to the library.

In the Reference Department, it was noticed with horror that the Sheffield collection of rare books was out on the shelves hampering the free use of necessary reference works, besides which they could easily be damaged by an unknowing reader. Piles of books, left in the basement without any written record, had to be sorted and the whole collection reclassified, catalogued and recorded.

The completion of the reorganization of Central Lending had provided the example for each of the branch libraries. Each year a selected team descended on one branch, staying there until all previous records had been relegated to oblivion and the remaining stock was reclassified in accordance with the practice at Central. Mr. J. Cranshaw remembers the branch libraries at Upperthorpe, Burngreave and Attercliffe in 1927 as being "arrid [sic] wastes of long forgotten books".[22] Lamb had told him that Central Lending and Highfields had been worse but Cranshaw found this difficult to imagine. There were too many scientific and technical books of the seventies and eighties and dust was piled high on volumes that were destined for burning. In spite of the limitations of the replacement fund, the staff found they could keep only about 25% of the book stocks that they examined.

In certain branches, children's corners with reading tables were arranged because there was little accommodation for junior libraries. The first separate children's library was opened at Walkley in November 1924. This was only possible because of the building that had been available. But the children's corners were made as attractive as possible in accordance with Lamb's views on "Freedom of choice in an atmosphere of beauty". Print displays were often a feature. So it was that brighter ideas came with the provision of books for children as well as adults. Many of the library staff were to remember the grimy books they had borrowed from their local libraries, as they contrasted them with the appealing volumes now being offered to the children.

The status of the Sheffield public libraries had already improved. It was just at this point that the partnership between Gordon and his deputy and the Libraries Committee under Alderman Simpson, which had produced such fruitful results, was ended. In the council elections of 1926, the Labour Party won a surprising victory and Alderman Simpson lost his office as chairman of the committee. Gordon, too, was leaving. He had applied and been accepted for the post of Chief Librarian at Leeds Public Library. To everyone's great satisfaction, however, Lamb succeeded him at Sheffield at a salary of £500 per annum, rising by increments of £25 to a maximum of £700 per annum. The *Sheffield Independent* congratulated the Libraries Committee on its choice of Lamb because of his wide experience of the reorganization of the library service when he was working under Gordon.[23] The decision was fully justified by the results. Lamb continued the consolidation of the Sheffield libraries and even expanded the service. The *Telegraph and Star* was later to say, "We are glad to note that the Gordon tradition is being maintained at the Free Libraries."[24]

Lamb now continued to practise the theory of librarianship which he held throughout his career as head of the Sheffield public libraries. He frequently stated, in lectures and in writing, that he thought the fundamental duty of the public libraries was "to provide books for people to read; to encourage the right use of books by a service and technique which will make these books productive".[25] He considered the average percentage of borrowers to the population—in the thirties, Lamb says, this was 15%—to be an extremely low figure. He fervently believed that the public libraries had a duty to reach at least half the population of the area they were serving. This could be achieved by a very careful selection of the book stock itself and surveys of the general interests of the locality. Lamb always set his aim rather high. Even today, the average percentage of borrowers in the country has not risen more than 10%. But the challenge was there—Lamb saw "a living lending service, not as series of buildings crammed with dead books, duplicated in all branches, because no one can imagine a library without such and such a book . . .".[26] He knew that the library clientèle had changed since his own youth. The numbers of less-dedicated readers had increased, and the average person came no longer for books to further his education, but came to wander around the library shelves until a title caught his eye. Reading was for recreation. Also, Lamb realized that there had sprung up a vast selection of material which libraries could not afford to ignore but which quickly became out of date. Trade journals, periodical literature on ephemeral subjects, works on economic problems—within a few months of publication much of this type of literature became worthless. Thus the librarian was faced with the need to reach a larger public and also to re-examine his policy of book provision on a usually inadequate book fund.

In Sheffield, Lamb practised his own solution. To encourage the city people, he provided many duplicates of standard popular works and he simplified the classification scheme to make it easier for readers to progress from the catalogue to the books on the shelves. He advocated a central pool of classical works that would be quickly available on request, but he thought that to have large sections of the duller "classics" in the branch libraries, where they would not earn their keep, was wasted effort. With posters outside the library and publicity in the press, Lamb hoped to draw more of the unconverted into the building both to see the attractive displays in order to arouse their interest and to be tempted towards the books themselves.

The work in improving the branches continued at the rate of one per year. Park branch was reopened with a children's library in December 1927; Tinsley was reopened in June 1928; and Hillsborough in April 1929. The book fund was still inadequate to stock these branches, but Lamb and his deputy found various means to use what grant they had to best advantage. The deputy librarian at that time recalls spending "three hectic days in Foyle's basement hunting for 'sixpennies' . . . many standard and semi-standard authors, dusty, but in tight covers and book jackets. On another occasion, Joe returned from Town with a famous publisher's list of 3/6d. and 2/6d. reprints which we could buy in sheets for 1/1d. and 10½d. provided we took 5,000".[27] That must have been a triumph.

However, there were other considerations. By the end of 1927 it was clear that the Central Public Library buildings were becoming more and more unsatisfactory due to the increase in the numbers of readers using its facilities and in the numbers of staff. At a meeting of the Institute of Public Administration in Sheffield, Lamb stated that the external squalor of the two buildings in Surrey Street was of less importance than their internal insufficiency, especially as the work of the Central Lending Library had increased by 370% since 1921.[28] In December, Lamb claimed that the library had reached the absolute limit of its capacity. He could see no way to extend the lending library except by using the newsroom.[29] The assistants were having to ask the readers to choose their books quickly and then leave because of the lack of space. The City Architect reported that the building was unsafe, especially the Music Hall, which could no longer bear the weight of the books stored within it. The Library Committee's recommendation that a new library should be provided for was turned down by the Council. It seemed as if the unhappy situation in Surrey Street was to continue. However, Alderman J. G. Graves reviewed the problem. He put forward the suggestion that there should be a new Central Library with an Art Gallery on the top floor. Lamb did not entirely approve of the idea of the Art Gallery—a judgement borne out today by the fact that the library, again overcrowded, cannot expand upwards. But under the circumstances he felt that the gift of £30,000 that Alderman Graves was offering towards the cost of the new building could not be ignored. The library portion of the building was to have £10,000 of this gift and the offer was very gratefully accepted.

"A Librarian's work is never done—that is if he carries out his work conscientiously."[30] Much later a colleague said of Lamb " . . . I began to understand the man, and to realise the grasp that he had of the many sides of library work, and to know that the Sheffield Libraries were his whole life".[31] In these years Lamb not only had a grasp of library matters, but he had the imagination to use what he knew towards the introduction of novel ways of library service. In 1928-9 Sheffield took part in a new kind of co-operative effort by becoming an outlier of the National Central Library. Attempts were also made to aid adult education within Sheffield. The library began an experimental scheme of co-operation with the BBC. Lectures were sponsored for those interested in historical, economic or social subjects and books were provided at these talks for home study. Wireless discussion groups were formed at Walkley branch library and later at Hillsborough, but these did not maintain the interest that their novelty had produced, for the talks were perhaps a little too advanced for many of the listeners. But the idea had been a good one for it showed that the library was helping to satisfy an expressed need for further education during the depression. More successful was the start of a service to the City General Hospital in 1931-2 and a co-operative scheme between the library, the Workers' Educational Association and the trades technical societies of the University. Lamb continued to have exhibitions set out in the library and to compile reading lists of selected titles. His awareness of the press was very evident throughout his career and he contrived to bring as much publicity to bear on the library as possible. A typical notice in the local press in 1928 informed readers that an "Attractive list for those interested in the outlawry of war has also been arranged. The list contains 28 books on disarmament, the League of Nations, International Government and International peace and war".[32]

In 1931, from the end of May to the beginning of August, Lamb spent a private holiday in the United States. Here, he satisfied a dream of seeing the Grand Canyon, which had been engendered in his boyhood by a drawing in a school geography book. And here, also, he suffered the anticlimax of arriving at Los Angeles in a temperature of 95° with a most unromantic cold in the head. But he also mixed business with pleasure by visiting as many of the important libraries as he could in that "Mecca of public librarianship". Lamb was especially interested in library building. He had been collaborating very closely with the City Architect with the plans of the new City Library in Sheffield and had, indeed, supplied extremely detailed drawings of the new furniture and equipment that he wanted there. From his own survey of American libraries in Cleveland, Philadelphia and Washington, among others, Lamb did not think that any ideas he had put into the new Sheffield blueprint need be altered. The *Sheffield Independent* had grave views over Lamb's trip and its supposed effects on the library service, and these had to be quelled by a sharp letter from the chairman of the Libraries Committee.

> I regret [he wrote] that you still appear to be under the misapprehension that we are trying to emulate the libraries of the USA, or the magnificent library building now under erection in Manchester. It is true that Mr. Lamb went (at his own expense) in order to see the library buildings in that country, but he viewed them in a very critical spirit and they suggested little that would show any practical improvement on the much less expensive plans already in hand. On the contrary his experience there enabled him to suggest administrative reorganisations, which made it possible to meet a 30% increase in output without adding to the staff.[33]

The amount of thought that Lamb put into the organization of the new library building was considerable. Even today, the library is basically adequate, though it has become fearfully overcrowded through expansion in every department. In the 1930's the design of the furniture and the fittings, to which Lamb had given much attention, were considered very functional and modern. The President of the American Library Association in a visit to Sheffield public libraries in 1935 expressed his admiration of the desks with their unique pigeon-holes for readers' belongings.

A scheme came to fruition in 1932 that had been very dear to Lamb's interests, and one in which he played an extremely prominent part. The Organization for the exchange of technical publications in Sheffield and District, later to be known as SINTO, was inaugurated in December. Several years before this, Lamb had been trying to persuade the city authorities and prominent men in industry in Sheffield that an information service was essential if the industries of the city were to compete successfully in the British market. He thought that as much specialized, technical information as possible should be available for consultation at a central depot where it could be examined by local firms. Even before these startling ideas were generally accepted, Lamb made friends with those industrialists who shared his views. Stories have been told of his holding friendly discussions with them in his library office as he sat with his feet on the desk and a cigar clamped between his teeth. Lamb allowed representatives of firms to by-pass many of the obsolete library regulations in order to borrow reference volumes that they needed. He used every opportunity to demonstrate the possibilities of the Commercial and Technical Library. In September 1932 he addressed the Association of Special Libraries and Information Bureaux on "The Public Library as an aid to Industry and Research". The next month he told the Sheffield trades technical societies, in a lecture, that, although there were 10,000 books and journals dealing with the local industries in the Commercial Department, there was surprisingly little demand for them.[34]

With the election of Alderman Samuel Osborn as chairman of the Libraries Committee in 1932, Lamb found an influential man in sympathy with his ideas. A start was immediately made in persuading rival firms to co-operate between themselves, the library and the research organizations within

Sheffield. On 12 December, nineteen representatives of the different companies appeared at a meeting to discuss the project—Lamb and his colleagues had inspired great interest in the scheme and overcome a great deal of suspicion. The interlending experiment began. Mr. Simons, the former information officer of Edgar Allen & Co. Ltd., recalls:

> Mr. Lamb did not merely inaugurate the Interchange Scheme, he *was* the Interchange Scheme, at all events until it was standing firmly on its own feet. I was always lost in admiration at the manner in which he manoeuvred puzzled and not always sympathetic Chairmen of Committee into blessing and facilitating the working of the scheme. He made things so clear, he was so persuasive and tactful, he argued so cogently, that only a fool could have failed to grasp what a noble work was about to be or was actually being done.[35]

At such a time, to have even thought of such a plan would have been creditable in itself, but to have bullied and convinced others—Lamb could use every means of persuasion on occasion—to follow shows the imagination and persistence of the man at a time when he must have been extremely busy with other matters. Justifiably the interchange scheme was a success and it has been imitated by many other cities.

A little earlier Lamb had applied for the vacant position of Chief Librarian at Liverpool. The salary was £900 per annum. His salary at Sheffield was £800.* Fortunately for Sheffield, Lamb did not obtain the post, although he was "runner-up" to the man who had been deputy in Liverpool. This disappointment did not daunt Lamb, and he flung himself, with characteristic energy, into increasing the prestige of the Sheffield public libraries. In order to provide for the interchange scheme, he realized that the information provided by the Commercial and Technical Department must be of the best quality. He was a pioneer in this field. In his desire for an efficient service, he did not select the specialist books himself. He brought into being a panel of experts who chose up-to-date material. This selection by persons really conversant with the subjects involved ensured that there was little biased or obsolete work on the library shelves. Another vital collection, aimed at industry, was the series of American and British patents, which was rehabilitated and properly maintained by Lamb and his staff. These were also available for reference along with the runs of current catalogues and handbooks collected from all over Britain and the Continent. Lamb's ideas regarding commercial and technical library provision brought a new conception of the value of scientific information to Sheffield industry and to the country. It was certainly through his initiative and forcefulness that the Sheffield city libraries came to be recognized as foremost in this field. Lamb was publicly praised for his work—in October 1951 he was

---

*Lamb applied because his wife wanted to be near St. Helens and her family. He says that his Chairman offered him an extra £100 if he would withdraw but that, "honest as usual, and equally daft", he told the Chairman there was not the remotest chance of Liverpool appointing him, but that he could not withdraw, even for £100—a fortune in those days.

asked to open the new commercial and technical library in Newcastle upon Tyne. In 1952 the Sheffield city libraries were made the first English library outside London to be a repository for the non-secret reports dealing with atomic energy research in Britain, the United States and Canada.

Meanwhile the construction of the new library building had been progressing and this was to be opened by the Duchess of York in July 1934. The teamwork among the staff that had been built up by Lamb and his predecessor was shown during the period of the change from the old buildings to the new: 150,000 books had to be moved twice and staff were obliged to work on half-days and on Sundays, but there was no lack of volunteers. The move took place without closing the library to the public at all. The deputy at that time remembers two members of staff, after a hard day's work transporting books between buildings in shallow bakers' trays, chanting with feeling, "Yo, heave ho! Four loads to go!"[36]

These achievements perhaps hide the fact that others did not believe as heartily in the advantages of a library service as the Chief Librarian. Britain was in the throes of the depression, and the city council, desperately trying to pare down the proposed budget, took up the attitude that the library expenditure could be cut with little loss to the citizens. This angered Lamb very much as an example of the outmoded attitude towards library service which was unfortunately still prevalent in many quarters. In 1932 he protested in print, "A cut of £6,000 has been demanded, which, with the £1,500 lost during the current year, will make a total reduction of £7,500 from a total of £39,000: a ruinous proportion. If this cut is enforced, it will largely nullify the work of the past few years."[37] It seemed to be fortunate that the new library building was already on the drawing boards, for the early 1930's would not have produced a grant from the city authorities. From 1931 to 1934 book accessions dropped to a quarter of the normal rate and book issues decreased in number. It was only after 1936 that the situation began to improve. The book stocks in Central Lending were gradually built up and the brighter, more attractive books encouraged readers to come to the new library building.

In 1934 Lamb had been obliged to turn down an invitation from the American Library Association to attend the conference in Montreal because the dates clashed with the opening of the new Sheffield Library building. However, in the next year, he was indeed given a token of honour nearer to home. The Libraries Committee decided to adopt standard practice and designate the Central Library as "the City Library" and Lamb as "the City Librarian". The Sheffield public libraries system had, at last, recognition within civic circles. At this time, when he was 45 years old, Lamb obtained the Fellowship of the Library Association. He had passed all the sectional examinations many years before, but did not have the appropriate language qualification to enable him to apply for the fellowship. He did not agree with the action of the Library Association in awarding the fellowship for war service and, in characteristic fashion, set himself to completing his qualifications. His fame as the chief of a most efficient library network was already assured, but Lamb had never been entirely satisfied with the Library Association itself. In 1941 he was appointed a member of its Council and later became Chairman. He served on many committees including the executive committee and those for education and publications, yet a senior colleague recalls that many thought that Lamb was "unduly critical" of the Library Association.[38] Lamb was always of a questioning disposition and this, along with his forceful temperament, must have brought him into conflict with the Association. He now no longer belongs to it.

However, the beginning of the Second World War was to interrupt the life of Britain. It is to Lamb's credit that he succeeded in his determination, throughout the war years, to keep the libraries open despite all the difficulties that faced him, the war-time restrictions and the diversion of professional staff into the services. It may even be said with pride that, under his guidance, the city libraries contributed greatly to the morale of the citizens, and, thereby, emerged in 1945 with increased prestige. In contrast to many other cities in Britain, use of the libraries in Sheffield rose during the war.[39] Books were bought to stock evening classes, while Crosspool became the first of a series of twelve library centres established for adults who could not venture to their nearest branches. Some 40,000 books were put into store to anticipate a similar book shortage to the one that had occurred after 1914. In two book recovery drives at least a million volumes were carefully examined. Later in the war, the wholesale destruction of books was carried out, especially in the London area, from fear of fire, and Lamb's vision in planning for this was remarkable. The junior libraries did close their doors, but in their place grew the co-operative effort between the libraries and the Education Committee. A "home service" was established whereby books were still supplied to the children. This had surprising results: although there had been a school library service before the war, it was these new developments which paved the way for the completely integrated service which established Sheffield as a leader in such matters.

Lamb's greatest contribution during these years was his part in the in-information service, which was set up to aid the people of Sheffield. He, himself, had always required a clear, direct answer to any problem and he believed that the same was owed to the citizens. In 1939 he became honorary secretary of the newly formed Sheffield Information Committee, whose aim was to supply accurate information in those troublous times, and to counter-act any rumours that might have been inspired by the enemy. Even more important was Lamb's role in building up a complete information service in the Central Library from practically nothing, after the air raids of 12/13 and 15/16 December 1940 when thousands of bewildered people needed urgent advice and comfort. The Social Assistance Department headquarters had been destroyed by the enemy attack. The Central Library miraculously escaped almost undamaged and, at very short notice, Lamb had been asked to convert it into a centre of post-raid rehabilitation. Under these circumstances, Lamb's drive and powers of organization are clearly shown. Mr. E. Simpson, Deputy City Librarian at that time, recalls:

> One can remember high officials from the Town Hall occupying Cataloguing Department, officers from various government departments in the Reference Library, and all the time there were huge queues of people waiting to report damage to their property or to obtain relief. Billeting, casualties, mortuaries, missing persons, telegrams from men overseas, lost property, evacuation, rest centres were only some of the 101 matters with which we had to deal. . . . The organisation from above was terrific. Out of it all came the "Where to go" guide, the Information Bureau, and a highly trained organisation designed to move into action immediately further air-raids . . . took place.[40]

Instructions to the inhabitants of Sheffield were broadcast from cars driven by voluntary workers, while other more necessary messages were distributed in leaflet form. Young trained cyclists were organized into a group to answer queries from worried citizens who lived at a distance from the town centre. Lamb was appointed BBC liaison officer in 1941 and elaborate secret plans were made in co-operation with the Invasion Committee—if the enemy should invade Sheffield at any time, all the information services were to be concentrated in the Central Library. Luckily, these well-rehearsed schemes never came into action. However, after the peace, the Government reviewed the need that had arisen in the country throughout the war for an efficient information service. It urged civic authorities to set up such services under their control. In Sheffield, the natural place for the civic information service was the Central Library and thus the work of Lamb and his colleagues during the war has been extended, and is with the city even today.

With the coming of peace, the development of the city libraries continued. Despite the post-war restrictions on building materials, blueprints were drawn up for new branches to cater for an estimated 37% of the population of Sheffield district which did not live near a permanent library. The home of Sir William Ellis, set in a beautiful park at Ecclesall, was converted into a very pleasant branch library. A prefabricated "hutment" was set up on a housing estate at Southey, and this branch was equipped with an initial bookstock of 10,000 volumes for adults and children. Junior libraries were converted from what had formerly been the newsrooms at Attercliffe and Tinsley. Later, in 1952, Manor branch library was completed. It had been begun just before the war, but had been abandoned until permission had been granted in 1950 to complete it. New plans were drawn up and the new building can be seen as a remarkable experiment in modern library planning. The man who had once advised every librarian to read Henry Gardner's

Paint researches and their practical application before redecorating a library[41] had been as deeply involved with this new building at Manor as he had been with the Central Library. There are floor-to-ceiling plate-glass walls, upholstered seats, shadowless artificial lighting and a cunning scheme of library helpers. This latter idea had been instituted to stop vandalism, which had been noticeable at Manor library before it was completed—it imposed discipline on the children through the children, and gave them a sense of pride in their junior library.

In July 1949 Mr. Lamb was honoured by the University of Sheffield when he was created an honorary MA at a degree ceremony. It might be said that the University was equally honoured by his somewhat reluctant acceptance. In his address, the Public Orator stated " . . . we may claim with pride that nowhere are the manifold opportunities and responsibilities of the office of Chief Librarian more imaginatively conceived, more brilliantly discharged than in Sheffield".[42] It is perhaps appropriate that the man who had begun work in the St. Helens Library when he was 14 should at last receive this distinction. Although he was not biased against graduates entering the library profession, Lamb did not consider that they should be given preferential treatment over non-graduates with professional qualifications.

> It may be excusable for a university man to argue that people are better for having had a university course; but the general inference to which it leads, and which is shown by the exclusive appointment of university candidates by committees over which the Universities have influence, that a university product must *always* be superior to a non-university candidate is not only an indefensible assumption, but a silly one.[43]

Lamb always preferred to base his judgement of a candidate for librarianship on that person's individuality and flair for the work in hand—his curiosity and his desire to learn. He was supporting those people who had not had the opportunity to go to university or college through lack of grants rather than through lack of ability. Many of these had entered librarianship and proved most successful. Lamb did not believe that possession of a university degree necessarily allowed a man to say he was "educated and cultured", and he felt only scorn for those who held this view.

However, within the field of education, Lamb considered that the public libraries had a great part to play. He quoted Lord Stamp: "You will be mentally more powerful if you know *where* to find knowledge instantly than if you stuff your head with facts. . . . The man who knows his way about a library is more effective today than the man who knows twenty of the books by heart."[44] Library visits for adults had been arranged in order to show them what services the library could offer, but even more important was the work with the children. Lamb had had experience of students, who hoped that the library staff would work for them. "It is common for university students practically to ask us to do a thesis for them."[45] So he thought that if schoolchildren could be taught the rudiments of cataloguing and classification, they would, at least, learn about the differing subjects held within the library and, at best, learn how to find out their own information. The idea had grown up before the war, until, with the co-operation of the Principal of the Central Day Commercial College in 1936, ninety-six pupils inaugurated an experimental class. Lamb did not intend that the teaching should be forced on the pupils, and he ensured that the instruction periods took the form of a quiz paper following a brief talk on the use of business books. Unfortunately, Lamb expected too much from the first classes and the course had to be reduced in length and be simplified during the war. But the scheme has expanded and has proved to be a very important part of the extension work of the city libraries. Instruction classes for boys and girls in their last or penultimate year at school had been held regularly in the Central Library from 1942 and in 1956 5338 pupils attended. At Manor branch library, in the same year, over 1500 pupils from five local schools worked in the Reference Room attempting to complete quizzes set by the librarian and his staff.

Another facet of Lamb's work was his organization of a Local History Department in the Central Library. His care of the Manuscript Collection led directly to the Fitzwilliam papers and archives being deposited in Sheffield in 1949. This was one of the most important collections in the country and the name of the Sheffield city libraries was now to spread into the world of scholarship. Lamb said at the time that it was an "Honour to Sheffield in that it shows confidence in the work of the Department of Local History, which has gained for itself such a reputation among historians and scholars".[46]

On 2 February 1949 he recorded a talk for the BBC "Eyewitness" on this loan of one of the biggest collections ever handed to a British city. The documents go back to the thirteenth century and include the correspondence of Edmund Burke, which had not been examined for over a hundred years. This series of letters made Sheffield the centre of research on Edmund Burke and his period. Lamb was perhaps less interested in the papers as historical manuscripts than in the fact that they would increase the prestige of his library system. But his appreciation of the archive material in his care, before this date, had made Sheffield a suitable repository for the Wentworth Woodhouse muniments. When the Fairbank collection was presented to the library in 1932, Lamb had an archivist appointed. He, himself, assisted in the preliminary work of classifying this collection. Soon after it was suggested that the Wentworth Woodhouse muniments should come to Sheffield, Lamb had already decided on ways of increasing the strong-room accommodation. He was ready, as always, to adapt the library requirements to a changing situation. Scholars from all over the world came to study the Burke Papers. Professor Copeland of Chicago collaborated with other researchers to compile a checklist of Burke's entire correspondence. A definitive edition of the correspondence has also passed beyond the planning stage—a great treasure had been brought to Sheffield.

In April 1951, Mr. Harold Wilson, then President of the Board of Trade, appointed a committee of eight to inquire into the law of copyright. Lamb was nominated as the only librarian on this committee. He told reporters that the last Copyright Act had been passed in 1911. Since then so many advances had been made in the use of technical reproduction that further scrutiny of this Act was urgently required.[47] Lamb undertook his duties with the thoroughness that characterized his work in general. Before the first meeting of the committee, he had studied the relevant documents, both British and foreign, that dealt with the Copyright Act. He attended almost all the committee meetings and examined bulky memoranda, containing evidence from such differing bodies as the British Museum and Danceland Publications Ltd., or questions such as the position in copyright of the broadcasts of the Grand National.[48] Lamb became completely knowledgeable about all aspects of copyright, especially those affecting libraries. His resolutions on the committee gained some privileges for librarians and removed many awkward restrictions. Fifty-seven meetings of the committee were held and seventy-seven organizations and individuals gave evidence. To be associated with the report submitted to the Board of Trade in 1952 could not have been easy, especially as Lamb had an active library system to control. He was, however, much concerned with the features of copyright uncovered by the commission—copyright which had once been limited to literary and artistic works could now cover a whole new range of interests. Later he was to dedicate his book, *Commercial and technical libraries*, to the chairman of the Copyright Committee—"To Sir Henry Gregory, KCMG, CB, with whom I was privileged to be associated in a difficult but agreeable task".[49]

All this time, while Lamb was so actively engaged in administrative work both within the city libraries and without, he was busy writing. He compiled numerous articles on library policy both for the local press and the national dailies. He wrote, for example, on "The public library and industry" in the *Manchester Guardian*.[50] Lamb could have had little time to write a large connected text, yet he managed eventually to publish a Library Association manual, *Commercial and technical libraries*, which appeared in 1955. Lamb was drawing on all his previous experience in this field. It was clear that he was one of the few people in the country who were expert in it. When the book was printed Lamb "had the satisfaction of noting how few librarians could be found competent to review it. For in this work, as elsewhere, he was a pioneer".[51] In his book Lamb discussed the vast range of topics relevant to technical and commercial libraries. Among other things, he mentioned their history, the practical training of their staff, information indexes, map

c

fittings and so on. Nothing was too insignificant to escape his notice. In his work Lamb put all the exactness of thought that he expected from himself and from others. Inaccuracies had to be eliminated. This attention to detail, along with his other commitments, kept the book for long in the manuscript stage. In 1930 the *Sheffield Daily Telegraph* reported, "At the present time he is engaged in writing a text book on library work."[52] Knowing that Lamb's interest in commercial libraries had begun even before this date, it is even possible that the "textbook" may have had some connection with these specialized departments. By 1939 he had sent questionnaires to libraries that claimed to have scientific sections such as Glasgow Mitchell Library and Dundee Public Library. However, time was pressing, and a colleague believes that the volume might never have been published in 1955, had not the 1951 edition of the *Reference catalogue of current literature* listed it as being already in print.[53] Nevertheless, the book is an extremely valuable one and has yet to be superseded.

Another of Lamb's smaller and more general works was a handbook printed for the Festival of Britain Year. This booklet, called *Sheffield, England*, was intended to give the city some favourable publicity by describing the story of Sheffield within a framework of attractive photographs of the area. It was aimed at those people whose ideas of Sheffield and the Peak District were coloured by the view from the railway line. Lamb had always thought that more could be done to advertise Sheffield, and, also, to make Sheffield better worth advertising by improving the amenities for visitors. The booklet was a very great success—"a first rate piece of work, which must have entailed a lot of homework for Mr. Lamb".[54] Copies were sent to various dignitaries in other towns, at home and abroad, and it is extremely interesting to see how Lamb dealt with the influx of town guides that were sent to the Central Library in return. Instead of relegating these valuable guides to some forgotten book stack, Lamb turned the opportunity to the advantage of the library by erecting a huge holiday exhibition in the Civic Information Department in February 1952. This collection was headed "Sunlit Beach— or Magic Mountain", and contained some 600 official handbooks from Britain and the Continent. Here again Lamb's flair for publicity was dramatically demonstrated.

The last example of Lamb's technique of publicity was shown in his planning of the celebrations for the centenary year of the city libraries in 1956. He wrote an illustrated *History of the city libraries* which was published in the summer. The actual centenary day was arranged to coincide with the opening of the new Woodseats branch library in July. It was a fitting climax to the work of Mr. Lamb. After 49 years in librarianship he was to retire. His last public appearance as City Librarian was at the official centenary luncheon in the Town Hall, honoured by the presence of the

Duke of Devonshire. Many of Lamb's former staff, now librarians themselves in various key posts throughout the country, had been invited to the luncheon. Lamb's old friend, Mr. R. J. Gordon, and the successor to Lamb in Sheffield, Mr. J. Bebbington, were also among the guests. This was not the only recognition of the hundred years of public library work in Sheffield. The Central Library was opened to the public for thorough inspection—groups of interested spectators were shown round the various workrooms and administrative departments, while members of staff gave talks on the services of the library. There was an important Centenary Exhibition in the civic information room which illustrated the advance of libraries and library techniques from 1856 to 1956. A small model public lending library of the late nineteenth century had been set up with a mahogany counter bearing a Cotgreave Indicator. Original books of the 1880's were shelved on high stacks to show the old, dull library bindings. The archaic printed catalogues and heavy ledgers of that early period in library history were shown on the counter. Lamb must have remembered the library desk at St. Helens when he examined this model.

Another display attempted to give a pictorial demonstration of public library development in the twentieth century, while a further section of the exhibition was devoted to the present-day facilities offered by the library. The very contrast between the two main exhibits could, in some sense, point out the achievements of Lamb and his colleagues. This was mainly demonstrated by a very modern and unusual device for those times. A film had been made for centenary year in co-operation with the library staff, a professional script writer and a local firm of photographers. This colourful film was projected through the screen of a television set, itself part of a model of a modern sitting room with two easy chairs facing the screen. The whole exhibit displayed books from the lending library in bright colourful jackets. The title of the film, *Books in hand*, was further carried through by suspending two pairs of model hands, holding open books, at eye-level above the chairs. The success of this documentary film was apparent during the 3-week period of the exhibition. Later,

> as a result of articles in the professional press, and other publicity, requests soon began to come in from organizations outside Sheffield. Altogether it was lent for showing outside the city in 30 Libraries and 11 other institutions in places as far apart as Orkney, Aberystwyth and Germany. Then it began to sell. Before the end of the year 29 copies had been bought by the British Council, two by other English institutions and two by foreign libraries.[55]

Lamb was now within weeks of retirement in August 1956. The Sheffield city libraries may have been his whole life, but he had several interests beyond librarianship. His interest in the theatre, for instance, is well known. He became chairman of the Sheffield Repertory Company in 1946, and he brought to this the same ruthless organization and efficiency as he did to the library system. He drafted and got through new Articles of Association, which reorganized the Board of Directors and their powers completely, and drafted a new administrative organization. As he had thought with the city libraries, so he thought with the theatre. He considered that if the theatre were made attractive and inviting, and all the draughts excluded, people would want to watch the productions. Lamb insisted that money should not be wasted unnecessarily but that the management should not skimp on the show. Today the Playhouse stands as further proof of Lamb's abilities of organization.

Less well publicized, perhaps, was Lamb's own personal delight in music. When he was young, he had played the piano, practising duets with his friend Tom. He had hoarded his money to hear Carmen, Lohengrin and Tannhäuser and this love of music remained with him. Lamb was also a Rotarian when he was in Sheffield.

Lamb's personality was extremely dynamic and forceful. He would never allow a member of his staff to be criticized by an outsider, but he did insist on absolute loyalty in return. He welded his staff into a body and he commanded their complete respect and admiration, despite his strict control of every aspect of administration. Because he demanded the best in himself, he asked for the best in others. Mr. Taylor of Central Lending remembers being lambasted by Lamb over what the latter thought was an unhappy headline in a local paper regarding the libraries. He could have been too exacting a man to work for in harmony, but he was always kindly to those experiencing a period of stress and he could always allow his annoyance and irritation to dissolve in laughter—especially at himself. He once announced to an audience that most people regarded librarians as congenital half-wits. After a pause he added, "They are probably right."[56]

In his 35 years in the Sheffield city libraries, Lamb had seen a great number of changes, many of which he had himself instituted. The presentation on his retirement on 16 August 1956 was a very sad yet proud occasion. Sheffield had lost a chief to whom even the Director General of the French National Library had paid tribute, pointing out that his fame as an organizing genius had spread not only in Britain but to the Continent.[57] From the dingy closed access rooms and the pitiful branch libraries, the Sheffield library system had been remoulded into one of the foremost systems in the country. Lamb was presented with a writing desk, made, typically enough, to his own design. But the student of librarianship will understand that "the many tributes paid to him at official and private gatherings could not adequately express the esteem in which he is held, nor can this Report do justice to the great value of his services to the City and to the profession of librarianship".[58]

NOTE. Mr. J. P. Lamb wrote a great amount of literary work and, in the main, I used his articles and letters as the basis for this study. I found them extremely useful and to the point. To fill out the picture, I have been greatly helped by the newspaper files concerning the public libraries in the Local History Department, Central Library, Sheffield, and by a magazine of essays, written by colleagues to honour Mr. Lamb on his retirement. A select number of the annual reports of Sheffield City Libraries also proved useful. I also received personal views of Mr. Lamb from Mr. R. J. Gordon, MA, FLA, former City Librarian of Leeds and friend of Mr. Lamb; Mr. H. M. Cashmore, MBE, FLA, City Librarian Emeritus of Birmingham; Mr. Arthur J. Avery, at one time a great friend of Mr. Lamb; Mr. W. A. Taylor, MC, FLA, City Librarian of Birmingham Public Libraries; Mr. H. C. Caistor, FLA, Chief Librarian, St. Helens; and Mr. Paul Sykes, DMA, FLA, Chief Librarian of Rochdale. My thanks are due to these gentlemen, who answered many of my queries.

In conclusion, I must thank the Sheffield City Librarian and his staff in the Reference Library and the Local History Department, who helped me in every way; and in particular Miss Mary Walton and Mr. C. W. Taylor, Central Library, who discussed Mr. Lamb's work with me and gave me many important clues to follow up.

REFERENCES

1. HUTCHINGS, F. G. B., J. P. Lamb, *Spellbound* **6,** 5 (1956).
2. LAMB, J. P., Libarrian when young, *Librarian* **45,** 2 (1956).
3. *Ibid.* 2 ff.
4. JAST, L. STANLEY, quoted by Lamb, *op. cit.* 4; also quoted by LAMB, J. P., Manor branch library, *LAR* **55,** 186 (1953).
5. LAMB, J. P., Librarian when young, *Librarian* **45,** 34 (1956).
6. *Ibid.* 35.
7. LAMB, J. P., A few facts for American readers, *Wilson Bull.* **8,** 513 (1934).
8. LAMB, J. P., Librarian when young, *Librarian* **45,** 36 (1956).
9. *Ibid.* 49 ff.
10. This information was received from Mr. A. J. Avery in a personal communication.
11. This opinion was received from Mr. H. M. Cashmore, MBE, FLA, in a personal communication.
12. LAMB, J. P., Librarian when young, *Librarian* **45,** 51 (1956).
13. *Note.* For an example of the way in which Gordon and Lamb thought alike, see their attitude towards the passing of the closed access system in GORDON, R. J., Presidential address, Library Association, *Papers and summaries of discussion at the Brighton conference* 2–3 (1947), and LAMB, J. P., Librarian when young, *Librarian* **45,** 52 (1956).
14. LAMB, J. P., *op. cit.* 51.
15. GORDON, R. J., A long look back, *Spellbound* **6,** 8 (1956).
16. *Ibid.* 8 ff.
17. LAMB, J. P., Librarian when young, *Librarian* **45,** 52 (1956).
18. LAMB, J. P., Gleanings from Yorkshire libraries, *Library World* **29,** 44 (1926).
19. LAMB, J. P., Reconstructing a city library system, *LAR*, n.s. **5,** 20 (1927).
20. OSBORN, T. E., Retrospect, *Spellbound* **6,** 7 (1956).
21. GORDON, R. J., A long look back, *Spellbound* **6,** 9 (1956).
22. CRANSHAW, J., Between the wars, *Spellbound* **6,** 10 (1956).
23. *Sheffield Independent*, 31 Jan. 1927.

24. *Telegraph and Star*, 27 Sept. 1927.
25. LAMB, J. P., Modern library organisation, *Library Assistant* **25,** 251 (1932).
26. *Ibid.*, 252.
27. CRANSHAW, J., Between the wars, *Spellbound* **6,** 10 (1956).
28. *Sheffield Telegraph*, 19 Nov. 1927.
29. *Ibid.*, 5 Dec. 1927.
30. Who's who in Sheffield, *Sheffield Daily Telegraph*, 11 Oct. 1930.
31. THORPE, J., Preface, *Spellbound* **6,** 2 (1956).
32. *Telegraph and Star*, 20 April 1928.
33. ALDERMAN BARTON, *Sheffield Independent*, 30 May 1932.
34. *Sheffield Telegraph*, 14 Oct. 1932.
35. SIMONS, E. N., Service to industry, *Spellbound* **6,** 13 (1956).
36. CRANSHAW, J., Between the wars, *Spellbound* **6,** 11 (1956).
37. LAMB, J. P., What of the future?, *Library World* **34,** 121 (1931–2).
38. This opinion was received from Mr. H. M. Cashmore, MBE, FLA, in a personal communication.
39. *Telegraph and Independent*, 17 Nov. 1939.
40. SIMPSON, E., The war years, *Spellbound* **6,** 19–20 (1956).
41. LAMB, J. P., The interior decoration of libraries, *Librarian* **22,** 68 (1932).
42. The University of Sheffield, *Forty-fourth annual report to the Court of Governors, 1948–9*, 102.
43. LAMB, J. P., The making of a librarian, *Library Assistant* **31,** 9 (1938).
44. LORD STAMP quoted by LAMB, J. P., Teaching the use of books and libraries, *LAR* **51,** 102 (1949).
45. LAMB, J. P., Address to Strathclyde Libraries Club, quoted by *Scottish Daily Express*, 9 Feb. 1950.
46. *The Star*, 28 Jan. 1949.
47. *Sheffield Telegraph*, 12 April 1951.
48. COLEHAN, P., A difficult but agreeable task, *Spellbound* **6,** 26 (1956).
49. LAMB, J. P., Dedication in *Commercial and technical libraries*, Allen & Unwin, 1955.
50. *Manchester Guardian*, 23 Dec. 1952.
51. OLLÉ, J. G., The professional writings of J. P. Lamb, *Spellbound* **6,** 27 (1956).
52. *Sheffield Daily Telegraph*, 11 Oct. 1930.
53. OLLÉ, J. G., The professional writings of J. P. Lamb, *Spellbound* **6,** 27 (1956).
54. *Sheffield Telegraph*, 2 July 1951.
55. Sheffield City Libraries, *One hundredth annual report, 1956–7*, 6.
56. HUTCHINGS, F. G. B., J. P. Lamb, *Spellbound* **6,** 5 (1956).
57. Reported by *The Star*, 4 May 1949.
58. Sheffield City Libraries, *One hundredth annual report, 1956–7*, 7.

2. TRADE LITERATURE:
ITS VALUE, ORGANIZATION AND EXPLOITATION

ELIZABETH B. SMITH

Librarian, Edinburgh School of Agriculture

INTRODUCTION

Innovation is the result of the application of existing knowledge to
the satisfaction of human needs. [1]

Even in the field of pure research, in the academic sense, "discovery" is
based on a subconscious plagiarism of existing ideas and processes. There
should, however, be a more conscious link between existing knowledge and
the inventor; between industrial activity and pure research. One way in
which industry plays its part in forging this link is in supplying a continuous
flow of information on new products and processes, in the form of "trade
literature". Librarians and information officers can help at the receiving
end of this by making this type of literature available for use by those who
would benefit most from it and from the information it conveys. There is
little evidence of effective communication between various branches of research through this medium in Great Britain, although in the USA, USSR
and Czechoslovakia, for instance, even university and national libraries are
performing their part in this co-operation by collecting the trade literature
produced by industry, thus giving students the opportunity of gaining a
balanced impression of industrial activity, side by side with their own
research.

The importance of trade catalogues as a means of conveying useful technical information will be investigated below, but this will not include pub-
lishers' catalogues (which can also be an extremely useful source of information), nor will house journals or instruction manuals be considered. The
subject coverage discussed will be mainly that of physics and its applied and
associated subjects. As the importance of trade information to chemists is
perhaps realized to a greater extent, and this field is certainly better docu-
mented, [2, 3, 4, 5] the applications and uses of trade literature in the field of
chemistry will not be discussed.

1. VALUE

The definition of a trade catalogue, according to one source,[6] is "a book or pamphlet, issued by a manufacturer or dealer, illustrating and describing his goods or products, and sometimes including, or accompanied by a price-list". This is distinguished from the "consolidated" or "union" trade catalogue, and from the trade journal or house journal. To consider how the most use can be made of these publications, it will be helpful first to define more clearly their nature and what information they are likely to contain.

The reason for a manufacturer publishing a technical brochure in the first instance is that he has produced a new product (or a modification of an existing product) or process which he wishes potential customers and research workers to know about. "Companies are spending more on technical brochures every year—sometimes as much as 50% of their advertising budget."[7] Such an outlay obviously anticipates some direct financial return, and this indicates the first use of trade literature—for promotion of sales. In a highly competitive structure of industry the competition aspect will also arise, and emphasize the need for as much information as possible on the product, its possible uses and application, and costs when possible (although these are seldom given in practice, due mainly to rapid fluctuations). So, for direct sales promotion alone, we find already a useful compilation of facts necessary for inclusion in a technical brochure.

It has also been suggested, however, that in recent years the trend in technical brochures has been towards using them "to help find new uses and develop new markets for a particular product, rather than just to help boost sales *per se*".[7] This indicates that brochures are intended for people engaged in research and development as well as for the person about to use the product as it stands. Much useful work may be sparked off by some of the more detailed information and ideas presented.

There has been a great deal of discussion on the question of what type of information should be contained in trade brochures, not the least of which took the form of a conference held in London, in 1959, entitled "Information in the building industry".[8] Mr. B. Agard Evans, one of the principal speakers, and a well-known voice in the industrial library world stated that "year by year trade literature is improving in presentation, and in its content of responsible information . . . : More and more it is recognized as a very important addition to the information files of practitioners." The main point which arose out of the discussion which followed, however, was that there seems to be a need for several levels of presentation of the information. People actually carrying out the task of setting up apparatus or assembling equipment do not want to plough through a mass of reading matter before they find the necessary practical instructions, while, on the other hand, someone at top level (in their case the architect) wants as much of the information relating to the product as possible. This is discussed in further detail in several papers from a conference held at the Production Engineering Research Association in June 1963.[9] Another point raised at this conference was that the technical writing of the brochures themselves is a very skilled operation, since not only must the author have the ability to make the text readable, but he must be in very close contact with the research team concerned in order to include as far as possible the theory behind its production, in order to bring out more fully the widest possible implications involved and convey them to a largely unknown body of potential consumers. It is clear that if a brochure is not going to be immediately filed in the waste-paper basket, it must contain sufficient technical information to appeal to specialists in the field, at the same time making it easily understood by members of the public with sufficient technical knowledge to be interested.

Apart from these practical indications and discussions on how much information should be presented in trade literature, there is also a British Standard[10] which, while dealing mainly with recommendations as to size and layout of the brochures, also gives an indication of the type of information they should convey.

To the "information-conscious" it must be obvious that there is a great deal of information contained in these brochures describing products and processes which may never be included in journal articles or textbooks, and which could be extremely valuable to research workers and students. Some of them are almost equivalent to a reference work on the subject. Several random examples of brochures containing useful information are listed in Appendix A. A good example of a reference work from this list is the British Aluminium Co. booklet *Aluminium—facts and figures*, which is "essentially a reference book for aluminium and its alloys". Some brochures also contain long bibliographies of references to technical literature.

Many more similar and perhaps better examples could be quoted. A list of the more important ones in the library of Boeing Airplane Co., Kansas, was compiled in 1947 and published in an article in *Library Journal*,[11] where they were referred to as "commercial reference sources". A comprehensive, annotated bibliography of these "reference aids" would be a very useful "tool" to be compiled now, and would perhaps encourage further use of them in libraries. It might also provide a greater stimulus for all manufacturers to include as much technical information as possible in their catalogues.

To take another American example, Dr. S. V. Billingsley (Technical Information Director, Interstate Electronics Corp., California) in 1960 published an article[12] emphasizing the value of the information contained in trade literature, in which she described "the harassed engineer, searching frantically for the characteristics of a piece of equipment" and "turning to the industrial librarian for help". The general opinion here also seemed to be that in the majority of cases they are unable to help, since most librarians seem to shy away from the idea of maintaining a file of manufacturers' literature. The reasons suggested in this article are that library schools do not teach librarians how to handle this material, and the physical character- istics of the material itself do not readily lend themselves to conventional library management, although Dr. Billingsley's experience is that "the value far exceeds the extra effort".

Apart from this value to industrial libraries of trade catalogues, there is also a great deal of information which might be of interest to technical students. For example, a student of physics taking even the elementary courses in electricity finds great difficulty in finding circuit diagrams for many of the laboratory problems. My own solution was to obtain a com- mercial publication of an electronics company on radio circuits, but some of the instrument catalogues (e.g. Cambridge Instrument Co., *Cambridge A.C. instruments for high frequencies*) would also have given explanations with clear diagrams on, say, the Carey Foster Bridge and its possible applications in various circuits, together with worked examples. Some, such as the *Manual of spring engineering* produced by the American Steel & Wire Co., even give sample problems and formulae, extremely useful for students, while the brochures of Ferodo Ltd. and the Bendix Aviation Corp. start right from the elementary introduction to friction and pressure respectively.

1.1. Foreign literature

One very important aspect of the subject which has not yet been men- tioned is the interest of information from abroad. Trade literature is perhaps even more important in this field than in any other, since delays in receiving foreign information, although greatly reduced now by the greater availability of foreign journals in this country through the National Lending Library for Science and Technology and its translation services, are still inevitable. It is not the delay in receiving the journal which is the setback now, but too often the language difficulties involved at the receiving end, in the case of the smaller firms at any rate. Trade literature, on the other hand, often tends to be of a more pictorial nature—firms can afford to illustrate their brochures to a greater extent than a journal with limited space attempting to accept as many articles as possible; and illustration in most cases takes the form of graphs and diagrams, tables of statistics and data. These are often used by translators as well, who find that they give up-to-date technical language for machinery or processes. This rapid dissemination of facts be- tween countries could also give an indication of the research which has already been undertaken, and help to avoid duplication of effort.

A very poignant comment on this subject was published in an OECD leaflet[13] where a list of quotations was given to stress the value of foreign information. One of the most striking examples was:

> Canadian Company [unspecified] . . . required information on a process used in Switzerland. Since the data was too complicated to obtain by mail, a vice-president of the company was assigned to make this trip. The company librarian, hearing of the situation accidentally, made a search and produced the information from the Company's own files

—unfortunate for the vice-president perhaps, but saving the company a great deal in time and money. Other similar examples were quoted.

Some people would argue that demand governs supply, and that if there is little call for this type of information there is not much point in devoting time, space and money to it. A very interesting answer to this type of comment was published in an article in *Technická knihovna* in 1960.[14] This was a description of the collection of trade literature in the Central Technical Library, Prague. The needs of industry were taken into account when collecting information for the files, and apart from normal sources the collection included information from, for example, Scandinavian and Japanese firms, using contacts by state export firms for acquiring the literature, and also occasions like the Trade Fair at Brno. It consisted mainly of foreign information in fact, and a table of the use made of it over a number of years was given, and is reproduced below:

Year	1950	1951	1952	1953	1954	1955	1956	1957	1958	1959
A	4329	5162	4294	3044	5090	5280	7027	14722	14268	18010
L	2944	5588	7919	7877	7810	23500	45212	44398	69230	82904

A = additions.   L = loans.

From an examination of these figures it can be seen quite clearly that as more material was added, the use of the collection increased substantially.

It will be interesting, in the light of this statement, to follow the figures for the Board of Trade Statistics and Market Intelligence Library collection (see section 2), for the next few years, to see whether they would show a similar trend. At the moment their "additions" (A) are approximately 3900 per year, and their "loans" (L) approximately 3000 per year, i.e. almost equivalent to the position in Prague in 1950; and they state in their brochure that "the collection of trade catalogues is growing rapidly".[15] No figures are available for previous years unfortunately.

1.2. Historical uses

The other, perhaps minor, importance of trade brochures, from the information point of view, is the importance to individual firms of keeping a file of the literature they themselves have produced over the years. This gives a very clear indication of the way in which the company has developed, and possibly how its interests have changed.

2. ORGANIZATION

One great difficulty in the organization of a file of trade literature is the enormous variety of sizes encountered. This is due mainly to the fact that since the literature is for publicity and advertising purposes, it is designed to create an impact on the receiver, and variations in size and shape make the brochure different from others.

> In an ideal world each manufactured product would be described on a separate sheet of paper of uniform size, with a standard layout giving all the information which a purchaser might require. It would be preclassified by some simple, universally agreed subject classification, so that it could be easily put away in a file from which it would readily pop up when required.[16]

The British Standards Institution has attempted to attain uniformity in this by making the recommendation[10] in 1955 that manufacturers should adhere to one of two sizes for trade literature:

(i)   297 × 210 mm (A4),
(ii) 210 × 148 mm (A5),

or multiples of these sizes.

In the building field, the first of these, which is equivalent to the international paper size A4, is now generally accepted as standard format for all building trade literature in the United Kingdom. This is important, since the A series of paper sizes is used in at least twenty-six countries, and "the importance to Britain of foreign trade makes it necessary that our practices should be in line with other countries".[17] Another standard[18] gives details of binders and recommends that holes be punched in the leaflets at a specified distance apart. The building industry have also tried to centralize classification of the literature and have adopted the Swedish SfB system for this purpose. This lays down standards for both size and classification of trade catalogues.

It must surely be the problem of maintaining such a collection which is the reason for the comparative neglect of this type of literature, as it is neither difficult nor expensive to acquire. For a library interested in a specific field, there are many methods of finding out which firms are likely to produce literature of interest, such as through buyers' guides or trade directories. There are also ways of finding out about the literature directly through scanning abstracts and advertisements in technical journals. Since the material is normally distributed free of charge, the only cost involved in building up a collection is that of a duplicated letter to the firms chosen with a request to be put on their mailing list. As an experiment to demonstrate the ease of obtaining the literature, I wrote to eleven firms whose booklets had been mentioned in the December 1963 issue of *Metallurgia*. The letter was written from a private address, giving no indication of the occupation or interests of the writer, or of the reason for requiring the publication. In nine cases out of the eleven, the desired booklets were sent; one firm included sets of data sheets in addition, and another a copy of their latest handbook which had appeared since the requested publication. It is therefore not difficult to start a collection. It is perhaps more difficult to make sure that the request to be put on a mailing list is being remembered, but most firms are only too glad to increase their publicity range.

The material, once collected, can be arranged in boxes or vertical files, according to preference, and can either be arranged alphabetically by name of manufacturer or by subject. There are differing views on which method is more satisfactory. Mr. V. C. Watts,[19] of the Production Engineering Research Association Library, states that from experience, they find that "filing the catalogues in subject order is much more economical than by manufacturer's name. Most of the users are interested in the product initially, rather than the name of the manufacturer." Similarly, R. L. Collison[20] agrees that "the ideal arrangement of trade catalogues is by specific subject, either alphabetical or classified". But this seems to be a matter on which opinions differ, as L. J. Anthony[21] considers that filing by subject is the "least useful from the user's point of view". My own view is that the actual filing is not so important from a retrieval point of view as the indexes to the collection, which will be discussed in section 3, and that probably filing by manufacturer's name is the simpler method. Since material must constantly be kept up to date, there will not be great accumulations of these brochures for one manufacturer, so if details of each product are desired, they can be kept with the folder itself. Very few of the catalogues sent out by manufacturers have a date on them, in fact, so it is important to date-stamp each one as it arrives. Because of the ephemeral nature of the material, and the fact that manufacturers are continually improving their products, or replacing them by newer models, this will be essential to the efficiency of a collection, as out-of-date material can be very misleading. Some manufacturers give helpful instructions on new catalogues, for example: GEC "Motor Control and Power Distribution Centres" carried the direction— "Switchgear Publication SP 530—superseding Technical Descriptions nos. 445 and 468". Others send out looseleaf supplements to existing catalogues. The process of "weeding" files and discarding out-of-date material can be very laborious but necessary.

2.1. Studies of individual libraries in Britain

It was hoped to obtain an indication of the number of libraries in this country actually maintaining a file of trade literature for comparative purposes. A survey of industrial libraries was made by Dr. D. J. Campbell, late Assistant Director of Aslib, in 1956, and the results collected and published in report form by Mr. C. W. Hanson, now Head of Research at Aslib, in 1960. [22] The questionnaire for the survey (sent to a representative selection of industrial libraries) had included several questions on trade literature, but due to several factors, the results on this particular question were not considered sufficiently representative to be published. Also, as the information related to 1956, it is now out of date and unavailable. The general impression gained, however, [23] was that whereas most firms indicated that they possessed collections of catalogues, virtually none of them were able to give any indication of number, or any further particulars. The implication was that the catalogue collection was not treated very methodically (thus producing a very interesting parallel with the situation as described by Dr. Billingsley in America) and trade catalogues were usually the "Cinderellas of the library".

In my own experience I have known several cases of the collection evolving naturally from the material which "blows in" to any large organization becoming too large to be filed cursorily in a spare drawer, and the responsibility for it being passed from one department to another until it is finally regarded as "hopeless" and is abandoned.

In spite of the difficulties enumerated, however, a number of libraries have persevered, realizing the value of having a file of this nature. The examples given below have been collected mostly from personal contact with the libraries mentioned, and it is hoped that they will be a representative selection of types of library, making no claim to be a comprehensive collection of libraries in the country maintaining a file of trade literature.

2.11. Industrial libraries

Libraries in this group will be considered as follows:

    (a) private firms,
    (b) research associations,
    (c) development associations,
    (d) trade associations.

(a) *Private firms.* "Most information departments develop from collections of reference books in the chief engineer's office. At some point, the need is felt for some control of the literature that is steadily building up." [24]

This was certainly my experience with a firm of consultant engineers in London employing about 120 engineers. This firm had recently moved to a new building and had decided that the time had come for a room to be set aside and called "The Library". Since trade literature was a most important source of information to them, and they had till then collected it in a very haphazard fashion, in individual offices, they adopted the SfB system together with its system of binders, classification and associated problems. Since this was a narrow field, SfB satisfied their requirements.

Another very specialized field is that of steel, in Sheffield. The library of the United Steel Cos., one of the biggest concerns, keeps a collection of literature on steel. This is a slightly easier problem, since different types of steel are given definite specification numbers, which makes retrieval easier by "subject", i.e. type of steel. They have invented their own system of numbering catalogues for lending purposes. The library here makes an attempt to collect the other trade literature which is brought into the firm, but I was told that the chief chemist keeps anything in his field in his office, similarly with the chief engineer and others.

Brown–Firth Research Laboratories also keep a collection, although as they are at present in very cramped quarters, awaiting removal to a new library building, they have recently thrown away much of the material they had and are starting a completely new file. This is again mostly literature on steel, but does include material from abroad (e.g. Canada, Sweden, America, Germany, Japan, France, etc.). This is filed by manufacturer's name, but the information is also digested on to card indexes—one of manufacturers, including a summary of the content of each brochure, and a trade-name index, as well as the "steel index" of specifications. It was noted here, however, that any other information which the brochure may contain, apart from steel specifications, is not indexed, e.g. technical information and data on processes in general. They are interested purely in the type of steel described. This firm also has a collection of their own literature, for historical purposes.

Unilever Research Laboratories are another organization whose library collects trade literature. The only details obtained on this were that the information from the collection will soon be included in their punched-card automated system for information retrieval.

In a different field entirely, British Nylon Spinners deal with the problem in a different way.[25] As they are suppliers of raw material to manufacturers, the importance of catalogues to them is perhaps not so great as to some. The purchasing section, however, which has no connection with the library, does maintain a large collection of catalogues, filed by names of manufacturers, but with no subject index ("purchasing staff quickly learn by experience which manufacturers handle which products, so such an index would not justify the cost of making it"). The technical library does collect selectively trade literature which gives technical information, and this is treated as pamphlet literature and not as a separate collection. In the case of technical manuals, these are collected from abroad, from the major yarn producers of the world, for comparison with their own publications, and again are treated as reference books or pamphlets. British Nylon Spinners do, however, maintain a file of their own trade literature for historical record purposes. This is kept quite separately, and is not used currently for the information it contains.

(b) *Research associations.* The two research associations I have chosen to represent this category both have very strong collections of trade literature. The aim of a research association is "to promote research in the field it represents, and to assist member firms in their own research programmes", and as has been pointed out, one method of promoting research is to use existing knowledge. Trade literature should and does therefore play an important part in a service of this sort.

The library of the Production Engineering Research Association (PERA) maintains a collection of approximately 40,000 trade catalogues,[19] about half of which are from abroad, "including most industrialized countries, i.e. USA, Canada, France, Germany, Italy, Holland, Japan, etc.". This is used very extensively by the library inquiry staff, and also by the research department and advisory staff. From information obtained from a member of PERA (Edgar Allen Ltd.) I understand that the collection is also used by them, as they do not collect trade literature themselves, but rely on PERA for technical data and information. Catalogues are also sent on loan when requested—about 10,000 annually.

The collection is filed in subject order, according to their own scheme, which will be compared with others in section 3.

The trade catalogue collection on scientific instruments in the library of the British Scientific Instrument Research Association (BSIRA) has been described very fully in a paper given by Mr. C. Pickup at a SIRA Symposium "Science and Information" held in 1963.[26] In this library the catalogues are filed under manufacturer's name, in alphabetical order of firm (approximately 2000 British firms and a similar number of foreign firms, in a separate sequence, attention being paid to foreign firms with British agents, and cross-references used). The catalogues are scanned and briefly indexed under subject matter ("Unfortunately, time does not permit the luxury of detailed indexing at this stage"). The resulting subject index contains approximately 4700 cards. There are, however, two supplementary indexes for named devices (these will also be discussed in section 3).

This collection is also used very extensively both for specific inquiries and for "state-of-the-art" surveys.

(c) *Development associations.* Their function is "largely promotional . . . organizations devoted to educating and encouraging users and potential customers in the proper and widest application of their products". This again can be greatly stimulated by the use of trade catalogues, since one of the best ways of promoting use or further application of a product is to let manufacturers and customers know what is being produced by competitors.

The Cement and Concrete Association has a very large library stock which includes a comprehensive collection of manufacturers' catalogues on building materials. "Local authorities . . . government departments, and universities . . . are supplied with scientific and technical information free of charge . . . in the interests of the cement and concrete industry generally."[24]

The Zinc Development Association and Lead Development Association Joint Library also attach importance to the information contained in trade literature.[27] If a catalogue contains technical information on the use of zinc and lead it will be abstracted, and published in either *Zinc Abstracts* or *Lead Abstracts*. The information is then recorded by a co-ordinate index system (unspecified) along with the other routine acquisitions of the library, and filed under a running number on the shelves.

In the case of catalogues giving details of competitor products, or containing largely commercial data which are not abstracted, the catalogues are simply filed alphabetically, by name of company (approximately 2000 catalogues at present, with no indexes).

The literature collected by the Aluminium Federation is also treated in two distinct ways.[28] One collection is maintained by the Advisory Services Department, and is purely a reference collection for the use of staff answering trade inquiries. This is filed in alphabetical order of firm, with a classified subject index. The other collection is kept by the library, where it is filed in classification order (according to UDC) and catalogues are sent on loan to inquirers wanting information on products or new treatments.

(d) *Trade associations*. The main function of these associations is "to represent their members in all matters concerning the legal, commercial and trading interests generally."[24] It is unusual to find an association of this nature with an organized library of any kind, although they do sometimes act as a clearing-house for commercial information, putting members in touch with people who can answer their inquiries rather than answering them themselves.

Under this broad heading, however, we can perhaps include the Engineering and Building Centre in Birmingham. Here manufacturers can display their products along with others where they can be assessed by potential buyers.

The Building Centre has adopted the SfB system, and all of the literature is classified by this, and filed under the classification, where brochures deal only with one subject. For larger catalogues covering many subjects, the contents are cross-referenced into a book on the SfB system (which is to be eventually replaced by a card index) and the catalogues placed on shelves alphabetically by name of manufacturer. It is found that they require a three-way cross-reference—first for the maker's name, then for the product

D

and thirdly for the Brand name.[29] Inquiries have been categorized in three groups by the Centre—business, private and students, and percentage inquiries are approximately 35, 35 and 30 respectively.

A similar situation exists in the engineering section where they have a catalogue library, classified by "products" rather than "firms", offering a wide selection to the inquirer. Literature of all exhibitors is displayed in containers, and distributed on request.[30]

The Design Centre in London gives a similar service, although the design index is rather unique. In this, details of each product accepted by the Centre are available. The index covers only goods manufactured in the United Kingdom. For each product the manufacturer completes an appropriate questionnaire form, which may be returned along with a leaflet or brochure on the product. The information supplied on the questionnaire is digested by the Centre, and a full factual description of it, plus photograph, is mounted on a card and the cards are filed in Roneodex Visible Index cabinets. The completed questionnaire and supporting literature are then filed separately for internal reference purposes. At present the index contains approximately 10,000 entries, representing 1400–1500 manufacturers.[31] The index is arranged in broad categories, e.g. brushes; clocks and watches; cutlery and flatware; domestic appliances, etc. Technical advisers have been appointed for each category and products are submitted to them whenever the Council's selection committees want further technical information.

2.12. Government department libraries

The Patent Office Library, where one would perhaps expect a comprehensive collection of trade literature on products for which patents had been accepted, does not in fact appear to deal systematically with this side of the subject. "Pamphlets and manufacturers' catalogues are included when of sufficient size and interest, but it has not been possible yet to make these comprehensive or even representative of all industrial activity."[24] Perhaps when the stock is reorganized and incorporated with that of the National Reference Library of Science and Invention this will be possible.

The collection of the Board of Trade Statistics and Market Intelligence Library is very important, as it consists entirely of foreign literature. Over 12,000 catalogues make up the collection at present. The library receives between 300 and 400 new additions each month, mostly as a result of requests made by United Kingdom firms for particular catalogues. All of these are available for reference, or for loan to firms who cannot visit the library.[32] They lend between 200 and 300 catalogues per month, mainly to United Kingdom manufacturers.

The Ministry of Public Building and Works Library also has an extensive collection, and at least two published descriptions of it are available.[16, 20]

The library attempts complete coverage in its field (i.e. building materials, building equipment, furniture and accessories) and the resulting trade catalogue collection is representative of approximately 8000 firms with details of about 16,000 products. The catalogues are arranged alphabetically by name of firm ("the only unequivocal arrangement for filing"), but there is also again a card index for manufacturers along with a separate index for trade names and one for subject. Each catalogue is date-stamped on arrival, and files are weeded periodically (one letter of the alphabet per month). Two notable features of this collection are first that two copies of each firm's catalogue are collected and filed—this would appear to be a good safeguard against loss, and would save the additional hazard of chasing up catalogues sent on loan. Secondly, a highly condensed account of the main features of the brochure are given on the back of the cards in the trade names index.

2.13. Public libraries

The three public libraries visited in connection with this study were Birmingham, Sheffield and Manchester, and I shall deal with them in that order, Birmingham being the easiest, as their collection was the one mentioned earlier which was first in the Commerce Department, then passed on to the Technical Library, and finally handed over—*en masse*—to the Engineering and Building Centre, where it has already been described.

Sheffield is a rather special case of a public library serving a very specialized industrial city—consequently their organized collection is limited to catalogues on steel. Again, as with United Steel, this simplifies indexing to a certain extent, and they find that a typist can quite easily pick out specification numbers from catalogues for transference to their steel index. Again here, catalogues are filed under name of manufacturer, and the index does include information on foreign steels. Apart from steel, however, the Technical Library also has much trade literature on its shelves in the form of manuals, some of which have been mentioned already in section 1, and also possesses a set of Sweet's Catalogues (1962) which was donated, and collections like the Architects' File and Builders' File.

Manchester Central Technical Library appear to be the most ambitious of the three as far as trade literature files are concerned. The collection at the moment includes only British firms, but it is hoped to include foreign manufacturers very soon. The brochures are classified by Dewey and filed in fairly broad subject groupings. There are two indexes to the collection—one of subject headings (since the files are distinguished by Dewey numbers) and one of firms. Although actual brochures from individual foreign firms are not received at the moment, many firms are represented by cumulated volumes of catalogues, e.g. CIBA, Indanthren (Frankfurt), Oerlikon

(Zurich), etc. Several of the more important British firms are represented in this way also, e.g. ICI, Gallenkamp, etc., and while these are not as up to date as the brochures themselves would be, and are not indexed for information retrieval, they are still valuable sources of information.

A description of the collection was published in 1964 by the library[33] which stated that there were over 13,500 catalogues at that time. An extract from their form-letter requesting literature from firms gives a good idea of the scope of the collection:

> . . . The collection is very well used by two distinct types of readers: those who are anxious to obtain information for business purposes, and secondly, by technical students, who are of course, interested in all new ideas, which are in many cases, only available through the medium of the catalogues issued by the manufacturer.

2.14. Academic libraries

The general impression gained from this type of library as regards trade literature is that being academic institutions, by its very nomenclature, "trade" or "sales" literature is quite outside their field. Perhaps it is the nomenclature which is unfortunate, as if they were more generally known as "technical brochures" more attention might be paid to them. There was one exception to this attitude that I did encounter, however, and, of course, there may be more of which I am unaware. The one I have seen is in the Science Library of Nottingham University.[34] The collection has been in existence for nearly 12 years, and covers any subjects considered to be of interest to the students. Selection is made on this basis, and catalogues are also acquired by donation from members of staff or following specific requests from students or staff. At present the collection consists of 554 items, indexed and filed by name of manufacturer. It was also stated that it was believed that good use was made of the collection, although no statistics were available.

No other examples of collections in academic libraries were investigated. Even in an applied science library, such as the one in Sheffield, where it would probably be of even greater interest to students and staff, any trade literature which they have in the library is filed with their pamphlet collection, and is mostly out of date and very haphazard in coverage.

Much more could be done in this field to assist academic research workers in knowing what products are already available in their field and, more important, what research work has already been done in industry. In this way, a much closer contact could be made between basic and applied research, and closer links with industrial activity could be of benefit to both sides. It should therefore be brought more forcibly to the attention of university libraries that although this information is perhaps in unconventional or inconvenient form, it nevertheless exists and should be exploited—particularly since it would not involve a heavy tax on the precious book grant.

2.2. Collections in other countries

Examples so far in this section have been taken from British libraries, but the situation abroad seems to be slightly more enlightened on the subject, although individual investigation of foreign collections has not been attempted.

The relative importance of trade literature in America seems to have been realized at least to a greater extent than in this country (although Dr. Billingsley in 1960[12] still regarded it as a neglected source of information in many libraries).

A list of American libraries maintaining collections is given in Appendix B.[35] The more significant collections mentioned are perhaps those of the Library of Congress (part of this collection—"170 feet" of catalogues, dated 1890–1920—was handed over to Midwest Interlibrary Center a few years ago)[36] and of the Carnegie Library of Pittsburgh (Technology Department here has maintained a very extensive collection of all types of trade literature for many years, and the Department will answer requests for information).[3] The fact that Columbia University Egleston Library and the University of Houston M. D. Anderson Memorial Library have collections of catalogues is also significant. We could equate these to similar establishments in this country to realize even more fully the difference in attitude, e.g. with the British Museum or some of the major university libraries.

The second list in the Appendix consists of holdings of libraries which not only include trade catalogues in their collections, but also use co-ordinate indexing systems for recording the information contained in them.[37] The Applied Science Corporation of Princeton is a particularly good example of a well-organized system. This serves a staff of 300 personnel (engineers and research workers) and occupies the time of two library staff plus typing help. The Uniterm system, or similar arrangement (in which each indexing term is represented by a card, on which code numbers for manufacturers are listed in ten columns, according to the last digit of the number), seems to suit this type of material, and is used in most of the libraries quoted. Details on use of Applied Science Corp. Library collection were that an average of fifteen searches a day is made for specific items, using four to five terms per search.

In the USSR, Moscow University library has a technical reading room, where students of technology, engineering, etc., can refer to all types of useful technical literature, including periodicals, standards . . . and trade catalogues.[38] While the competition aspect does not affect internal industrial activity in Russia, they obviously still realize the need for knowledge about products and processes of other countries on which to base their further research.

The collection of the Central Technical Library, Prague, which is approximately equivalent to a university library, has already been discussed, but there is a further description, referred to in *Library Science Abstracts*, 1962, in a Hungarian journal.[39] The abstract quotes the collection as including 180,000 catalogues, classified by UDC and recorded on hand-sorted marginal punched cards, retrieved by semi-automatic selection.

Also mentioned was a large collection of trade catalogues in the Textile Machine Institute, Karl Marx Stadt (GDR), and a central collection for the metallurgy and engineering industries in Hungary.

Compared with the collections described in this country, these isolated examples seem to be more significant indications that the importance of information in trade catalogues has been realized to a greater extent abroad than here, and that some of the larger libraries have taken methodical steps towards having a well-organized collection.

3. EXPLOITATION

A collection of trade catalogues, like any other library collection, is of little use in itself if users are not aware of the fund of information it contains. There are several ways in which a library can make this information more easily accessible to the user.

The passive approach is to provide a subject index for the material so that inquirers who know what they are looking for can find whether the collection includes any information on it and, if so, can be directed to the literature of manufacturers who cover it. Too often, however, potential users do not think of unusual sources for information. The more active or promoting role therefore is to produce and even publish surveys or bibliographies from the collection, on specific subjects, or to include information from trade literature in bulletins of abstracts, or technical journals.

Of the collections investigated, the more unusual types of index were the following:

(1) *United Steel Cos.*—the difference here was due to the different nature of the material, namely steel specifications. "Subject indexing" in this context involves simply listing by specification.

(2) *BSIRA*—apart from an index for subject and for trade names here, they also have what they call a "family index" for groups of devices, which show a family resemblance in their names;[26] e.g. at present this is in four sections, and includes over 1000 "meters", 800 "trons", 500 "scopes" and 300 "graphs".

(3) *Design Centre*—information from the literature is digested on to Roneo-dex visible index cards together with photographs, so that in fact in many cases reference to the literature itself is not necessary.

(4) *ZDA/LDA Joint Library*—this library was the only one of those examined which was using a co-ordinate indexing system for trade literature, and even in this case it was simply being treated with the rest of the library materials.

3.1. Indexing

My own view on indexing a collection of this type is that the fewer operations it can be reduced to, the better, since the material itself costs little or nothing, and its "life" in general is short. The most complex of the schemes specially designed for trade literature which were examined was certainly the SfB system. An outline of the main divisions used in this scheme is given in Appendix C. Even from this brief extract from the schedules it is apparent that a reasonable knowledge of the field concerned, as well as of indexing theory, would be necessary for anyone attempting to classify material by this scheme; and even presupposing this knowledge, I would suggest that a great deal of experience with the scheme itself would be needed before the indexing or finding of literature by means of it would achieve any degree of efficiency.

Another specialized scheme was drawn up in the Engineering Library of Iowa State College in 1933[40] based on a decimal division of classes (see Appendix C). For example, the classification numbers for chemical engineering trade literature range from 40.00000 to 49.99999 (chemical engineering being the fourth group in the division of engineering at Iowa). The classes are arranged according to unit operations, i.e. the ten basic groups are types of process, e.g. heat processing, divided into subgroups becoming more specific, e.g. calcination and roasting. The next decimal place is used for classes of equipment. It is only at this second decimal place that the actual catalogue can first appear. A third place, used for more specific type of equipment, then appears; a fourth for manufacturer and a fifth in the event of one manufacturer issuing several pamphlets on a similar subject. All this is no doubt very ingenious, but its limitations are fairly obvious, and its complexity formidable.

The systems in use at PERA and the Ministry of Public Buildings and Works Library (Appendix C) are much simpler in operation, both for indexer and user. These two systems are based on an alphabetical arrangement of subjects, similar to a trade directory. Each subject or topic is given a number, and decimal places are used for further subdivision where necessary.

The final simplification of this type of index is to eliminate all decimal placings and cross-references, and have purely a "dictionary" of words and phrases used by the indexer. This type of index involves a certain amount of time and patience while the collection is being built up, but once a collection has been established, it is advisable to add as few terms as possible. This type of listing is not, of course, a new idea, being the basis of any list of subject headings or thesaurus. The important aspect of it, however, is the reduction in ambiguity, and the adaptability of the scheme to use in individual libraries.

The American system of "Uniterm" cards employs this principle, and the fact that it has been adopted for collections of trade catalogues in some American libraries (Appendix B) indicates that it is a suitable medium for this type of material. In this system, names of manufacturers are coded with a running number, and cards are then made out for each "concept" or indexing term. Each brochure is examined, indexing terms are noted (anything from 3 to 50 terms per brochure), and the code number of the manufacturer written on each card. (Details of this system in practical use in the library of the Applied Science Corporation, Princeton, are described fully in the publication previously mentioned in this connection.[37])

For libraries in this country wishing to collect trade literature methodically, I would suggest that this basic type of system would be the most economical from the time aspect. Information could be recorded on feature cards, similar to Uniterm cards—one for each indexing term chosen, together with additional terms such as bibliography, data, properties, installation, etc., which could be applied in all subjects, and also trade names (thus eliminating the need for a separate sequence). Instead of listing code numbers of manufacturers on each card, "Peek-a-boo" cards would be more flexible, holes being assigned to manufacturers, since checking for coincident holes would be quicker than checking matching numbers on various cards, especially for a file of any size.

3.2. Commercial exploitation of trade catalogues

This aspect of the subject has only been mentioned in passing so far. Under this heading are included services such as Sweet's Cataloging Service in the United States, or Standard Catalogues Company in this country, which collect catalogues from many manufacturers and present them for sale in a uniform classified order (in the case of Sweet's, in 17 volumes). The "Architects' File" and "Builders' File" give the same service on payment. Two new services of a slightly different nature have been started in this country recently, one by the New Products Centre, and the other by Materials Data Ltd. The first claims to act as a "central clearing house of information about new products and processes . . . as they come on the market anywhere in the world", covering the "whole range of the manufacturing industry". A journal is issued monthly—*New Products International*, which includes abstracts of literature about the world's new products and processes in the previous month. Taking the November 1964 issue as a specimen, 56% of the products represented are from the United Kingdom, which seems to be slightly unbalanced in view of the world trade position. The United States accounts for 23% of the entries—less than half the United Kingdom representation. In fact, the United Kingdom, USA, France, West Germany, Belgium and Switzerland collectively account for 96% of the products, leaving the remaining 4% for information from the USSR and eight other countries. This is only one issue, of course, but it claims to be representative of all new products and processes produced during the preceding month. Materials Data has not been established long enough to give similar details of use, but it is more of an information service rather than a clearing house for the actual catalogues. Uniformly prepared data sheets are produced, recording the properties of metals and alloys, with a comprehensive index. These are presented on feature cards, which, together with a set of manufacturers' cards, are hired to libraries or companies. This would mean that each company could have its own collection of information from trade catalogues without handling the material itself. I was told also[41] that information is constantly kept up to date, this service being included in the annual cost of hiring. The cards, from specimen samples, appear to be extremely comprehensive, and contain much valuable information.

This type of service may well be of great value where staff is in short supply, but I feel that individual eccentricities in firms can be satisfied more easily by someone connected with the firm.

3.3. Surveys, bibliographies and abstracts

The other active and promoting role in the exploitation of trade literature is by surveys, abstracts, etc.

British Scientific Instruments Research Association compile surveys periodically in their field. These are usually produced in tabular form, containing as much relevant information as possible, on the basis of work in hand on a particular problem. Surveys already available may be used as a guide, but when a new one is produced, it is given a number, a card is placed in the subject index referring to that number, and all previous cards appertaining to that survey are removed or destroyed. This type of survey is what is generally known as a "state-of-the-art" survey and can be extremely valuable in searching time, for while no two inquiries are phrased in exactly the same way, or require the same information, they do often overlap to a certain extent, and a previous review of this nature can provide a basis to work on, and eliminate much unnecessary duplication of effort.

Surveys of this type are also published in journals, e.g. *Control* and *British Communications and Electronics*.

Another very valuable aspect of this is the fact that some trade catalogues do in fact include relevant bibliographies from technical literature, e.g.

Mond Nickel Co., *Magnetic properties of the nickel–iron alloys*, 55 references, American Magnesium Corp., *Designing with magnesium*, 62 references.

Abstracting of information from trade literature is perhaps more common, however, and equally valuable, as this type of material is not covered in general by abstracting periodicals (with the exception of *Zinc Abstracts* and *Lead Abstracts* which have already been mentioned). Some of the more outstanding technical journals which provide this service are listed in Appendix D, with some details.

Again, this is only a selection, but shows that even comparatively "learned" journals are paying attention to the importance of the information contained in trade literature.

This type of service could be of great assistance to librarians in building up a collection of catalogues and in bringing the materials to the attention of users. Since the literature is in most cases distributed free of charge, and information would only be of interest fairly soon after it was available, it would be unreasonable to expect any central lending collection to provide information. It is therefore up to individual libraries to make this available.

3.4. Economics

The economics of the question are also quite encouraging. It is a well-known fact that in the majority of special libraries, much more outlay is made on staff salaries than on actual materials, and this would also be the case for trade literature. If the suggested systems for indexing were adopted, however, one member of staff with some technical background could spot index terms in a number of documents in a reasonably short time, and the remainder of the work (i.e. punching, filing, etc.) could be done by clerical assistants. Outlay on material is virtually nil. Equipment for storage and retrieval of information from the material would not demand much more financial outlay.

More libraries, and particularly academic libraries serving large proportions of science or technical students and research workers, might well consider the advantages of maintaining a file of trade catalogues which would help to bridge the gap in communication which still seems to exist between industrial activity and academic research.

APPENDIX A

Examples of trade literature almost equivalent to textbooks on various subjects.

1. ALLEGHENY LUDLUM STEEL CORP.
    Stainless steel handbook, 1956. 120 pp.
    Includes technical data and information, e.g. on selection, analysis, properties, and fabrication of various types of steel, and tables, reference material and index.

2. ALUMINIUM DEVELOPMENT ASSOCIATION
   Aluminium rainwater goods. 40 pp. 10s. 6d.
   Properties, description of goods in service (ref. to British Standards) designs, installations, diagrams, data, etc.

3. AMERICAN MAGNESIUM CORP.
   Designing with magnesium, 1943. 161 pp.
   Sales talk, i.e. advantage of magnesium over other metals, etc., choice of fabrication, properties, plus bibliography (62 references), tables and index.

4. AMERICAN STEEL AND WIRE CO.
   Manual of spring engineering, 1941. 130 pp.
   Includes (among engineering data suggested in the title, and information on various types of spring) formulae and problems on springs.

5. W. AND T. AVERY LTD.
   The Avery business, 1730–1918, 1949. 86 pp.
   History of Company. Bibliography (22 references)—mainly to historical items.

6. BENDIX AVIATION CORP. BENDIX PRODUCTS DIV.
   ABC of vacuum power brakes, 1942. 132 pp.
   Theory of pressure, history of the Company and its use and expansion of the theory, details on present products.

7. BRITISH ALUMINIUM CO. LTD.
   Aluminium—facts and figures, 1959. 162 pp.
   Details of compositions, physical and mechanical properties, etc.; accompanied by a series of "application brochures" suggesting possible applications in various fields.

8. BRITISH METAL SINTERINGS ASSOCIATION
   Metal sinterings: a guide to their application in industry. 32 pp.
   Theory of process, with diagrams and illustrations; advantages, applications (photographs), properties, graphs, etc. Information requirements for manufacturer.

9. FERODO LTD.
   Friction materials for engineers, 1961. 54 pp.
   Details of materials, including much theory, accompanied by formulae, tables, etc., plus data sheets.

10. FIRTH–BROWN LTD.
    (i)   *MITIA carbide tips and tools,* 1949. 104 pp.
          Spiral-bound—details of tools, data, etc.
    (ii) *Small tool products,* 1933. 500 pp.
          Hard-bound—arranged in sections; diagrams, data, etc.

11. MOND NICKEL CO. LTD.
    (i)   *Transformation characteristics of direct-hardening nickel–alloy steels,* 91 pp.
          All theory, graphs, etc. Bibliography (86 references).
    (ii) *S.G. Iron in steelworks plant,* 21 pp.

12. HENRY WIGGIN AND CO. LTD.
    (i)   *Wiggin nickel alloys v. fluorine and fluorine compounds,* 1959. 40 pp.
          Corrosion problems, generation, use, etc.; hydrofluoric acid, future of fluorine chemistry; details of service for further information, e.g. access to data, etc.
    (ii) *Wiggin nickel alloys v. caustic alkalies.*
          Similar to above, with industrial applications.

APPENDIX B

(i) Examples of American libraries having collections of trade catalogues.[27] (Statistics given in parentheses are indications of the overall amount of literature which includes the special collection but is not necessarily limited to it.)

1. LIBRARY OF CONGRESS
   No information as to size or scope of collection.

2. CHICAGO HISTORICAL SOCIETY LIBRARY
   No information.

3. COLUMBIA UNIVERSITY, EGLESTON LIBRARY
    Vols.: 200,000 American manufacturers' catalogues.
4. UNION CARBIDE AND CARBON CORP., PURCHASING DEPT. LIBRARY
    Vols.: 1500.
5. BLAW–KNOX CO. CHEMICAL PLANTS DIV. LIBRARY
    Vols.: 1000.
6. CARNEGIE LIBRARY OF PITTSBURGH
    Vols.: 23,589 catalogued.
7. RUST ENGINEERING CO. LIBRARY
    Vols.: 730.
8. UNIVERSITY OF HOUSTON, M. D. ANDERSON MEMORIAL LIBRARY
    Vols.: 1000.
9. YOUNG RADIATOR CO.
    3500 manufacturers' catalogues, indexed.

(ii) Further American examples, where information was given on methods of storage and retrieval of information from the collections.[28]

1. APPLIED SCIENCE CORP. OF PRINCETON
    Product literature files—brochures, pamphlets, etc.—on electronics, 5500 manufacturers with approximately twenty pieces of literature each.
    Uniterm system for indexing—approximately 3500 Uniterms. Three to fifty terms used per document.
    Additions: about 200 items per week.
2. BAY AREA AIR POLLUTION CONTROL DISTRICT
    Uniterm file for trade literature.
3. CONVAIR (DIV. OF GENERAL DYNAMICS CORP. POMONA)
    Brochures, sales literature.
    Omnidex cards. Twenty entries on average per document.
    6000 terms at present—approximately 3·9 per accession.
    Searching by Peek-a-Boo techniques.
4. FOOD MACHINERY AND CHEMICAL CORP.
    Sales brochures, technical bulletins from other companies.
    Indexed by machine-sorted, punched-card system (IBM).
    Dictionary of subject-indexing terms—approximately 6–15 subject term codes punched into each card—about 1000 terms so far (maximum for card 2100).
    Author or corporate author also coded and punched in card.
5. MERCK, SHARP AND DOHME RES. LABS. (DIV. OF MERCK AND CO. INC.)
    Trade literature.
    Alphabetical dictionary of both specific and generic terms.
    See also section 1.[15]
6. INTERSTATE ELECTRONICS CORP.
    Approximately 35,000 brochures from 7000 companies.
    Additions: about twenty new companies per week.
    Subject index on Roladex—approximately 7000 subject cards, with 30,000 entries on seven Roladexes.

APPENDIX C

Outline of various systems in use for the classification of trade literature (see section 3).

1. SfB—outline of main tables

Principal divisions
A   Theory
B   Practice
C   Earthwork

D	Materials
E–X	Construction
(1)–(8)	Functional elements
(9)	Buildings

Each principal division is divided into—

Main groups
e.g.

D	Materials : general
Da	Materials : properties
Db	Materials : testing, etc.

or

(9)	Buildings
(91)	Engineering works and agricultural buildings
(92)	Civic, administrative, public, commercial and office buildings, etc.

Some main groups are then divided into—

Subgroups
e.g.

Dp	Materials, aggregates and fills : general
Dpl	Aggregate : mineral
Dp2	Aggregates : bricks, concrete, etc.
Dp5	Fills : shavings
Dp6	Fills : powders, etc.

The subgroups are not further subdivided by SfB notation, but guidance is given on how best to divide the subjects by—

Name sections
e.g.

Bb5	Power plant : general
Bb6	Power plant : pneumatic
Bb5	Power plant : steam, etc.

Further suggestions are also made if still more subdivision is required.

2. IOWA STATE COLLEGE, ENGINEERING LIBRARY—outline of scheme for the cataloguing of chemical engineering trade literature according to unit operations.

General groups

40	General catalogs
41	Building
42	Power plant operation
43	Heat processing, etc.

Subgroups
e.g.

40.0	Chemical engineering
.1	Chemical and food processing
.2	Hardware supplies
.3	Laboratory supplies, etc.

43.0	Annealing and tempering
.1	Autoclaving and sterilization
.2	Gas power
.3	Liquid fuel power, etc.

Further divisions are made according to—

Class of equipment

e.g.

43.3	Drying
.30	General and theory
.31	Agitated driers
.32	Board driers, etc.

Type of equipment

e.g.

47.49	Valves
.491	Angle
.492	Globe, etc.

Manufacturer

e.g.

47.4910	Angle valves—CRANE CO.
.4912	Angle valves—GLOBE MFR. CO., etc.

And *similar pamphlets* from same manufacturer

e.g.

47.31030	Centrifugal pumps—GOULD PUMPS INC.
.31031	Centrifugal pumps (selection charts)—GOULD PUMPS INC., etc.

3. MINISTRY OF WORKS PUBLIC BUILDING AND WORKS LIBRARY

Subject index for trade catalogues.

101	Abattoir equipment
102	Abrasives
103	Acetylene (other than welding)
104	Acoustical treatments (*see also* : Tiles : Acoustic), etc.
112	Alloys
113	Aluminium
.1	Foil
.2	Windows, doors, roofing
.3	Sections
.4	Alloys
.5	Paint and surface finishes
.6	Other products
	Anchors (*see* cramps, dowels and anchors)
114	Anodizing, etc.

4. PRODUCTION ENGINEERING RESEARCH ASSOCIATION LIBRARY

Subject divisions for trade catalogues.

1.	Air equipment
2.	Abrasives
3.	Acetylene equipment
4.	Adhesives, etc.

with subdivisions for each heading

e.g.

2.	Abrasives
2.1	Miscellaneous
2.2	Cloth, paper and discs
2.3	Powders and pastes, etc.

Also, a third digit denoting position of catalogue in section (since this collection is filed by subject)

i.e. 2.2/1, 2.2/2, etc.

APPENDIX D

Examples of periodicals which abstract information from trade literature.

Engineer. Section entitled "New Products and Processes" giving brief notes on each, with readers' card service for more information.
  Also reports of new brochures. For example:
    1963. STONE MANGANESE MARINE LTD.
    Propellor and watertight door brochure.
      Also a general leaflet, which gives particulars of the Company's products in twelve languages, etc.
Engineering. Similar section entitled "New Plant and Equipment" with readers' card service for further information.
Instrument Review. Section entitled "Instrument Digest".
  Abstract of literature, with photographs, and again a reply-card system.
  Also, under the section "Literature" are included details of new leaflets, including those from foreign companies, giving addresses.
Metallurgia: the British Journal of Metals. A monthly list, under "Current Literature" of recent trade publications.
R & D: Research and Development for Industry. Section on "New Brochures", with abstract of information and address of firm, along with an *R & D* number "for further information".
Machines Françaises (publication in French, English, German and Spanish).
  "Review of the foreign technical press."
  "The review . . . will be glad to give all information on machines of French manufacture" but also includes features on British, German and Spanish machinery.
Schweizer Archiv für angewandte Wissenschaft und Technik. In the section "Buchbesprechungen", one or two trade manuals are mentioned. For example:
    Katalog über Lehren und Erdmasse published by the firm Kunkel–Voba, Gesellschaft für Messtechnik und Präzisionstechnik.

REFERENCES

1. ADVISORY COUNCIL ON SCIENTIFIC POLICY, *Annual report, 1963–4,* Cmnd. 2538, 1964.
2. BOTTLE, R. T. (Ed.), *Use of the chemical literature,* Butterworth, 1962.
3. CRANE, E. J., *et al., Guide to the literature of chemistry,* 2nd ed., Wiley, 1957.
4. GOULD, R. F. (Ed.), *Searching the chemical literature,* Advances in Chemistry Series, no. 33, American Chemical Society, 1961.
5. MELLON, M. G., *Chemical publications: their nature and use,* 3rd ed., McGraw-Hill, 1958.
6. MORLEY, L. H., *Contributions toward a special library glossary,* 2nd ed., New York, Special Libraries Association, 1950.
7. ANON., Companies put new zip into old sales tool, *Chem. Eng. News,* **38,** 34–6 (1960).
8. AGARD EVANS, B., and MARTIN, W. K., Information in the building industry, *Aslib Proc.* **12,** 51–84 (1960).
9. PERA, *Publications for industry,* Procs. Conf. 25–27 June 1963, unpublished.
10. BRITISH STANDARDS INSTITUTION, *Sizes of manufacturers' trade and technical literature,* B.S. 1311, 1955.
11. MOORE, M., and HOLLEMAN, W. R., Commercial reference sources, *Libr. J.* **72,** 1599–1601 (1947).
12. BILLINGSLEY, S. V., Manufacturers' literature: an information goldmine, *Sci-Tech News,* 8–9 (1960).
13. ORGANIZATION FOR ECONOMIC CO-OPERATION AND DEVELOPMENT, *Does your firm need its own information service?,* 1962.
14. PETERA, J., Ve službách budování socialismu: 15 let práce Knihovny vysokých škol technických v Praze (In the service of the construction of socialism: 15 years of work in libraries of Technical High Schools in Prague), *Technická knihovna,* 49–59 (1960).

15. BOARD OF TRADE, *Statistics and market intelligence library* (1962).
16. AGARD EVANS, B., and CHILD, P. J., Trade literature, *in* BURKETT, J., and MORGAN, T. S. (Eds.), *Special materials in the library*, 1963.
17. DIXON, K., Producing trade and technical literature, *Insulation*, **7**, 81–2 (1963).
18. BRITISH STANDARDS INSTITUTION, *Dimensions of folders and files for correspondence filing*, B.S. 1467, 1957.
19. WATTS, V. C., Production Engineering Research Association, private communication (1964).
20. COLLISON, R. L., *The treatment of special material in libraries*, 2nd ed., Aslib, 1957.
21. ANTHONY, L. J., Filing and storing material, *in* ASLIB, *Handbook of special librarianship and information work*, 2nd ed., 1964.
22. HANSON, C. W. (Ed.), *Survey of information/library units . . .* , Aslib, 1960.
23. HANSON, C. W., Aslib Research Dept., private communication (1964).
24. IRWIN, R., and STAVELEY, R. (Eds.), *Libraries of London*, 2nd ed., Library Association, 1961.
25. ASHWORTH, W., British Nylon Spinners Ltd., private communication (1964).
26. PICKUP, C., Scientific instruments, accessories and components: their commercial sources, *in* SIRA Symposium, Science and information, 1963, unpublished.
27. BLAGDEN, J., Zinc Development and Lead Development Association Joint Library, private communication (1964).
28. BARNES, W. C. E., Aluminium Federation, private communication (1964).
29. MATHEWS, E. P., Birmingham Building Centre, private communication (1964).
30. PLASKETT, A., Birmingham Engineering Centre, private communication (1964).
31. PURVES, M. E., Design Centre, private communication (1964).
32. HARVEY, J. M., Board of Trade Statistics and Market Intelligence Library, private communication (1964).
33. MANCHESTER PUBLIC LIBRARY, *What's available in the technical library*, 1964.
34. OUGH, C. J., Nottingham University Science Library, private communication (1965).
35. ASH, L., *comp.* Subject collections, 2nd ed., Bowker (1961).
36. BUDINGTON, W. S., The paradoxical trade catalog, *Spec. Lib.* **46**, 113–17 (1955).
37. NATIONAL SCIENCE FOUNDATION, *Non-conventional technical information services in current use*, 1958, 1959, 1962.
38. PYSHNOVA, T. P., Obsluzhivanie v chitalnykh zalakh universitetskitch bibliotek (Collections in the reading-room in the university library), *Biblioteki SSSR*, 76 (1964).
39. PARANYI, G., A prospektustár—újtípusú speciális múszaki könyvtár (The trade catalogue collection—a new type of special library), *Müszaki könyvtárosok tájékozatója*, **9**, 4–18 (1962).
40. VILBRANDT, F. C., The cataloguing of chemical engineering trade literature according to unit operations, *J. Chem. Educ.* **10**, 354 (1933).
41. BAKER, G. G., Materials Data Ltd., private communication (1965).

3. A SURVEY OF THE PROVISION AND USE OF LIBRARY SERVICES IN CERTAIN LONDON PRISONS

PENELOPE A. ROWLINSON

Staffordshire County Library

ABSTRACT

Four prison libraries have been studied in this survey—those in Holloway prison for women, and in Pentonville, Wandsworth, and Wormwood Scrubs prisons for men. It is believed that they constitute a representative sample of the prisons in London. It is hoped that they will also, to some extent, exemplify the conditions existing throughout England and Wales.

All four of these prison libraries are now the responsibility of their local public library, which buys books for them out of a capitation grant made by the Prison Department of the Home Office. It also supervises the organization of the prison library and acts as consultant. It does not actually supply the staff to run the library, although it does provide professional staff as advisers.

All routine work is carried out by selected prisoners, under the supervision of the library officer.

The libraries contain quite large permanent stocks, and the books are in good condition and of varied types. Prisoners also have access through a request service to all the books in the system which serves them. Censorship is not very strict, and most tastes can be accommodated.

It was found that extremely good use is made of the library service. Nearly all prisoners join the library, and most borrow a considerable number of books. Some progress towards more solid reading was noticed— particularly amongst those serving long sentences. In Pentonville and Holloway, this progress is assisted by the advice of the professional librarians who make frequent visits.

The library service in the most progressive prisons is fast becoming quite as good as at branches outside, but shortage of money and staff are hampering further progress. The contribution made by the Prison Department is not adequate to cover the service provided at some prisons, and certainly does not encourage expansion.

HISTORICAL PERSPECTIVE

The Prison Act of 1877 vested ownership and control of all local prisons in the Secretary of State. Thenceforward all prisons, both convict and local, were effectively under one administration, and it became possible to formulate and carry through a uniform policy.

The prison library service is very closely linked with the concepts of education and reformation.

Prisons were for long regarded as places of retribution or, at best, of detention. Books could have no place in a system designed to make life as unpleasant as possible.

The eighteenth century had seen a movement towards prison reform. But it was Mrs. Elizabeth Fry who, at the beginning of the nineteenth century, really started the movement for education and rehabilitation. Mrs. Fry aimed at a reformative training which included plenty of useful work and attention to education and to religious instruction; she wanted a library to be provided.

For another half century the movement towards good prison libraries advanced extremely slowly. Then, after the Prison Act of 1877, attention was given to the prisoners' education, and basic instruction in reading, writing and arithmetic was given. A prisoner was allowed to borrow a library book when he had reached a specified standard of reading. A little later, the progressive stage system of sentences was introduced, and the fuller use of library books was one of the privileges granted to the prisoner as he progressed.

The Gladstone Committee Report of 1895 underlined the importance of education for prisoners. One of the recommendations of the Departmental Committee (1910) on the supply of books to prisoners was that a 1s. 3d. capitation grant for books should be paid for the entire prison population. The committee also recommended the provision of bound copies of illustrated periodicals for illiterates, and of quality weekly and monthly reviews.

In the 1920's, thanks largely to the financial generosity of the Carnegie United Kingdom Trust, an educational library was created and housed at Wakefield. This still acts as a centre to which requests for educational books may be sent. The post of librarian officer was created at each prison in 1934.

In 1938 East Suffolk County Library supplied a loan collection to Hollesley Bay Borstal Institution. The collection was increased in the early years of the war, and the local authority applied for a grant towards expenses, which they received in 1942 at a rate of 2s. per head of average population. This was a notable step towards the present-day close co-operation between public libraries and prison libraries.

War-time conditions provided a further impetus. As many classes were discontinued, the demand for books increased. However, it was almost impossible to buy non-fiction cheaply. Circumstances therefore forced the Prison Commissioners to seek to co-operate actively with the public library service. In 1944, with the approval of the Library Association and the County Libraries Section, Durham County Library took over the library at Durham Prison.

The public libraries at first sent in collections of books, which they exchanged at regular intervals. As rate-supported institutions, they could not purchase books which they did not intend to make available to the whole community. So a capitation grant was essential. In 1948 this was increased to 5s.

THE PRESENT DAY

Today the responsibility for the provision of books for prisoners rests with the Prison Commissioners.

There are two ways in which they can satisfy this obligation. The first is to provide the service themselves. In this case they provide a collection of books in the prison. This is supplemented by the Educational Library at Wakefield, which is intended to receive requests from all prisons.

The other method open to the Commissioners is to invite the local authority to co-operate in providing a library service, and to pay the authority a capitation grant towards the cost. The Wakefield Library is still available for use, if required. This is now the more frequently used method.

In the 1960 report, *Prisons and borstals*, the Commissioners said of the co-operation with local authorities: "This development has greatly increased the facilities and prisoners are encouraged from the beginning of their sentence to make full use of them."

The idea of allowing prisoners only very restricted reading matter during the first stages of their sentence has disappeared. Thus, in theory at least, the prisoner gets as good a service as the citizen borrowing from any branch library.

Writing in 1952, Sir Lionel Fox said, in *The English prison and borstal systems:* " . . . It ought to be, and in no long time will be, possible to say that (saving the often unsuitable premises) any prisoner may get as good a library service inside a prison as out."

EXPLANATORY NOTE

During the course of this survey, four of the London prisons were studied particularly, namely Holloway, Pentonville, Wandsworth and Wormwood Scrubs.

Holloway is a prison for women. Because of the smaller number of women prisoners, many different classes of offender are housed in separate parts of the same prison. Holloway has local prison accommodation for 534 women, with a daily average population of 303 (figures as at 31 December 1963). Every prisoner, on committal, is sent to a local prison, and the majority of prisoners have to remain there, as they are ineligible for transfer. In Holloway there is also regional prison accommodation for 81, with a daily average population of 57. Regional prisons are training institutions for selected prisoners serving a sentence of 12 months or more. Personality is the criterion upon which the selection is based. These prisoners have training facilities and plenty of work. Holloway also acts as a central prison, with a daily average of 7 plus an average of 8 preventive detainees. Central prisons are theoretically for those serving sentences of 3 years or more; however, in practice overcrowding usually prevents these prisons accommodating recidivists serving less than 5 years. There is also accommodation in Holloway for corrective trainees, although there were none in during 1963. Corrective training is a sentence, from 2 to 4 years, given to younger recidivists over 21 who are still considered trainable. Holloway also contains borstal accommodation for 54 girls, with a daily average of 19.

Pentonville has local prison accommodation for 956 men, with a daily average population of 1250. It is also a corrective training prison, with a daily average of 1.

Wandsworth has local accommodation for 1123 men, with a daily average of 1499. It also contains a regional prison acting as an allocation centre. This part has accommodation for 37, with a daily average of 26. However, the prisoners only stay for a very short time before being sent to the prison in which they will serve the remainder of their sentence.

Wormwood Scrubs has local accommodation for 644 men, with a daily average of 642 plus 67 young prisoners. It has central accommodation for 323 men, with a daily average of 326. It also has a borstal for 317 boys, with a daily average of 309.

Out of a total prison accommodation for 20,593 men, Pentonville, Wandsworth and Wormwood Scrubs have, between them, accommodation for 3083 men. Holloway has places for 615 women out of a total of 1274 places.

HOLLOWAY

Since 1 April 1960, Islington public libraries have been responsible for the supply of books to Holloway Prison.

Before this date, Islington public libraries deposited in the prison a small selection of 450 books to supplement the prison's own collection. The prison could also call upon the resources of the Wakefield Educational Library.

The section of the prison library containing Islington's books was open for 2 hours each week, and a member of the public libraries' staff was in attendance to advise readers and to take special requests for books. The loan collection was mainly used for recreational reading. Each prisoner was allowed to borrow two volumes at a time. The librarian reported a weekly issue of 110–130 volumes in 1956–7, and of about 150 in 1957–8.

This loan collection must have improved considerably the prison's library resources. However, Islington had been conscious, for some time before 1960, of the limitations of the service which they were able to provide. They were unable, in particular, to cope with the persistent demand for new books.

In his annual report for 1959–60, the Chief Librarian comments:

> Our contribution towards the reading demands of those in Holloway Prison has, in the past, been small. . . . We have been conscious of the inadequacy of this arrangement but have hitherto been unable to improve it.
>
> However, we are now pleased to report that we have been asked to take over responsibility for the supply of books to Holloway Prison.

Since 1960 Islington has treated Holloway prison library as one of its branch libraries.

The prison library is hampered by lack of space. It is the size of three cells knocked together, with access to a fourth cell which is used as an office. Extra stock has to be stored in several, separate locked cells. However, the library is due for enlargement in the very near future. It is expected to be about seven cells. The space can only be increased lengthwise, due to the structure of the building—cells along a corridor. This may mean that expansion would eventually lead to the creation of a rather awkwardly shaped room. The library can expand in one direction only, as it is situated next to a landing which cannot be used—this will also eventually limit the size; however, this problem is unlikely to arise for some considerable time.

The library is situated in an open wing of the prison. Small collections are also housed in the borstal wing, in the hospital and in a wing where women are given housecraft training. The other readers come to the main library. It is not basically an attractive room, being rather dark and having dull paintwork. However, the library officer makes it extremely pleasant with bulbs and flowers. The present writer visited the library shortly after Christmas, when it had been decorated to look most attractive; not only were there flowers and plants, but also small decorated tinsel trees and strings of tinsel across the ceiling.

The books form a permanent collection, as at the branch libraries. The stock, on 31 March 1964, totalled 10,228 volumes, composed of 6832 fiction and 3396 non-fiction. A high proportion of these books has plastic jackets, which helps to improve the appearance of the library. Books are either bought new, or are sent from Islington's stock provided that they have at least 6 months' life. Quite frequently borrowers outside would not look at a rather dull-looking copy which a prisoner would appreciate; nevertheless, torn or dilapidated copies are never used. The other source of supply is from prisoners themselves. They are permitted, at the Governor's discretion, to have books sent in by friends provided that the books become the property of the prison library when the prisoner has read them. However, many of these books are paperbacks, and not necessarily of great use to the library.

The life of the books is reported as good: probably better than in an average branch. Mutilation is almost unknown. However, a collection of shabby books, which are uncatalogued, is kept for receptions, and, occasionally for very disturbed women. It has been found that the greatest risk of damage to books is in a woman's first 24 hours in prison. At reception she is given four books to occupy her for the short while until she can come to choose some herself. The woman will probably be extremely confused and may show her distress by destroying whatever comes to hand in her cell—library books being an obvious target.

Prisons are one of the very few communities in which every member normally belongs to the library. At reception, every prisoner receives her books, and most make considerable use of the library thereafter. The readers are allowed open access to the books. They may borrow an unlimited number of books with no restrictions of type of book. They visit the library weekly, and, although they may keep books longer than a week, they are expected to bring the books in for renewal so that they can be accounted for. The total issues for 1963–4 were 56,560.

A simple charging method is used. The reader's number is entered on the book card and the running number of the book is entered on the reader's cell card. The woman needs a cell card because a list must be kept of the articles she is permitted to have in her cell.

A library officer is in charge of the library. She is assisted by two prisoners. These assistants are usually stars, i.e. first offenders, who are generally considered fortunate as it is pleasant work. The officer and her assistants carry out all the library routines. A senior librarian from Islington public libraries visits the prison once a week. She can then give advice to the officer on any problems of organization, she can give valuable assistance to individual readers and she can take any special requests. Specialized requirements are supplied from the public library stock, just as requests are supplied to any reader. It should be noted that, despite weekly visits by the professional librarian, it is essential that the library officer should be enthusiastic and efficient. The pleasant atmosphere and attractive decoration in this library are very largely attributable to the officer.

Fiction forms the greatest demand. This is often because there is a very large number of women serving short sentences, and there are also those awaiting transfer to other prisons; these women do not usually settle down to serious reading. Indeed, some of them are confused and need help with choosing even the very light fiction. Romances and thrillers are very popular, so are spine-chillers—Dennis Wheatley being particularly popular in this field. But plenty of the more solid fiction is read, including classics. The popularity of a book is always increased if it is filmed. Among the non-fiction, biographies are very well liked—especially the lives of film stars and actors. Accounts of war experiences are also enjoyed, as are such works as picture books of London. Poetry is far more popular than in most branch libraries. Music scores are also borrowed.

The library itself does not take any newspapers or periodicals. A representative selection is supplied to each wing. However, the women can buy them out of their earnings or can have them sent in by friends. They are allowed one daily and one evening paper, one Sunday paper and two weeklies. These are selected from an approved list, which is quite comprehensive and includes the most popular women's magazines. If the woman has a paper regularly, she has it sent in direct from one of several selected newsagents. All newspapers are sent to the library, and, from there, distributed to the various wings. There is no need to examine the papers that come from the newsagents. However, any papers or books that come from friends have to be searched in the library before distribution to ensure that nothing is concealed within them—such as tobacco. A newspaper or magazine is not issued until the old copy is returned. Back numbers of old magazines are bound, mainly at Parkhurst Prison. Old copies of *Woman* and similar magazines are in great demand. The public library also provides back numbers of illustrated magazines, which are bound and issued to illiterate women. Foreign language magazines are also very useful in supplementing the book stock suitable for foreigners.

Facilities are available for prisoners to take special educational courses leading to GCE, various diplomas, or even to a degree. The public library can be particularly useful here in supplying the less frequently used books of a specialized nature. The Wakefield Educational Library is not used. However, women prisoners work for examinations far more rarely than men. Xenia Field, in *Under lock and key: a study of women in prison*, writes: "Although there are far fewer illiterate women in prison than men, the general intelligence is considerably lower. It is rare for a woman prisoner to work for the GCE. There was only one candidate in 1961 for this exam, although all facilities were available, and no candidate during 1962."

Censorship is in the hands of the Governor. When library censorship was part of the chaplain's duties, it was often very restrictive—any mention of sex or the use of any vulgar language automatically excluded a book from the library. Now, however, a much more liberal attitude is adopted, although some books are still withheld. Books about true crime or living criminals are not permitted, as it is felt that they foster the idea that the criminal is a glamorous individual, and also because disciplinary problems might arise should the criminal come into prison. Books dwelling excessively upon sex are also excluded. Law books are provided for a woman who is making an appeal, but otherwise they are limited—particularly as they are generally very expensive, and quickly become out of date. Works of medicine and psychology are treated very cautiously, because people confined for long periods are apt to brood upon imagined symptoms. Until comparatively recently, detective stories were not permitted, however unrealistic the treatment of the story might be; but now fictional detective stories are widely read. It is thought that the women would read these stories outside, and that their husbands and boy friends are probably reading them, so it helps them to maintain more normal contacts.

Thus the women get a very similar library service in prison to that which they would receive if they were members of their public library outside.

PENTONVILLE

Islington public libraries have been responsible for providing the entire library service to Pentonville Prison since 1947. Before this date the public library had provided a loan collection of 1000 volumes, with five copies of each book. This loan collection proved unworkable through difficulties in changing collections and because a large enough collection was impracticable.

When the public library took over full responsibility in 1947, they discovered that the books belonging to the prison were in a tattered state, such as they themselves would certainly have discarded. They began to build up a deposit collection, which superseded the prison's collection.

They started gradually, acquiring an understanding of the problems peculiar to prison communities and fostering interest amongst the male members of the public library staff. There was already a library room, with a library officer in charge. The public library established a charging routine. They gave advice to those prisoners who could afford to have books sent in to them by friends. They obtained additional shelving and put up displays and notices, and they increased the number of books allowed per man.

The library consists of seven cells, and therefore has seven windows along one side. The furniture and fittings were made in the prison. There are two doors. The borrowers come in through one, and the assistants are seated at an enclosed counter on their left. Borrowers leave by the other door. The fiction is arranged around the walls, and the non-fiction on island shelves, which have display fittings on them. Reserved or returned books, or those in any other special category, are put on shelves behind the issue desk. The catalogues are also behind the issue desk and available to the staff only. Displays and guides help to make the library attractive.

It is believed that 100% of prisoners use the library. The total stock on 31 March 1964 was over 23,000 volumes, forming a permanent deposit collection. Most books now have plastic jackets, which form another aid to an attractive library. Binding is mostly carried out in Parkhurst Prison.

The men are allowed to borrow as many books as they wish. Over 6000 books are borrowed per week. This means that the average issue is just under five books per man per week.

The total book issues from Islington public libraries in 1963–4 were 2,718,230. Of these, 249,124 were issued from Pentonville.

TABLE 1. *Comparative table of stock and issues, 1963–4*

Service point	Adult lending stock	Adult lending issues
Central	73,640	404,982
North	33,557	248,936
West	23,167	134,771
South	27,709	228,517
Archway	21,383	233,797
Mildmay	15,764	129,145
Arthur Simpson	24,898	192,014
Pentonville	over 23,000	249,124
Holloway Prison	10,228	56,560

It may be seen from Table 1 that the issues from Pentonville Library compare very favourably with those from branches with a book stock of similar size.

There is a considerable variety in the books stocked. Books may be purchased new by the public library, out of the capitation grant. Important books are purchased new—e.g. Churchill's writings, or Chester Wilmot's *The struggle for Europe*. Sports books are bought, as these are extremely popular. Popular non-fiction is also bought, such as Rawicz's *The long walk*. Books for illiterates are bought, as are the ever-popular cowboy stories, and as are some Pelicans—the complete *Pelican history of England* was bought and then reinforced by the library staff.

Books with approximately 6 months' life in them may be transferred from other branches. But no dilapidated or tattered books are sent. Fiction is transferred, so are editions of works that have been replaced but are still useful.

Other sources are books that are sent in to prisoners, which must be handed over to the library after use, and gifts—particularly from philanthropic and religious organizations.

Books last at least as well as in an ordinary branch library. The main risk of destruction or mutilation is by prisoners at reception, so a collection of the oldest books is made available to these men.

The library is run by the library officer, with the assistance of selected prisoners. Prison libraries are probably unique in their freedom from staff shortage. A senior member of the public library's professional staff visits the prison library every working day to act as readers' adviser and to give any professional advice that may be necessary to the officer—such as the establishment of various library routines. The prison library is open at lunch time and for a few hours during the evening. The professional librarian visits at lunch time.

The inmate assistants are chosen on their intelligence, experience and record. They may, of course, have worked in a prison library before, because, with the exception of prisoners awaiting transfer, they are not first offenders.

The officer and his assistants carry out all the routines of the library—including cataloguing. The job is considered as a privilege, being one of the most congenial in the prison.

The library routine is fairly simple. Each man may have, within reason, as many books as he can read. Sometimes it is quite obvious that a man could not read the number of books he has chosen, and the officer may have to use his discretion in keeping back books which are required by a serious reader. It is not unknown, for example, for someone to take books merely because they will look decorative in his cell. There is open access to the books. A book card and ticket charging system is used, similar to that used in many public libraries. The book card has the number, title and author of the book on it, and the prisoner's number and the date borrowed are recorded on the card. The prisoner also has his own card, recording the number of each book and the date borrowed. These details supplement those on his "permitted articles" card, which states what he may have in his cell. His own books, periodicals and newspapers are also recorded on his "permitted articles" card.

The catalogues are simple, but effective, and they enable the stock to be used efficiently. They are used only by the staff, who are likely to understand more fully than the borrowers the information contained in them.

The books are not shelved until after each session's group of men has left the library. This ensures that all books, however popular, circulate round the prison, with men being able to see them, regardless of the day on which they visit the library.

Displays are regularly looked after and changed, so that readers' attention is drawn to individual books or to particular subjects.

Special requests noted by the readers' adviser or the prison library staff are satisfied, as at a branch library, from the public library's stock whenever possible. The public library attempts to cover any deficiencies. The national inter-lending service is occasionally used, mainly for foreign books for aliens. The central pool of books at Wakefield is never used. It is extremely unlikely that Wakefield would have any books not in the public library stock. Some language groups are helped by loan collections from outside organizations. But normally it is difficult to provide sufficient books for aliens.

The library itself does not take any newspapers or periodicals, although a selection is distributed in association rooms. But the men are allowed to buy newspapers and periodicals out of their earnings. About 30% receive daily newspapers. They may also have sent in by friends books, newspapers and magazines, at the Governor's discretion. Books sent in must be surrendered to the library once the prisoner has read them. They are mainly paperbacks. Newspapers and periodicals are administered by the library staff, and are issued on a one-for-one basis. A man is not permitted to lend a magazine to another or to cut anything out of it. Prisoners, having no personal possessions, often tend to hoard anything that they can acquire; and it is frequently a source of irritation to have to surrender a magazine.

Reading taste corresponds quite closely to that which one would expect to find in an all-male community. There are, nevertheless, certain special problems. About 3% remain totally illiterate. A further 3% of the population is able to read simple comics, but cannot progress towards the "Easy Reader" stage. These men, together with a few foreigners who cannot read or write English, place a great strain on the library's magazine resources.

A considerable number of the remaining men are not normally book readers. The first demand of these men is for cowboys and thrillers. There are never sufficient cowboy stories to meet the demand. However, thrillers are more plentiful, and these are often used in displays designed to help those who are unused to books and libraries.

Once they have settled down, most readers tend to choose a good solid novel with strong narrative interest, and preferably with one or two "high spots". As they have more unoccupied time than the general public library user, the men will often read books of more than average length. American novelists are particularly appreciated. Among the most popular novelists the librarian notes Hervey Allen, Nigel Balchin, H. E. Bates, Erskine Caldwell (and Taylor Caldwell, to a lesser extent), Theodore Dreiser, C. S. Forester, Louis Golding, Ernest Hemingway, Sinclair Lewis, Eric Linklater, Somerset Maugham, J. B. Priestley, John Steinbeck, Dennis Wheatley and Vaughan Wilkins; and there has been a marked revival of interest in the older works of P. G. Wodehouse.

Those men with a really long stretch to serve finally tend to turn away from novels to "true life" stories—biographies, travel books and war stories.

Amongst the non-fiction books, sports books are extremely popular. Boxing and football books are the favourites, followed by racing and cricket. War stories are plentiful and widely read. Biographies and travel books are the other most popular types.

In a closed community information is passed on very rapidly. A recommendation to one reader can virtually be regarded as a recommendation to the whole community. Advice from the librarian is almost invariably received with much gratitude, and great confidence is placed in it. Book lists are passed from one reader to another. The man who has been in for some time frequently recommends books he has enjoyed to newer members of the community. Prison visitors also sometimes recommend books—but these are usually confined to the instructive or improving type of work.

As many of the men take newspapers, and even more have access to news in some way, readers often know about interesting new books. Thus, in various ways, many readers are quite well informed about what they would like to read. It should be borne in mind, however, that they rarely have an opportunity to browse amongst the books because such a large number of men have to pass through the library in a limited time. Therefore, ways of helping them to find quickly a suitable book are particularly valuable.

Men often study very thoroughly books about their civilian work. They may also attempt to learn or improve a foreign language. Correspondence courses such as Pitman's are provided, at public expense, for those serving a sentence long enough to enable them to complete a course. Men with their own resources may choose their own correspondence schools. Lecture meetings are available in the prison, and have constant waiting lists. There are also classes for illiterates. The tutor organizer is usually responsible for the supply of books to classes. But the library gives every assistance with special requests for students. Sets of plays are provided for play-reading groups. Music is borrowed for study and for reading. There is a never-failing demand for dictionaries, which tend to be borrowed on a semi-permanent basis, as an aid to ambitious reading, to letter writing or to study. Atlases are also extremely popular.

When Islington public libraries first took responsibility for the Pentonville Library, censorship of any sort was frowned upon. It was felt that any book considered suitable for Islington's other readers was suitable for the Pentonville Library. However, persistent demand caused by morbid interest soon made it clear that certain books were unsuitable for inclusion in the stock. When these works were worn out, they were not replaced. Books are rarely withdrawn; they are simply not replaced. *Fabian of the Yard* was withdrawn, however, at the Commissioners' request. Amongst the books not replaced because of the morbid interest shown in them were Joan Henry's *Yield to the night*, Motley's *Knock on any door*, H. Patterson and E. Conrad's *Scotsboro' boy*, Raymond's *We, the accused*, G. J. Seaton's *Scars are my passport*, and R. W. Thorp's *Viper: confessions of a drug addict*.

However, there is extremely little censorship. Medical and psychological books are chosen with great care in case men who are in their cells for long stretches imagine that they have all the symptoms described. Books containing photographs of nudes are avoided.

It can be seen, therefore, that the library at Pentonville provides extremely well for the requirements of its users. The men can call on a good deposit collection backed up by the entire resources of Islington public libraries and, indeed, if necessary, of the national inter-lending system. They have an excellent advisory service at their disposal. The stage is, in fact, rapidly being reached at which Islington may have seriously to consider how good a service they should provide. Quite obviously the capitation grant which they receive does not cover the handsome provisions which they make. The capitation grant is spent on the deposit collection at the prison. But the prisoners can call on a much larger book stock than this. Also, the grant is spent entirely on books, and the staff for the advisory service are provided by the borough. The staff have to visit the prison library during their lunch hour, and are therefore paid overtime as well as travelling time. Clearly the public library is to be congratulated upon its service. Equally clearly the Prison Commissioners could not provide a similar service on the capitation grant. It remains to be seen how much further the public library feels it can develop its service to the prison without jeopardizing the interests of its other readers unless it receives a more realistic financial contribution.

WANDSWORTH

Wandsworth Borough Library took responsibility for the library in Wandsworth prison some 3 years ago.

The library consists of converted cells in the main cell block. It is small; but it should be noted that only ten to fifteen readers are ever in it at one time. It has a very pleasant appearance, with attractive posters and guides. The staff take great pride in the library's appearance, and keep all the books straight and in their correct order. There is no area furnished with easy chairs and set aside for relaxation; but this is because the readers would not have time to use it.

It is believed that at least 80% of the prisoners use the library. Every prisoner may visit the library once a fortnight. Because of the large numbers to pass through the library, men are allowed to stay there only 10 minutes. If the situation permits, a prisoner who obviously needs more time may be allowed to stay longer. But very many men can easily change their books in 5–10 minutes, particularly if they read light fiction only. There is open access to the books. The men are allowed seven books each, which are issued for a fortnight, but may be renewed if necessary. Issues are recorded in a register, noting the prisoner's number and the book's number. The total issues for 1963–4 were 400,400 books.

The book stock numbers approximately 19,000 volumes at present; 3763 new books were added during the year ending 31 March 1964. When the public library took responsibility some 3 years ago, they had to start virtually from scratch. There were very few books in the library, and these were tattered and old. The stock has, therefore, had to be built up. But it is now reasonably strong. This means that more stock revision is now possible. The stock is permanent at present; but it is hoped that it will be possible eventually to build up a loan stock which may be sent to other libraries.

Both fiction and non-fiction are stocked. The books may be bought new for the prison library, or they may be sent second-hand from branches of the public library. In the second case, only clean books are ever sent. In general the books remain in good condition for longer in the prison library than they do in branch libraries. Only a very few prisoners ever mutilate books—partly because they appreciate the library service and partly because they lose remission if they do mutilate books.

The library is run by library officers assisted by prisoners. There are periodical visits by the Chief Assistant of Wandsworth Borough Library. He collaborates with the chaplain and the officers over such matters as book selection. He also gives professional advice and supervises such library routines as cataloguing. Under this system, good relations between the public library and the library officers are essential, as the latter could easily undo all the public library's work between the visits of the Chief Assistant. The prison library has fortunately always so far been staffed with capable and enthusiastic officers. The officers have a short training in library organization at the public library, and can advise and help their readers to a limited extent. But they cannot be expected to perform the functions of a pro-fessional librarian. The public library realizes that there is a need for far more frequent visits to the prison; but staff is not available. They would like to see daily visits, or at least three visits of 4 hours each week.

The library officers are assisted by prisoners. There is a very big ratio of staff to books. The assistants are chosen for their intelligence and experience. They are all highly intelligent, and some are graduates. As Wandsworth is mainly for third and fourth offenders, there may well be inmates who have worked in a prison library before. However, during the time that the public library has been responsible for the prison library, none of the library assistants has ever returned to the prison. This may be purely coincidence, but it is also possible that some rehabilitative effect has been achieved. The men are glad to be employed in the library because it is pleasant work. They also spend less time confined to their cells. They enjoy, too, a very noticeable freedom of speech with the officers, who treat them more or less as equals. The prisoners carry out all the routines of the library. They issue the books, keep the library tidy and attractive, make guide cards and notices, and catalogue and classify the stock.

It is estimated that about 60% of the users of the library read light fiction only—Westerns being the most popular of all. There is a direct system of book reservation from the central library for any reader who requires a particular book that is not in stock at the prison. The public library does not send inter-library loans direct to the prison because it does not feel that its responsibility to the lending library permits this. However, in special circumstances, the book may be sent to the library officer who is then personally responsible for it. Nevertheless, with this exception, the request system for the prison library operates in the same way as for any branch library.

The tutors of the Educational Department run educational courses and supply the necessary books. If any more books are needed, the library will supply them. But the public library does not know the reason for or the origin of the requests passed on to it. The library officers have some opportunity to guide readers who are following a course of study, but the Chief Assistant from the public library cannot visit often enough to do this sort of advisory work. Similarly, special books used in the classes for illiterates are not stocked by the library but are supplied by the Education Department.

Special foreign books sometimes have to be supplied, if there are, for example, Hungarian or Polish prisoners who cannot speak English.

The library does not take any newspapers or periodicals. It is supplied by the public library with some old copies of illustrated magazines, such as *Illustrated London News*, for poor readers. About 700 newspapers a day are bought by prisoners out of their own money. The checking, searching and distribution of these papers is all organized by the library.

Prisoners may have books and periodicals sent in to them by friends at the Governor's discretion, provided that they are handed over to the library when the man has read them. However, the practice is frowned upon. It causes a great deal of extra work in the library, as each book has to be approved and searched. Such books as are sent in are mainly paperbacks, not all of which reach the prisoners. Very few of them reach the library afterwards. The aim is to build a library collection strong enough to remove the need for extra books to be sent in.

Censorship is not strict. However, certain types of book are not permitted. Medical books and works on psychology are excluded in the men's own interest; books on such skills as rope-making or ju-jitsu are excluded as a safety precaution; and true crime or escape stories (but not fictitious ones) are forbidden on the grounds that they make the offender feel that he is important and in order to prevent any difficulties should a criminal who has been the subject of a book appear in the prison.

The men in prison certainly read more than they do outside. It is not known whether the habit of reading remains permanently after a prison sentence. Many only ever read light fiction, but some do progress. The more intelligent men read very deeply. There is a bigger demand for classical authors and classical poets than there is in most branch libraries.

Problems are bound to arise in a prison library because discipline and restraint have to be maintained, and this adds to the administrative difficulties. There are special problems, such as passing the men through the library very quickly; but problems arise in any special community—such as a hospital. One sometimes needs to be firm with borrowers in a public library, and this is even more essential in a prison library. But the prisoners must not be treated as people apart, as their library needs are basically the same as anyone else's.

Much could be achieved through the library. Even with insufficient liaison between the prison and the public library, the library has helped in the rehabilitation of some men. With qualified staff permanently available for advice, one could expect that a great deal more might be achieved. This liaison between the prison and the public libraries is of extreme importance; and a permanent member of the public library staff is urgently needed for the prison library. It is felt to be very satisfying work. With a qualified librarian as adviser, a prison library could be one of the best types of library in the country; there is a very high ratio of staff to books: the library is the main interest of the assistants for very long hours: and they have a great pride in its appearance and efficiency.

The Borough Librarian, in his annual report for 1963–4, comments: "With the prisoners confined to their cells for so many hours of the day and night the library service is obviously one of the most important factors in their daily life and any steps which could be taken to improve it would be a good investment."

WORMWOOD SCRUBS

The library at Wormwood Scrubs is the responsibility of Hammersmith public libraries who try to run it as if it were one of their branch libraries.

The public library has had responsibility for the Wormwood Scrubs Library for about 3 years. Before this, the prison had its own collection, and could call upon the Wakefield Educational Library.

The library is small, but it is now quite attractive, with good notices and posters. The book stock numbers 20,000 volumes. Of these, 12,000 have been supplied by the public library and 8000 remain from the old prison stock. These remaining books are gradually being replaced.

The books form a permanent collection at the prison. The life of the books is generally longer than at an average branch library.

It is estimated that almost all the prisoners use the library. However, Wormwood Scrubs does house a borstal institution for a daily average population of 309 boys. These boys do not use the main library, but have a separate library of their own, run by the borstal's education authorities. The public library has no connection with the borstal library.

The men have open access to the books. They may visit the library once a week, and are allowed to borrow six books at a time. The books are issued, as in many public libraries, by the Brown charging system, with the addition of a cell card. Each man is required to have a cell card showing what articles he is permitted to have in his cell. In addition to the records maintained in the library itself, the numbers of the books he has borrowed and the date issued must be entered upon the man's cell card.

The organization of the prison library is carried out by a library officer. He has received a month's training course at the public library, learning methods and techniques. He is assisted by prisoners. One of the assistant lending librarians of Hammersmith public libraries has special responsibilities for supervising and visiting the prison library. He visits the library at irregular intervals—usually once every 5 or 6 weeks.

The prisoners are chosen to work in the library on the basis of record, intelligence and experience. Library work is regarded as one of the most pleasant jobs in the prison, and cataloguing is one of the best paid—it is therefore considered something of a privilege to be chosen.

These prisoners perform all routine tasks such as charging and discharging books or tidying shelves. The original stock from the public library was already catalogued and classified for them. But all new fiction is now catalogued in the prison library—the cataloguers work on precedent set by the original collection. Non-fiction is catalogued and classified by public library staff. Book selection is also carried out by the professional staff at the public library.

Westerns and science fiction are the most popular books. Accounts of war-time experiences are widely read, and crime stories are well received.

Quite a number of men follow educational courses while they are in prison. Although many men are in Wormwood Scrubs for a very short time only, whilst awaiting transfer, it is also a central prison, which houses men who are serving really long sentences. About 2000 men are following prison courses. These may be of an academic nature, they may be of a vocational nature or they may be more simply the pursuit of an interest. About twenty men are following English extension courses. A few of the inmates already have degrees.

As the librarian from the public library is only able to visit the prison rather infrequently, he is clearly not in a position to give advice to the men which would help them to follow their courses. The education officer is responsible for the supply of books essential to courses. However, the library deals with requests from students for additional books as it would those coming from any branch, and men are allowed any reasonable number of books needed for their studies.

The library itself does not take any newspapers or periodicals. However, it does bind back numbers of illustrated magazines for illiterates and poor readers. The men themselves may buy newspapers and periodicals out of their earnings. They are allowed to take one morning and one evening paper a day and two periodicals a week.

There is a bindery in the prison. This is, naturally, very useful to the library, as they can send off what books they like and expect the work to be carried out to their requirements. The bindery is, of course, run by trained craftsmen.

Hammersmith public libraries have not had responsibility for Wormwood Scrubs Library for very long. They are obviously still building it up—e.g. they have not yet completed the replacement of the original prison stock. They are hampered by lack of space—they have only a small room, much of which is taken up by the working area for the staff.

However, the insufficient liaison between the prison and the public libraries is the greatest barrier to further progress. Although the public library is maintaining an efficient administrative link, there is no readers' advice service. This could not be expected, when the librarian is able to visit the prison only every 5 or 6 weeks. Nor can the public library hope to provide such an advisory service until it has sufficient trained staff free to operate it. The difficulty is probably partly financial and partly one of staff shortage. This situation could, to some extent, be alleviated by an increased grant from the Prison Department. As the situation stands, money could only be spent on extra staff at the expense of the book stock, and the stock is not yet strong enough to justify this. It is very clear, however, that a very friendly spirit exists between the prison and the public library. Not only do they co-operate well over their work, but the public library has sent teams to play, for example, cricket matches against the prisoners. A climate of feeling seems to exist in which really good results could be hoped for if the present service were developed so that it took on a more directly personal aspect.

SUMMARY AND CONCLUSIONS

Almost all prisoners make some use of their prison library. Of the four London prisons studied particularly, two claimed 100% membership, one 95–100%, and the other at least 80%. Issues are generally high. But even those issue figures which are available do not accurately assess the use made of the books. Of these four prisons, Holloway alone is not overcrowded. The other three have more prisoners than cells. Therefore, in many cases, men may read at least twice as many books as they are known to have borrowed. Even where cells are not shared, it is recognized that books are somehow passed around, so that often a prisoner does not return the book he borrowed. With this volume of reading, both recorded and unrecorded, it is clear that the library is a very busy and active department of the prison.

At the moment, Pentonville is alone in possessing reasonably spacious premises, but Holloway should soon be enlarged. This shortage of space is naturally a disadvantage, as it has an adverse effect on any attempt to make the library attractive, and it hampers the expansion of the book stock. However, the disadvantage is not as acute as it would be in a public library, as, for disciplinary reasons, a limited number of readers only is ever present at one time.

The libraries do not usually occupy attractive premises, but great efforts have been made to improve their appearance by the use of displays and posters and, in Holloway at least, flowers. The staff take great pride in maintaining the pleasant and orderly appearance of their library.

There is usually just one library for the whole prison—although a few rather more dilapidated books may be deposited at reception. Holloway is an exception in this respect as it also has a small collection in the borstal wing, in the hospital, and in the wing in which women are receiving domestic training.

Holloway Prison has the smallest daily average population—375 women— and the smallest book stock—10,228 volumes; i.e. about 27 books per head of average population. Wormwood Scrubs has a daily average of 1035 men and a stock of 20,000 books; this allows about 19 books per head. Pentonville has a daily average of 1251 men and a stock of over 23,000 books—about 18 per head. Wandsworth's daily average population is 1525, and the book stock numbers approximately 19,000 volumes—which is about 12 books per head. One should take into account perhaps the fact that Holloway and Wormwood Scrubs both receive the very long-term prisoners —Holloway has a daily average of 15 and Wormwood Scrubs of 326. These prisoners are likely to require a more varied book stock to cater for their needs throughout their sentence.

Book stocks form permanent collections in the prisons, and include both fiction and non-fiction. Books may be bought new, especially for the prison library; they may be transferred from branches; they are sometimes donated; or they may be books which have passed to the library after a prisoner has had them sent in to him.

Books receive very heavy wear. Due to the "grape-vine", a book which has been enjoyed by one reader will soon be in very heavy demand. There is also considerable "hidden" use, as a book may be issued only once but read by all the borrower's friends. However, there is very little mutilation indeed. Sir Lionel Fox, writing in *The English prison and borstal systems* (1952), comments: "An encouraging lesson from this development of prison libraries has been that it has practically killed the nasty and endemic prison disease of mutilating and scribbling in library-books, perhaps because these outlets for repressed resentments are no longer needed, perhaps because prisoners will live up to a good standard as easily as down to a bad one."

Prisoners may pay weekly visits to the library, except in Wandsworth, where the visits are fortnightly. The time which they are permitted to spend in the library is variable—Wandsworth being the least liberal and allowing only 10 minutes as a rule (but allowances should be made for the fact that Wandsworth has the largest population). Time restrictions are the result of shortage of discipline officers to supervise the prisoners, and of the very large numbers who have to pass through the library in the limited time which will not disrupt work or other routines. Although the unlimited borrowing found at Holloway and Pentonville is the ideal, the restriction to six books at Wormwood Scrubs is not unreasonable, as it has been found that men in Pentonville borrow an average of five books a week. However, when one considers the amount of leisure a prisoner has, the allowance of seven books a fortnight at Wandsworth leaves room for improvement.

There is now open access in all prison libraries. This is a great improvement on the situation described by "D. H. H." in "Prisoners need books", *Library Assistant*, Jan.–Feb. 1945. He states that in the prisons of which he was an inmate during the early 1940's, books were changed during the man's absence. Normally, the reader took what he was given. If he was privileged, he might ask for particular books, but usually stock was so old and catalogues so confused that it was very uncertain whether he would receive his requests.

Brendan Behan (*Borstal boy*, 1958) also discovered that the library service was rather "hit-and-miss", when he was imprisoned in Walton Jail because of his IRA activities. Books were often just handed out at random unless the librarian was obliging—in which case a prisoner might be more fortunate over his books.

> The librarian was not an undecent sort, and brought me books by Dickens that I had asked for. It was not much good asking for modern authors because they did not have any. It was my belief they bought the books for the prison by weight. I once got a *Chums* annual for 1917 and a Selfridge's furniture catalogue for my non-fiction or educational book. But when I explained to the librarian that I could not read the Selfridge's furniture catalogue and that I had had the *Chums* before, which was not true, he changed them for me. He gave *The Mayor of Casterbridge* by Hardy and *The Moonstone* by Wilkie Collins.

In all four prisons the reader has access to all the books in the responsible public library system by means of a request service which supplements the permanent stock. Wandsworth Borough Library will not lend books borrowed from other libraries (except very occasionally if the library officer takes personal responsibility); the other public libraries do not make great use of the inter-lending system on the prisons' behalf, but they are willing to do so if it is really necessary.

The libraries do not buy newspapers or magazines, but they are responsible for the large task of checking and allocating those purchased by individual prisoners. The number of books sent in to prisoners is no longer very high. As they are generally paperbacks, very few of these books ever reach the library in a state fit for addition to stock. The aim to build up such good libraries that extra books become unnecessary seems well on the way to realization.

Illiterates and poor readers, and also non-English-speaking prisoners, create special problems. Such people do not usually visit public libraries, but they do wish to use prison libraries. Illustrated magazines are invaluable in catering for these prisoners.

Censorship is in the hands of the Governor, and is not particularly strict. It tended to be more severe when it was the chaplain's responsibility. Nowadays, the aim is to encourage reading. Sir Lionel Fox writes in *The English prison and borstal systems:* "Since the War, everything has been done to encourage a full and intelligent use of the prison library. . . . The present wish is to encourage reading, not to restrict it."

It is easy to see the reason behind such censorship as does exist. It is quite genuinely in the prisoner's own interest to keep certain books from him while he is in prison. It is also quite fairly arguable that other types of book may be prejudicial to discipline—including those which foster the idea that a criminal is an important and exciting individual.

Prison libraries are not staffed by professional librarians, but the ratio of staff to books is very high. Selected prisoners, under the supervision of a library officer, perform all routine tasks. These tasks are simplified as far as possible. Professional assistance is provided by the public library staff—to an extent which varies considerably from one authority to another.

Many readers borrow only light fiction—particularly if they are serving a short sentence. But it should be remembered that many will not previously have done much reading at all—except, perhaps, of newspapers—and will almost certainly not have been library users. Nevertheless, many prisoners do move on to good solid novels, and the non-fiction section is also well used. The more intelligent and the long-term prisoners often read very deeply. This fact is noted in *Prisons and borstals 1963: report on the work of the Prison Department in the year 1963:*

> . . . Men in prison are often more prepared to read deeply than is sometimes thought. A Roman Catholic priest writes, "One of the visiting missionaries was quite amazed when a young 'lifer' told him that he had read all the works of Thomas Merton, and even more so when the man said that he had read one volume three times before he could properly understand it."

Men and women in prison certainly read more than they do outside. It is not known whether this habit is maintained after the prisoner's release. (This might perhaps be the subject of a valuable survey.) However, it does not seem unreasonable to hope that some prisoners at least keep the habit throughout their lives.

The advisory service provided by the public library varies very considerably. In every case, a senior member of the professional staff has responsibility for this service. However, at Wandsworth and Wormwood Scrubs they visit the prison only "periodically"—which means about once a month in the former case and once every 5 or 6 weeks in the latter. At the opposite end of the scale is Pentonville, which receives daily visits. In between these extremes is Holloway with weekly visits. Only Pentonville and Holloway have a true readers' advice service. The professional librarians visiting Wandsworth and Wormwood Scrubs take the requests received by the officers, but do not visit frequently enough to give advice direct to readers. They are mainly concerned with helping the staff. They are therefore very valuable consultants and liaison officers, but not readers' advisers. The problem is one of finance and staffing. It is extremely costly to supply staff as frequently as Islington does for Pentonville and Holloway. Islington itself has difficulty in finding enough staff to do the work. Some staff may be un-suited to the work, and others are not interested in undertaking it—and senior members of the staff only are used. In his report for the 3 years ended 31 March 1964, the Chief Librarian, writing about Holloway, says: "Our own staff problems are reflected in the staffing of the prison library. In October, 1963, we had eight of our senior staff on the rota for visiting the prison library; by March, 1964, five of the eight had resigned to take posts elsewhere and two more are going shortly."

The readers' advice service at Pentonville is undoubtedly the best. But one should remember that the public libraries in question have been re-sponsible for the other three prison libraries for a few years only—whereas Islington has the benefit of many years' experience at Pentonville. The readers' adviser at Pentonville, and to a rather lesser extent at Holloway, is able to build up a real relationship with the readers. His advice is freely sought and greatly appreciated. It is the readers' adviser's task to help the readers to make maximum use of the stock in the prison and to supplement this stock from the public library where necessary.

The advisers at Pentonville and Holloway all find that they may have to give help on a very simple level—perhaps to a recently received prisoner who is too confused to choose even the lightest fiction. On the other hand, they may be able to give more detailed advice about an ambitious course of reading.

It is sincerely to be hoped that the other libraries can overcome their financial and staffing problems, so that they can provide a true readers' advice service such as Islington offers.

It is important to help the short-term prisoners to reorientate themselves so that they can use the library profitably. Yet it is, perhaps, with the long-sentence prisoners that the most hopeful work, in the long view, can be undertaken. Although the librarian cannot hope to reform all prisoners, it is much more than possible that he will make a considerable contribution to the rehabilitation of at least a few.

In 1853, the Reverend Joseph Kingsmill, Chaplain of Pentonville, said: "To confer the advantages of a superior education on criminals, I hold to be wrong in principle." (Quoted from Fox's *The English prison and borstal systems*.)

Nowadays, considerable emphasis is placed upon education. Xenia Field, in *Under lock and key: a study of women in prison*, writes: "Sir Lionel Fox gave education in prisons a new high priority. All Governors were advised that the purpose of prison training was not primarily to inculcate particular skills, but to train the whole man. Education was no longer to be treated as "a thing apart, but must be related to the whole scheme".

The prison library service is very closely linked with the education service. The idea of education itself springs directly from the wish to effect moral reform and rehabilitation. This wish has not always been accepted. The House of Lords Committee of 1863 said: "We do not consider that the moral reformation of the offender holds the primary place in the prison system."

Happily, it has now been officially accepted that reformation and rehabilitation would benefit not only the prisoner but also society. Rule 6 of the Prison Rules, 1949, states: "The purposes of training and treatment of convicted prisoners shall be to establish in them the will to lead a good and useful life on discharge, and to fit them to do so."

It has, then, been recognized officially that it is desirable to educate prisoners. The concept of education is interpreted in several different ways. Hugh J. Klare, in *Anatomy of prison* (1960), feels that establishing the will to lead a good life is one of the most important functions of prison training: "You can *make* a man behave in a certain way while he is in prison, but it is much more difficult to make him *want* to behave in that way. Yet it is only when a man genuinely wants to change that there is real hope of rehabilitation. To create this want in him should be one of the principal aims of imprisonment."

Prisons and borstals: statement of policy and practice in the administration of prisons and borstal institutions in England and Wales (4th ed., 1960) also stresses this same aspect. It adds to it the ideas of counteracting mental stagnation and of providing more valuable matter for thought and conversation than would otherwise be found in prison. It quotes the words of the Gladstone Committee of 1895 that education should "awaken the higher susceptibilities of prisoners".

Education can also be understood in a more limited sense. It is no use encouraging in a prisoner the will to lead a useful life if one does not help him to acquire the means to do so. So education may equip him in this way. The Manchester City Librarian, in his annual report for 1962–3, writes: "Used to its best advantage a prison sentence can be a unique opportunity for a man to re-educate himself, or learn a trade or a job."

It is obvious that the prison library can play a very large part in all these aspects of education. Perhaps the easiest to satisfy is the need for books that teach a trade. The prisoner may choose to teach himself a trade independently, or he may wish to supplement a correspondence course or a class held in the prison. The libraries surveyed are all both willing and able to meet any such demands.

The other aims of education are rather less clearly defined. Mental stagnation will be overcome, and higher susceptibilities awakened, in different people by different methods. But the library is in an excellent position to attempt to carry out these objectives.

Mental stagnation is a serious problem. The Statutory Rules of 1949 provide that: "Every prisoner shall be required to engage in useful work for not more than ten hours a day, of which so far as practicable at least eight hours shall be spent in associated or other work outside the cells."

Unfortunately, it is often impossible to provide 8 hours of work outside the cells. Suitable work is usually in short supply, and the shortage of prison officers drastically reduces the hours for which a prisoner can be outside his cell. It is particularly difficult to provide suitable work for local prisons, and all four of the prisons surveyed are at least partially local prisons. This means that prisoners are liable to spend very long periods in their cells—with a correspondingly high risk of mental stagnation. The Manchester City Librarian writes, in the report quoted above: "Books are an essential part of a prisoner's life. Working only a few hours each day, often on a monotonous job which gives little satisfaction, a prisoner has ample time for reading."

The public library staff were unanimous in feeling that the library service is greatly appreciated by prisoners. The prisoners nearly always read more and to a deeper level than they would outside. A recommendation to one inmate is virtually a recommendation to all, as books are discussed and book lists circulate rapidly and widely. Those men and women who buy newspapers often read the book reviews and come to the library armed with a list of requests. One prisoner, nearing discharge, asked the librarian, who by this time knew his taste quite thoroughly, for a list of the sort of books he had liked, so that he could pass it on to his brother who was serving a sentence elsewhere. This passing on of lists, discussion of favourite books and interest in book reviews—these are all indications that the library is a source of considerable interest and pleasure to the readers. Pat Webster, writing about the Pentonville Library in the NALGO journal *Public Service* (Nov. 1956, pp. 322–3), expressed the opinion that most prisoners find the library a great comfort and help, and that the "Prison library service will help him to 'do his bird easy'."

So keen is the interest shown by some prisoners that Islington public libraries foresee the time when they may have seriously to consider how complete their service can be. One of the main problems has arisen in the last few years, since prisoners have been allowed to buy newspapers. In these papers they see reviews of new books—particularly new novels—and put in a request for them. If the book sounds good, a considerable number of men will ask for the same work. The public library cannot buy sufficient copies exclusively for the prison to satisfy rapidly the very large demand. To lend copies from the other branches entails a great deal of work, and, therefore, of expense. Besides this, it takes out of more general circulation a book which is extremely likely to be in great demand in the whole system. Is it really justifiable to restrict in this way the use of popular books, especially as the people who would be deprived of the books are those who pay rates towards the provision of the books? Some libraries already refuse to reserve fiction until it is 6 months old. In this case, the prisoners are receiving a better service than ratepayers in some areas. Although it could be argued that, because of their hours of enforced idleness, people in prison often have greater need of books than the average person outside, it could equally well be argued that those who have contributed the least towards the expense of the service should not receive the most favourable treatment. However, this question of the payment of rates can concern many other classes of population—such as students. But it does seem likely that some policy decision will have to be made in the foreseeable future.

Closely related to this problem of popular new books is the question of the man who reads only in a limited field. With such a lot of time at his disposal, a prisoner can cover a great deal of ground. If he wishes to read in a limited field, can he expect to exhaust that field? He may be studying some relatively obscure subject which could involve the library in much expense, purchasing or borrowing additional material. He may only be reading, for example, war stories—but can he expect the library to be stocked with large numbers of them for his benefit?

The capitation grant is spent by Islington purely on books; it does not begin to cover staff costs. But, even so, the amount of money available for book purchase for the prisons is painfully small. In 1963–4 Islington public libraries spent, over the system, £36,248 on books, pamphlets and prints—this is 21·58% of its total expenditure; 94·36% of its total income was derived from the general rate, 4·93% from library receipts, and 0·71%—or £1191—from all other sources, which includes the capitation grants for prisoners at Holloway and Pentonville. It can be seen from these figures that it would be unreasonable not to consider whether there is sufficient justification for expanding services to the prison when this might mean checking to some extent expansion in fields which more directly affect the ratepayers.

Charles J. Perrine outlines his views on prison libraries in "A correctional institution's library service": an address delivered at the 3rd Annual Workshop Programme for Directors of Education in New Jersey Institutions, held at the Public and School Library Services Bureau, Trenton, NJ, 11 March 1955:

> The library in a correctional institution must be conceived as a cultural center for the community of men within prison walls. If it is to be worth its salt, then its influence must permeate all aspects of institutional life and be functionally related to the needs, interests, hopes, and aspirations of the population using its services. . . . The library as a cultural center must serve as a guidance agency with the ultimate aim of establishing

good reading habits and providing services which will inculcate in the individual a realization of the practical value of reading as a positive and wise use of leisure time and as a means for self-development vocationally and in his pattern of living. . . .

The library Perrine envisages is more culturally than educationally biased. Of course, culture is part of education, and this idea of a cultural centre certainly fits in with the accepted British idea of overcoming mental stagnation and of awakening the prisoners' higher susceptibilities. He does not seem to envisage, however, quite such a close link with the general educational services as there is in Britain.

Perrine goes on to give a full and detailed list of suggestions for a good prison library. Many of these suggestions are already in general operation in this country—such as the provision of attractive fiction and biographies to develop a perception of different ways of life or of arts and crafts books to help to foster latent talent. Other facilities are already provided by other bodies—e.g. Perrine suggests lectures on such topics as civilian jobs or current events, these are already provided—the Field Lectures are a notable provision in this sphere. Another such suggestion is that a variety of good papers and magazines should be available—although only a few are provided in association rooms, more can be bought. Some of the suggestions put forward by Perrine are acceptable in principle, but have not actually been adopted in any of the libraries surveyed. One such suggestion is the provision of record collections and the formation of music groups, which, he believes, will sublimate and enrich the prisoners' fantasies; music scores only are available in these London prisons. He also suggests that picture and pamphlet collections, which emphasize design, should be provided, in order to further the aesthetic development of the inmates' faculties.

In one respect, present English views differ sharply from those expressed by Perrine. He states that: "The provision of books on religion, philosophy, psychology, physiology, or special problems such as alcoholism, anxiety, and fears offer safety valves whereby tensions and hostilities may be released through vicarious reading experiences."

With the exception of books on religion and philosophy, the general tendency in this country is to restrict the provision of such books, and to select with extreme caution those provided. It is usually accepted that release of feelings and emotions can be attained through vicarious experiences in reading fiction or poetry. Indeed, it is partly on these grounds that censorship has been relaxed on such books as those with a considerable interest in sex. But it is felt that it is too dangerous to allow unrestricted access to books on psychology or medicine or related subjects. It is believed that such works are far more likely to arouse fears and brooding amongst the prisoners than to afford them any release of feelings.

One point which Perrine does not mention, but which seems to be linked more closely with the cultural than the educational side of library service, is that the member of the public library staff is often extremely valuable simply because he is not a prison official. He wears no uniform and is not directly responsible for discipline, therefore the readers can more easily accept him as a friend. In his report for 1959–60, the Chief Librarian of Islington public libraries comments on the importance of this unofficial and personal relationship:

> The attendance of members of the library staff each day has a significance far beyond the mere supply of personal requests, valuable though that may be, inasmuch as these visits create an atmosphere of personal relationship completely devoid of officialdom. The hard work and enthusiasm of the librarians justly earns the gratitude of hundreds of inmates every year.

Even if there were no other, the existence of this unofficial relationship is one excellent reason for applauding the very clear trend towards giving responsibility for prison libraries to the public library services.

Libraries taken over from the Prison Department are usually understocked. The stock is often in poor condition, because the limited resources have not justified discarding books. Educational book provision is well below the standard set by public libraries, as the Wakefield Educational Library is not large enough, and is generally thought to be slow. Routines are probably less well organized, in the absence of a professional librarian. (The suggestion of the committee, appointed by the Library Association in 1936, that a professional librarian should be appointed to co-ordinate the whole prison library service, was shelved indefinitely.)

Prison life inevitably creates certain problems, and so prison libraries have some special situations to handle—such as the supervision of readers and the particular, limited times for using the library. But prisoners are not extraordinary beings, and a prison library can quite conveniently and efficiently be run as a branch of a public library.

All four libraries surveyed have been greatly improved since the public library has taken over responsibility for them. Islington public libraries have shown at Pentonville, in particular, what a valuable and worthwhile service can be provided by an enthusiastic authority with reasonable funds and sufficient staff to implement its ideas.

Unfortunately, not all public library services are able to do this—even once they acquire Islington's experience. The public library would not always be able to afford to provide staff out of its own funds. In this case the valuable link provided by an outside librarian working in close co-operation with the library officer would have to be sacrificed, as the capitation grant is already inadequate for books. Indeed, it could well be argued that it is not morally justifiable to send to the prison such of the public library's discards as are in reasonably good condition. If books are not good enough for the general public, is it fair to treat them as good enough for prisoners? Whatever the justice of this practice, it is, at present, absolutely essential in all these prison libraries if an adequate stock is to be maintained in them.

A much more generous capitation grant is needed. The entire grant is usually spent on book purchase for the prison collection. Even so, a large proportion of the stock is not bought from the grant, but transferred from other branches in the system. Nor is any provision made for the much-used request service. But, even more important, it does not pay for the staff.

The provision of books and of the facilities for borrowing them is very valuable. But the concept of educating and developing the whole man can only be furthered if professional advice is readily available to help the prisoner to read fruitfully and purposefully.

The Prison Department is, in fact, availing itself of an excellent service at a relatively small cost to itself. It seems only reasonable to hope that the Department will soon increase its grant to public libraries, so that the prison library service may become financially self-supporting, instead of relying so heavily upon the generosity of the public library service.

ACKNOWLEDGEMENTS

A substantial proportion of the material for this survey was obtained from personal interviews with members of the staff of the public libraries responsible for these four prisons, to whom I am extremely grateful.

My thanks are due to Mr. C. A. Elliott, FLA, Chief Librarian and Curator of Islington public libraries, and to Miss F. W. Lines, FLA, Senior Assistant of North Branch, and Mr. R. H. Crumpton, the Lending Librarian, who gave me much valuable information about Holloway and Pentonville prisons. Thanks are also due to Mr. E. V. Corbett, FLA, Borough Librarian of Wandsworth Borough Library, and to Mr. E. C. Transom, ALA, his Chief Assistant; also to Mr. G. C. J. Parker, FLA, Chief Librarian of the Metropolitan Borough of Hammersmith public libraries, and to Mr. Adams, his Assistant Lending Librarian.

BIBLIOGRAPHY

The material connected with this study falls into two categories. In the first group are included general works about the prison system in England and Wales. The second group comprises works with more direct relevance to prison libraries.

1. The prison system

CLEMMER, DONALD, *The prison community*, Holt, 1940.
FIELD, XENIA, *Under lock and key: a study of women in prison*, Parrish, 1963.
FOX, Sir LIONEL WRAY, *The English prison and borstal systems*, Routledge, 1952.
KLARE, HUGH JOHN, *Anatomy of prison*, Hutchinson, 1960.
MORRIS, TERENCE, and MORRIS, PAULINE, *Pentonville: a sociological study of an English prison*, Routledge, 1963.

HOME OFFICE, PRISON DEPARTMENT, *Prisons and borstals: statement of policy and practice in the administration of prisons and borstal institutions in England and Wales*, 4th ed., HMSO, 1960.

HOME OFFICE, PRISON DEPARTMENT, *Prisons and borstals 1963: report on the work of the Prison Department in the year 1963*, HMSO, 1963.

Also:

BEHAN, BRENDAN, *Borstal boy*, Hutchinson, 1958; this is an autobiographical account, which sheds interesting light on the atmosphere and conditions in prison; but it is rather out of date.

2. Prison Libraries

D. H. H., Prisoners need books, *Library Assistant*, Jan.–Feb. 1945.

ISLINGTON PUBLIC LIBRARIES, Reports of the Chief Librarian and Curator for the years 1956–7, 1957–8, 1959–60, and 1961–4.

MANCHESTER PUBLIC LIBRARIES, Reports of the City Librarian on the work of the libraries for the year ended 31 March 1962 and for the year ended 31 March 1963.

PERRINE, CHARLES J., "A correctional institution's library service": an address delivered at the 3rd Annual Workshop Programme for Directors of Education in New Jersey Institutions, held at the Public and School Library Services Bureau, Trenton, NJ, on the 11 March 1955. *Wilson Libr. Bull.*, Nov. 1955.

WANDSWORTH BOROUGH COUNCIL, *Annual report of the Borough Librarian for the year ended 31st March, 1964*.

WATSON, RICHARD F., *Prison libraries*, Library Association, 1951.

WEBSTER, PAT, Five books a week from this prison library help the Pentonville man to "do his bird easy", *Public Service* (NALGO journal), 322 (Nov. 1956).

4. LIBRARY SERVICE FOR UNDERGRADUATES

M. W. MOSS

University Library, University of Keele

THE separate undergraduate library has come to be widely accepted in America as a principle of university librarianship, and new libraries of this kind are being planned every year. The universities of Indiana, Chicago and Illinois, for example, are proposing to accept this solution to their library space problems and other universities are considering it. Indeed, in preparing for the predicted peak enrolments of 1970, some American universities are even contemplating the development of separate campuses for undergraduates, each with its own library.

Library provision on this scale is still a long way off in Britain, but interest in undergraduate libraries is particularly relevant at the present time and likely to become even more so if the present rate of expansion continues. Moreover, in the autumn of 1964 the first effects of the post-war bulge began to be felt in the universities. Allowing for differences in administrative and teaching methods, much can be learned from American experiment and experience with this and other types of library, and information could be extremely valuable for university libraries in this country, since a good deal of what applies to the American university situation today could well be applicable here within the next 10 years or so.

Library service for undergraduate students is a complex subject with very wide implications. The present study represents an attempt to place the undergraduate library in perspective in relation to the broader context of library service to the university community in general. This necessitates discussion of some of the origins of its development and its characteristics as typified by several such libraries which are already very well established in the United States. In addition to these general observations some consideration will be given to the various arguments generally adopted in order to defend or to oppose this type of library, as the case may be. Finally, possible future trends in undergraduate library service in Great Britain will be briefly reviewed against the background of the planned expansion of universities which is now well under way in this country.

The writer would like to express his thanks to the staff of the Sheffield and Liverpool University Libraries for obtaining useful material that was not readily available.

SOME GENERAL CONSIDERATIONS
ON UNDERGRADUATE LIBRARY SERVICE

The establishment of the separate undergraduate library within the last 20 years is the outcome of a variety of factors, some of which are particularly pertinent to the American university and college scene, but probably the most important of these is a long and growing awareness of the neglect of student needs in terms of book provision and library service in general. Since its first appearance on the American scene in the form of the Lamont Library at Harvard, the separate undergraduate library has come to represent, however controversially, a belief on the part of some librarians at least that the undergraduate reader has special needs of his own which can only be met satisfactorily with special facilities and a positive attempt to improve library service to this type of reader by providing the facilities which are thought to be necessary.

However, Harvard's Lamont Library, although perhaps the ultimate in undergraduate provision, is only one form of a service which over the years has been open to a diversity of interpretations, usually based on the size and scope of the institution concerned and the funds available. It is a tribute to Harvard that it was the first among the great American universities to attack this problem and that it did so, not under the pressure of increased enrolment, and not because circumstances forced it, but because it wished to improve library service to undergraduates despite the increasing demands of scholarship. It should be remembered in this connection that at Harvard the graduate students outnumber the undergraduates and that the Widener Library and the many branch libraries offer far more by way of library facilities than is available at most universities to serve much larger student bodies.

Thus Harvard was a pioneer in this respect and it was the Lamont gift that made it possible for not just a separate room but a separate building to be created. In the main, the American universities which followed Harvard's example in establishing a separate undergraduate library seem to have done so first and foremost under the pressures of local needs and circumstances rather than of any obligation to the student body, although it is those very needs and circumstances which have helped a good deal in focusing so much thoughtful attention on the problems of undergraduate library provision. These circumstances naturally vary considerably from institution to institution and it is not surprising, therefore, that even when one bears in mind that financial resources too are not very evenly distributed, librarians themselves have adopted a variety of solutions to what many now regard as the same basic problem.

In consequence, as is not uncommon, much of the theory of undergraduate library service has tended to follow rather than precede the practice and some of it has little or no bearing on current developments. It is difficult, therefore, to speak of a concept in relation to undergraduate library service in any but the broadest terms. In addition to the evidence of different approaches to the problem, the matter is further complicated by the fact that many teaching staff and a number of university librarians have grave doubts as to the wisdom of making special separate provision for undergraduate students, whether on one floor in the main library or in a completely separate building.[1] These librarians and university teachers feel that the work each is trying to carry out for the benefit of the undergraduate would be seriously hampered if special provision were made for the students, that the separation of students into graduate and undergraduate is a formal, institutional issue, and that the use of libraries should be independent of the status of the student. There is also apparent the fear that the student would lose much of the value that comes with the complete facilities of the main collection. These are all valid objections which warrant examination and will be discussed at a later stage.

Two brief examples may serve here to indicate different approaches to the problem of serving a large student population. The construction of the Michigan Library in 1958 with a bookstock of about 100,000 volumes represents one attempt to meet the special needs of the undergraduate. Here a separate building with a carefully selected student collection is provided. The construction of the Fondren Library at the Rice Institute in Texas several years earlier represents an entirely different approach to the problem, dictated, of course, by entirely different local circumstances. At Rice all library holdings, comprising some half million volumes, have been housed in a single building and no distinction whatever is made between undergraduate and research collections. Both of these decisions were made deliberately after considerable study of the needs of the different institutions.

In Great Britain there is nothing at present of the nature or scope of the Michigan Undergraduate Library, for example, but separate undergraduate reading rooms exist at Glasgow, Liverpool and Oxford, and the undergraduate reading room equipped with a good working collection and housed within the main library building is becoming increasingly common. These are all rather extreme examples and the comparison between British and American undergraduate provision is hardly a fair one, but in spite of the tendency to work out the problem in terms of the unique needs of each institution, some consideration of the modern university and the practices and experience of its library may help to provide certain common denominators of value in assessing the nature and purpose of the undergraduate library as it is known today.

Discussion of the advisability of special libraries for undergraduates appears earlier in the literature of librarianship than one might suppose. As long ago as 1608 when Thomas James was appointed to Bodley's Library,

G

he suggested the establishment of an undergraduate library to help the younger students. But Sir Thomas Bodley was opposed to the idea, and in a letter to James he pointed out that another keeper would be needed and that books used by the younger students might also be required by the more senior students at times. He concluded by saying that he believed there was much to be said against such a library.[2] The matter rested there for many years until the Radcliffe Camera, the building near the Bodleian which it had occupied since 1749, was finally attached to the Bodleian itself as an undergraduate reading room.

In the seventeenth and eighteenth centuries when there was only a handful of universities in Britain, the chief duty of librarians seems to have been the preservation of the scholarly collections from theft or loss, and the emphasis in the university library was very much on advanced study and research, since this was the gauge by which a university and its library had come to be judged. This marked emphasis upon research and conservation as being the prime functions of the university library persists to the present day, and not only affects the service offered by the university library but also makes no allowance for the social revolution which has taken place in British universities since the end of the last war. Even with the establishment of a number of provincial universities in the late nineteenth and early twentieth centuries, the history of British university librarianship is marked by constant underestimating of rate of growth and student numbers in terms of library buildings, and by little or no allowance for different and changing patterns of university teaching and library use. A major result of this failure to keep pace with educational developments is the general inadequacy today of university library buildings, book collections and service to readers. Only now with the growing awareness of present and long-standing deficiencies and the very real possibility that in the near future a re-examination of commonly accepted ideas and attitudes will be called for are steps gradually being taken to remedy the shortcomings apparent at all levels of university library service, and particularly at the all-important undergraduate level.

In the United States, although university teaching, administrative methods and student habits are different in some ways from those in Britain, many of the problems which have been and are being resolved there are results of the pressures of conditions and needs which this country's university libraries also will probably have to face in the not-too-distant future. Not the least of American university problems is the accommodation of rapidly increasing student numbers and the maintenance of a good library service for them, in addition to meeting the considerable demands of teaching staff and graduate students. This dilemma has been a familiar one to American university librarians for many years, and it is the undergraduate library which has been one of their most important means of attempting to resolve it. To some extent, therefore, since Britain has at present nothing in the order of a Lamont or Michigan student library, we must rely upon the practical experience of foreign precedent with certain reservations, and the full significance of the undergraduate library is perhaps best appreciated in the broad American context. If one can speak of a concept in relation to the development of the undergraduate library, the Americans have at least interpreted that concept in their own way according to their circumstances and have translated it into practical terms during the past 15 years.

American university libraries remained small until well into the nineteenth century, but have developed rapidly since then, particularly during the last 30 years. They have sought means of providing for research within the main library and space within the library for teaching and research to be carried out in close connection with books. A new library for the Johns Hopkins University in Baltimore, opened in 1914, is regarded by many as the starting point of modern university library planning since it was the first real attempt to elaborate a plan in accordance with the functions of the library. It provided a series of rooms for teaching departments adjacent to the stack on each side and communicating with its appropriate sections, and a general reading room across the end of the stack and also in direct communication with it. A year later, in 1915, Harvard opened its Widener Library which was the first to provide "carrels" or study cubicles in the stack itself. A large number of American university libraries were built in the following 15 years or so and the various principles of planning which gradually emerged from a good deal of experimental design included the segregation in a "reserved reading room" of large numbers of junior students doing their prescribed reading.

In Britain during the 1930's a number of universities had undergraduate reading rooms which were usually merely a room set aside for students who were carrying out their own reading but not consulting library books, as, for example, at Bedford College, London. Generally speaking, these rooms were housed in the main library building, though at Oxford and Glasgow they were separate, and while some contained a "general collection" or a "small selection of current books", others contained no books whatsoever and the student was more or less left to his own devices. If such collections were provided they were thought of almost entirely in terms of prescribed reading material or "the most wanted books". Moreover, librarians came to realize that a large number of these students using their libraries did not consult the books on the shelves but came only for their own study because they had nowhere else to go where they could read their notes or their own books, and this encouraged some librarians to provide reading rooms without any books, not only to cater for this type of student use of library facilities, but also as a means of preserving the hard-pressed library itself very much more for those who needed it for advanced study and research. This development is quite understandable in the circumstances, for if the undergraduate was not permitted to enter the stacks and made no use of any books available to him, there was little or nothing to justify his presence in the library in terms of the limited approach to library service for undergraduates at this time. In the United States, too, the provision of separate rooms or halls for undergraduate reading, although sometimes stocked with a reasonable number of books and placed in close proximity to the appropriate teaching departments for the convenience of users, was still largely a concession to neglected students and a means by which heavily burdened university libraries, greatly in need of extension, could find some measure of relief from the sheer pressure of student numbers.

Some idea of the approach adopted by librarians to student library service and their concept of the function of the university library can be obtained from the following statement which was contributed to a report on a survey of libraries made by the Library Association during the years 1936 to 1937. "It is not the librarian's primary function to cater for the needs of those who do not wish to use his collections, although, as has already been indicated, some so-called 'reference rooms' are tending to become mere reading rooms."[3]

However, if this seems an oversimplification of the state of undergraduate library service before, and indeed after, the last war, it must be remembered that even those librarians who were keenly aware of the need to improve their service to students were greatly compromised not only by their very definite obligations to the university, its teaching staff and graduate students for building as good a research collection as possible, but also by the constant stringency of financial resources which made even these important obligations virtually impossible to carry out to the full.

On the realization by the Americans during the 1930's that university libraries were favouring their senior classes of users with such devices as closed stacks, carrels, extended borrowing privileges for seniors and often small specialized branch libraries with restricted use, all at the expense of the intellectual development of the average undergraduate, some attempt was made to redress the balance by establishing browsing rooms, various types of better-stocked reading rooms, and also reserved reading rooms containing multiple copies of a few thousand books in very heavy demand which could be borrowed for a very short period only or not removed from the library at all. While representing a step in the right direction, it could hardly be said, however, that these devices represented an adequate effort to provide good overall library service to the undergraduate student body.

But clearly the university has an obligation to offer its undergraduate students the opportunity of acquiring a sound education. They usually comprise by far the largest section of the university's population, and after all, they are the potential graduate students and teaching staff as well as the future professional and civic leaders of the community. As one American librarian put it a few years ago: "A university which recognizes no obligation to these students is dishonest in accepting their money and their time."[4] As has already been said, the excellence of a university library has traditionally been measured by the strength of its research collections, and by the early 1950's many American librarians were ready to admit that this emphasis upon the acquisition of materials necessary for research was one of the major contributory factors in the neglect of the needs of the undergraduate over the years. The small American college library, realistically aware that it could not attempt to provide research material, in concentrating upon the best possible integration of the library with the academic programme of its institution was in fact fulfilling its responsibilities to the undergraduate much more successfully in many cases than the more renowned library of the larger university. Moreover, the lack of adequate library facilities, together with large student enrolments, gradually lead to the lecture-plus-textbook method of teaching and to the development of an examination system that determines the manner in which students study. Students quickly learn that the best way to study for the type of examination papers set is to confine one's reading to the assignments and to do the reading shortly before the examination. This causes library use to be largely confined to a few titles and to a few days in the term. Study of attendance records in American university reserve rooms has shown this practice to be extremely widespread.[5]

Large lecture classes breed impersonal student–teaching staff relations and seem to make students liable to resist the efforts of the faculty to teach. Lecturers are sometimes heard to complain that the vast majority of their students have no interest in learning and have declined in quality. Others recognize the unwillingness of the student to learn, but attribute this to the failure of the university to offer an interesting and demanding curriculum rather than to lack of ability in the student. In many cases the scepticism of the lecturer towards his students may be met by a growing scepticism on their part towards his lecturing ability and recommended reading, and the university librarian will very swiftly become aware of the resulting strain and conflict.

As a result of this highly unsatisfactory state of affairs, university libraries and instruction methods became the focus of keen attention among university librarians, and serious efforts began to be made to take into account the teaching as well as the research needs of the university, the aim being to make possible the fuller use of the library as a tool for instruction. This concept of the university library has been widely held in America for many years, and in some ways the undergraduate library is essentially an extension of it, but most British university libraries are only just beginning to feel that it is a function within their sphere of influence.

In America the increasing occupation with the teaching function of the library and the attempt to balance the trend in intensive specialization by introducing more general material of the kind associated with liberal arts studies led to the establishment or improvement of undergraduate reading room collections, browsing rooms, reference service and the general availability of books themselves. The problems of undergraduate library service were now arising essentially from the inclusion of the libraries' mass instructional and special research services in a single building. Most of the older and larger American university libraries were fixed architecturally and could not often overcome the limitations of their design. Thus, at a time when the ratio of number of readers per book was rising at a faster rate than ever before, libraries were finding it extremely difficult to enlarge central libraries sufficiently to handle these students.

In addition to main buildings being physically inadequate for satisfactory service to both undergraduate and research student, there was a growing feeling that a number of other characteristics of the large university library were totally unsuited to the needs of the undergraduate reader. These characteristics merit some consideration here since the awareness of them has exerted considerable influence upon the nature and scope of the undergraduate library itself.

The first feature of the university library which is regarded as being unable to function efficiently in relation to the undergraduate user is the sheer bulk of the book collection. This is not so applicable to British universities at present, but in America there are at least twenty-five universities with a bookstock in excess of 1 million volumes and almost as many more with a stock of half to three-quarters of a million volumes. Many librarians believe that it is no service to the undergraduate student with a problem to solve or an essay to write, particularly to the first-year student, to turn him loose among a huge collection which, in any case, consists largely of research materials. They argue that his needs are best met with a collection of material prescribed by lecturers together with a good selection of standard works and alternative treatises to cover his supplementary needs, maintaining that to offer anything much larger at this stage probably confuses and daunts rather than helps him, especially if, as is all too frequently the case, he has come up from a school which had no library worth the name, and from a home where books and reading were not regarded as an integral part of life. This latter point may be a very significant one in view of the very wide variety of social backgrounds from which today's students come when entering university. Moreover, there is some evidence, in British universities at least, that students' first experience of the library is a mildly traumatic one and that they tend to be overawed by its resources. [6] Equally, it may be argued that if freshmen find the university library "intimidating" when they first enter and attempt to use it, it may be not so much the library's size but rather their inability to find their way about and exploit its resources which is responsible, in which case the answer would seem to lie in librarians and teaching staff co-operating more closely in educating students in the use of the library.

Another feature of the large university library, considered to make it unsuitable for undergraduate use and allied to the one just mentioned, lies in the nature of the book collection itself. It is characteristically a research collection, and as such it contains a far greater variety of books on every subject than any undergraduate could possibly have been accustomed to previously through his school and public library. Some of these books are by competent authors and some are not. Some are general treatments of a subject and some are intensive studies of a highly specialized aspect of a field of knowledge. Some are authoritative and lasting statements, while others may already have been superseded by numerous other titles, all of which have been collected by the library in the interests of scholarship. A great many items have no immediate historical, literary, critical or synthesizing value but have been acquired as the raw materials for future research, and the reasons for their presence in the collection may be fully appreciated only by the scholar or librarian.

Furthermore, teaching staff today cannot afford to build personal collections, as they did a generation ago, and quite naturally lean heavily on the library for their book and journal needs. Expansion in student numbers entails a corresponding increase in the numbers of staff, and as each newly appointed member of staff brings with him his own special research interest, which must be catered for both retrospectively and currently, the cumulative burden upon the library's book funds becomes extremely severe. It is also maintained that while inter-library lending causes the research student to suffer constant frustrations and delays in obtaining required material, so, too, does the practice of permitting large numbers of undergraduates to have direct access to the stacks and to borrow from them. Evidence of the extent to which this is true is extremely difficult to come by, but the increasing emphasis laid upon independent investigation by undergraduates, especially in their final year, and the growing distinction, particularly in America, between research and non-research degrees for graduate students is resulting not only in the undergraduate using more graduate books, but the graduate using more undergraduate books.

However, in spite of these basic problems it may be argued on educational grounds that the freshman should be educated to use a large research collection from the start of his university career, not only so that should he eventually decide to undertake research he will be reasonably well equipped to handle the library's full resources, but also so that he might develop during these undergraduate years a sound sense of judgement in collating the investigations of others and in the weighing up of opinion.[7]

Leonard Jolley conveys the importance of this experience very clearly in the following words: "Perhaps the most important lesson the student can take away from his university career is to have learned to treat books not as sources of authority but as instruments to think with and this is a lesson which cannot be imparted in the lecture theatre but must be slowly and painfully acquired by daily toil in the library."[8]

Another characteristic of the large university library likely to discourage rather than encourage its use by undergraduates is the nature of the catalogue. As this provides the key to these huge and varied collections, it may of necessity be so large and so complex that it simply serves to hamper the students' efficient use of the collections. A number of surveys of library use by undergraduates carried out in British universities, for example, show a marked reluctance on the part of students to use the catalogue except as a last resort, and a general tendency for them to rely on a sense of location and to go directly to the shelves to search for what they require.

This unsystematic and time-wasting method of approach caused the Lamont Undergraduate Library to decide from the beginning to reduce bibliographical detail in its catalogues to a minimum so as not to form a barrier between student and books.

A further feature of the university library likely to deter undergraduates and which is far more relevant to the American situation at present than to the British, where a good deal of scope for development exists, is the question of reference staff. Qualified advisory staff, who normally might be expected to help the undergraduate overcome some of the difficulties already named, may be so occupied in meeting the demands of the graduate students and teaching staff that undergraduate needs are either ignored or given cursory attention. Also, the kind of staff assembled for research library purposes is not necessarily the kind of staff that can work most effectively with younger students. At Harvard, before the establishment of the Lamont Library, it was found that undergraduates, on the one hand, and graduates and teaching staff, on the other, were all competing in the Widener Library for reference service and that it was invariably the case that the student or teacher engaged on research monopolized the service at the expense of the undergraduate. In consequence, care was aken to ensure a readily available reference service for undergraduates when the Lamont Library was planned.[9] The real function of such a service is to assist the self-educator, to train the student to train himself, and the staff must always be available to give assistance to the student at each successive stage towards the full bibliographical control of his subject.

Finally, considerations of size both in terms of holdings and of student numbers usually make it expedient for the large university library to close its stacks to undergraduates, thus depriving them of free access to books.

Similar considerations frequently lead, particularly in the United States, to the establishment of reserve book rooms and other devices that may not be educationally satisfactory. In the past, if the stack has been open at all to readers, it has in the main been for the research worker on account of the obvious advantages of enabling him to work in close proximity to his material. The stack was thus considered the place of study for the research worker, and it was argued that while stack books were available to all who applied for them, indiscriminate access to the shelves would simply defeat its own ends in a large university. However, since the Second World War almost all the newer British and American university library buildings have provided open stacks, and some of the older libraries, such as Northwestern in the United States, have opened theirs. The chief argument for this practice is the belief in the widening of the student's academic interests resulting from browsing and direct contact with books and in the discouraging of his heavy reliance upon textbooks and prescribed reading for his work. This ready accessibility of books to students was one of the main objectives in setting up the Lamont Library and was assured by the basic plan of the building with its open alcove-type stacks standing between the entrances and the reading areas.[10] Shelving the majority of required reading on open shelves has the advantage of enabling undergraduates to help themselves, and shelving these books with the rest of the collection has the added advantage of continuously acquainting the student with other books on the same subject. In such circumstances browsing among books should become a part of the daily student routine and this leads to scanning books that catch the eye, and thus the reading habit is launched.

Given, of course, that national libraries must maintain closed stacks, the arguments against open stacks in university libraries apply mainly to those with huge and valuable research collections such as the Bodleian Library, though open stacks have several practical implications which should not be overlooked. For instance, there is the inevitable cost of keeping shelves in order, the possibility of annoyance to research workers with carrels in the stack, and the obvious disadvantages of reliance on the classification system as a guide to resources. Local conditions, methods of administration, physical facilities and the habits of students are elements that must also be considered in this question. Nevertheless, in discussing this same problem over 20 years ago, a British university and college library manual probably arrived at the most reasonable conclusion when it stated:

> If once it is established that the open stack benefits many (and probably most) readers while handicapping none, the administrative drawbacks can hardly be considered important. It is true that books will be frequently misplaced and that from time to time large moves will have to be undertaken but these objections apply hardly less to reading rooms, and must in any case be outweighed by the interests of readers.[11]

THE UNDERGRADUATE LIBRARY

The various difficulties, already discussed, which are encountered by the average undergraduate student when he attempts to use a university library of even moderate size are frequently used as the basis of arguments in favour of the undergraduate library, whether comprising an entire floor of the main library or a completely separate building, and correspondingly they have influenced, perhaps dictated, the general conception of such a library. They are, however, largely practical considerations related to the contention that in some situations the problem of providing adequate physical facilities for library service to undergraduate students may be solved most efficiently and even economically by a separate building. On the whole the larger, older and poorly designed or inflexible library buildings are the ones which tend to find themselves in this predicament. Both shelf space and reading space are at a premium, and efficient library service to the student community becomes increasingly difficult, if not impossible, to maintain as demands upon stock and library staff grow progressively heavier. Because limited funds often make it impossible to buy multiple copies of books, to give them shelf space and to provide adequate reading space for the students, the teaching staff have no option but to rely more and more heavily on textbooks for the course work. At Michigan, for example, before the opening of its undergraduate library in 1958, this kind of situation made it quite possible for a student to spend 4 years as an undergraduate at the university without once entering the general library building. [12]

The other justification for special provision for undergraduates is more theoretical and relates to the role of the library and the librarian in the education of the undergraduate student. If the latter seems more difficult to defend, the cause may be an unconscious, perhaps even conscious, diffidence on the part of librarians regarding their own importance for the educational process. However, as one American librarian has written: "A university education should awaken a student's curiosity and train his mind to enable him to continue educating himself throughout his lifetime. If the habit of reading is to be acquired at university then every opportunity in that direction must be made attractive. In this the library can exert leadership." [13]

The inadequacies of existing library facilities can also have a serious effect on the service provided for graduates and teaching staff, since if undergraduates turn to specialized departmental libraries for their needs, these libraries, which are frequently designed almost wholly for the convenience of research workers, immediately have a divided function. In any case, the idea of providing a series of scattered undergraduate departmental reading rooms is usually rejected on the grounds that none of them would contain an adequate collection or provide satisfactory service for its users and that the cost of setting up such a network would go far towards paying for a much more effective library for undergraduate use. When the Lamont Library was still in the planning stage, Keyes Metcalf stated that one of its main objectives was "To concentrate as far as is practicable the library service for undergraduates in a central location",[14] the general idea being that by concentrating the books and other materials needed by the undergraduates in one building, by providing as many copies of each book as are needed, and by employing an energetic staff to work intelligently with both faculty and students, it should be possible to bring the library in closer contact with the students' course work and the interests aroused in the lecture room, and to induce the students to give more attention to books that exercise the intellect and the imagination. Such a library with its accent entirely upon service to undergraduates would afford teaching staff much greater freedom in shaping their courses as they should, and also serve as an intellectual centre for the undergraduate student body.

Although it may seem to be a means of transforming necessity into virtue, the undergraduate library represents a positive and painstaking effort to correct the various deficiencies in library service to students which have become painfully apparent over the years. It means a library building specifically planned and administered to be of maximum benefit to undergraduate students, based on the premises that the library should be as important as the lecturer in undergraduate education, the one complementing the other, and that any undergraduate may realize his potentiality for developing a life-long interest in reading good books and in continued self-education long after his university career is over if the library assists him and makes the whole process attractive. The undergraduate library thus seeks to introduce the student to books, to lead him to form good reading habits, to assist him with his set work and to teach him really to use the library to the full.

The siting and planning of the undergraduate library will, of course, vary a good deal from university to university, and are largely governed by local circumstances, but one or two general remarks may be made on these aspects. While existing buildings may make it impossible for the undergraduate library to be the geographical centre of the university, it should certainly be the intellectual centre of the undergraduate community and be sited as strategically as possible in relation to the various teaching departments, particularly those of the humanities and social sciences which are likely to use it the most by the very nature of their work and its heavy reliance upon books rather than equipment. It is also desirable that the undergraduate library building is located in close proximity to the main university library, since it is generally agreed that the undergraduate should not be restricted to his own library, and it is hoped that his experience in the undergraduate library will encourage him to make advantageous use of the research collections. He should be welcomed at all branches of the university library system when he has a serious purpose in using them. Likewise, the proximity of the undergraduate library to the main research library has distinct advantages for scholars and teaching staff. At Lamont, for instance, periodicals are not allowed to leave the building and they are frequently consulted by scholars who find that the required volumes from the Widener Research Library are out on loan. The same applies to much of the apparently "standard" material at Lamont since its collection is far more than a student textbook collection. This overlapping of use between the undergraduate and main libraries, while obviously highly desirable in theory, could well produce numerous practical difficulties including serious interference with the essential function of each of the two libraries, so careful planning is needed to reduce such interference to a minimum and to strike a reasonable balance between the two.

The actual planning of the undergraduate library building will again vary according to existing conditions and the preferences of the librarian concerned as developments in the United States have shown, but there do seem to exist a number of important factors which should be taken into account in any situation. In these days of unparalleled growth of universities, declared as national policy, the first essential of any library building is flexibility. Modular planning can achieve this to a surprising degree allowing for expansion both outwards and upwards, for any necessary internal re-arrangements and for any modifications caused by shift of emphasis in the teaching pattern of the university. The internal layout of book stacks, study facilities and services will of course largely depend upon the planning of the librarian in conjunction with the architect. However, in recent years library building, planning and equipment have come to revolve around readers whose claims for materials and services are becoming increasingly heavy and varied. For instance, the proportion of the student population for which it is thought desirable to provide seats has tended to rise[15] and the allowance of square feet per person desirable in reading areas has gone up, especially where informal arrangement is intended. At the same time, it is generally agreed that access to collections must be easier than before. These standards have suggested larger capacities, and, more significantly, they seek to put users close to the materials they require. The guiding force behind all this spaciousness, comfort, ample study space and ease of access is the desire to encourage students to examine and use their study material at will, and, where desired, in consultation with their instructors or with librarians. As the idea has spread, great reading rooms have tended to become outmoded in favour of study cubicles and reading alcoves distributed throughout the book stacks, and reference departments have tended to be divorced from those that remain, while reserve book sections too have assumed less importance.

This stress upon availability of materials is reflected by the fact that the second main objective of Lamont, as seen by Keyes Metcalf, was simply "to make books readily accessible to the students".[16] This was achieved in Lamont's case by the basic plan of the building which provides an alcove-type stack through the centre, open on one side to the major reading areas and on the other to the entrances, the reference room and special collections. Users of the library, almost as often as they enter, move from one room to another, or leave, can hardly avoid passing through corridors or alcoves lined with books. Availability implies not only open shelves but a minimization of all other barriers between readers and books. In the context of the undergraduate library, enormous catalogues such as those used in the great research libraries are invaluable keys for scholars, but are necessarily so complex that they are deemed discouraging and time-consuming barriers to undergraduates, and at Lamont, Minnesota and New Mexico the catalogue is small in physical proportions and the cataloguing itself is kept to a minimum. Moreover, facilities are provided for by-passing it wherever possible in the form of visible indexes of reserved books, annotated copies of reading lists and at Lamont a simplified classification system based upon Dewey.

The general problem of reserve books exists in most academic libraries but is particularly relevant to the undergraduate library. Every undergraduate library will have to keep a certain number of heavily used books on reserve, but this number should be kept to an absolute minimum and as many books as possible shelved with the main open-shelf collection. Close co-operation between teaching and library staff in deciding which books to reserve and for how long should help to assure fuller use and circulation of the general collection. In order for the library to function smoothly in relation to student assignments, it is important for it to have in good time lists of required course readings, and if these are provided early enough, the library is in a position to obtain titles not already owned, to procure additional copies, or to replace those which may be lost or missing.

Changing objectives of the university, or at least changing methods of achieving these, have offered the library an increasingly significant place in the education of the undergraduate. This has not been primarily because of the development of courses in general education, with their aim to provide a broad and common intellectual experience at the university level, but rather because of the efforts to engage students actively in learning for themselves. Lectures, textbooks and examinations have been supplemented by methods of challenging students to take a larger share in their education.

If sensitivity and reflection and the ability to analyse and to judge are to be fostered at university, both lecturer and student must turn to books that encourage them to think and to feel for themselves. They must investigate primary and secondary sources where originality of thought and expression may be encountered.

This emphasis upon undergraduates' use of books other than textbooks makes the reserve collection totally inadequate for them. In America, and increasingly in Britain, the library has been and seems likely to continue to be primarily responsible for providing the duplicates necessary in courses that do not rely on textbooks and anthologies but seek to take the student to original works in as close to the original form as possible. This has brought about the expansion of student collections in both size and scope.

The undergraduate library should hold books on open shelves in sufficient quantity to reflect the entire undergraduate curriculum, including books of general interest.[17] Books, here interpreted in the widest sense, preferably should be brought together not by format and process but by content and idea to serve groups of related departments of instruction. The collection of the undergraduate library is formed to meet most of the needs of the under-graduate student and usually comprises an extensive open-shelf collection of reserve books, collateral readings, the main periodicals in each field, bibliographies, reference works, and a careful selection of books for general cultural and recreational reading which is often housed separately. It has been suggested that the collection be "an ideal collection roughly comparable to the library of a truly cultivated man", with its own simplified catalogue, its own librarian and its own reading area.

The University of Michigan, for example, intends to build up its under-graduate collection to somewhere between 100,000 and 150,000 volumes, allowing for necessary duplication, and then to maintain it at that level with careful and systematic weeding.[18] It is important that such a collection should never be considered as completed. Special funds must always be available for continued experimentation with new books to fill gaps, to replace obsolete or unsuitable material, to add better translations, better editions, and more up-to-date secondary works, and, in general, to effect changes according to the pattern and emphasis of the teaching programme. The available reading must not be fixed or restricted in any way if courses and teaching staff are to remain vigorous and stimulating. As has already been said, the bulk of the collection should be readily accessible to students with only specially assigned books on very heavy demand placed on overnight reserve to enable them to circulate as widely as possible in a limited period.

Another important feature of the undergraduate library is the reference service. Intelligent and sympathetic reference staff are a great asset in such a library since their efforts are focused on a definite clientele, with whose projects and problems they can become familiar. Reference advice can suggest where and how to find works on one's subject and what books and articles may possibly be helpful, but not usually, one would think, exactly what to read, as this is duplicating the effort of the teaching staff. It is not so much finding facts and answering questions for inquirers which is the primary task, although many such queries have to be answered, but the reference staff should aim through the inquiries made to educate the student to help himself. To this end a substantial collection of bibliographies and reference books is required on the open shelves, where they are accessible to both staff and students. It is important for this collection to be as comprehensive as possible since, as the Director of the University of Michigan Library has said: "The problem of helping a student halfway to an answer and then referring him to the General Library for additional assistance becomes intolerable in practice if not in theory."[19] The opening of the Lamont Library at Harvard made reference service more readily available to undergraduates than it had been in the Widener Library where faculty members, visiting scholars and graduate students tended to monopolize it. After the library had been subjected to 12 months' use it was noticed that there had been a gradual but distinct rise in the number and quality of reference questions and the rise has continued steadily since then. It is hoped that this will continue as students develop the habit of turning to librarians for bibliographical help.[20]

Careful introduction of freshmen to the library is particularly important, as are introductions to the layout of the stacks and of the reserves as well as to the catalogue, circulation practices and reference shelves. The professional librarian is constantly astonished to find how ignorant most students and many teachers are of the means of acquiring the knowledge they require. The process of finding things out demands skills which have to be taught and this must be pointed out. Thus the introduction of the student to the library is not something which is done once and for all. It is a continuous process which may well last beyond the student's university career and which becomes the more obviously valuable the longer it is carried on. These services are in accord with the general educational policy of encouraging students from the beginning to know and to use good books.

In spite of the difficulties and costs, the reason for having an undergraduate collection and library service, whether in the main library or completely separate, is the furtherance of student self-education and the university should recognize the relevant services as a necessary charge upon it for making possible the kind of education that it believes in and promises to offer. Undergraduates are no longer simply pupils, and the possibilities for intellectual initiative should not be postponed to the graduate stage or even to the final undergraduate year. Independent investigation (rather than research) by undergraduates is becoming increasingly common in both British and American universities, whether for a paper in an advanced course, for a special project or reading course, or as a requirement for an honours degree, and this is intended to further some of the main ends as seminar discussion based on challenging reading materials. In a more specialized and individual way it should encourage critically responsible inquiry and the capacity through analysis to formulate and to support conclusions. Such investigation must necessarily relate to a particular topic, usually in a special departmental field, and this reinforces the demands upon the undergraduate collection. As well as the fairly standard material already discussed, it is useful therefore to have a few of the leading specialized journals on hand for occasional articles, and, more important, for book reviews and bibliographical surveys. The student should become at least familiar with what these are and how they can serve both in exploratory reading in a field and in specific inquiry. It is unlikely that even the largest undergraduate collection by present standards would be able to cater for all the needs of the student engaged upon this kind of independent investigation and so he must be permitted to make use of the much greater resources of the main research library whenever the occasion demands. This is the case, for instance, at the Michigan, Lamont and Columbia undergraduate libraries.

The wide and consistent use of imaginative and thought-provoking books as instruments of education should, it is hoped, direct the interest of undergraduates beyond the completion of the assignment. If curricular and library services encourage first-hand acquaintance with creative and scholarly works through group discussion and individual inquiry and through open shelves and convenient arrangements for reading in and out of the library, librarian and teaching staff should anticipate, if these things are being well done, not only an increase in ability to read perceptively and discriminatingly but also curiosity and enjoyment in reading and in having books to read.[21]

In addition to the undergraduate library's provision of books and other material for curricular and general background reading purposes, the ease of access to its stacks, the facilities for overnight loan and reference inquiries, and ample reading space, devices for the encouragement of extra-curricular reading are also becoming an accepted library responsibility, especially in the United States. Such reading is usually housed in what is known as the "browsing room" with shelves of standard and recent literature, or in lounge-like comfort in a wing of a regular reading room with strategically placed shelves for new accessions or for a rental collection of contemporary fiction, drama, poetry and essays, for example. Conveniently placed shelves or stands for current journals or attractive and accessible periodical rooms may also further casual reading and the pursuit of special interests. Undergraduate reading of one kind or another may be encouraged to some extent by the smallest detail that makes any reader more comfortable and may be discouraged at least slightly by the mildest annoyance or smallest inconvenience. Hence the growing emphasis in recent years upon lighting, air-conditioning, the use of colour and library furniture. Other features of the undergraduate library which are designed for the comfort and convenience of readers and which warrant serious consideration when such a library is being planned are typing cubicles, smoking areas and refreshment facilities.

Books are the staple of libraries, but more than books may be expected of them. Now that courses in the history and interpretative analysis of art and music are becoming common, attention is being given to provision for the first-hand acquaintance of students with works of the visual arts and music. Lamont, for instance, provides a number of special rooms where facilities for listening to music, poetry and drama related to various courses are made available. The Michigan Undergraduate Library includes a small multi-purpose room equipped with 200 stacking chairs, motion picture projectors, and public address system for use by the students for lectures, discussion groups, the showing of films, or "for any affair which concerns undergraduates and the library".[22] Librarians are by no means unanimously of the opinion that it is desirable to provide such rooms in a library, but a very reasonable case may be made out for these facilities as valuable adjuncts to the teaching programme, and if they are to be provided, it is perhaps preferable to centralize them as part of the general service to students in the undergraduate library where the appropriate reading materials are available. However, it may still be argued that libraries, on the one hand, and art and music departments, on the other, are natural alternatives and perhaps rivals for this responsibility, particularly if no special library for undergraduates exists.

The initiative of the librarian is needed to assist or encourage the teaching staff to make the library the centre of study and of educational resources, at least in the humanities and social sciences. (A special problem is presented in the natural sciences by the power of laboratories to draw books away from the central library into departmental or special libraries.) He can certainly collaborate with lecturers in improving the book collections by making suggestions of purchases that will give better balance between areas in a field or will further a department's long-range plans for source materials or standard sets, for example.

Considerable tact may also be required to lead teaching staff and curriculum towards more reliance on the library and less on textbooks. The university librarian has more immediate acquaintance with the students' use of the collections than have most of the academic staff; but of greater importance for his influence is the rapport that he has established through his work with the library committee and with individual members of the teaching staff. He is clearly in a stronger position if he is a member of the various faculty committees, and stronger still if he does some teaching, though this rarely seems the case.

The presence of the undergraduate library on the campus has a number of other implications, most of which seem to be borne out by American experience at least. The most important and perhaps most obvious of these is its direct effect upon the students and teaching staff for whom it is intended. Without in any way curtailing the undergraduate's access to the great research collections, state universities like Colorado, Florida State, Michigan, Nebraska, New Mexico, Oklahoma and the municipal University of

Cincinnati have shown that carefully selected and attractively housed under-graduate libraries have not only increased support for lecture-room instruc-tion but have stimulated considerable voluntary reading, and in connection with the latter a revival of "lists of books every college graduate should have read" before receiving his degree is making its presence felt on the campus. Twelve months after it opened the Lamont Library reported that while borrowings from the main research library dropped only slightly during that period, the total for the research and undergraduate libraries combined was 37,000 volumes greater than the research library's figure for 1948 when Lamont was not yet available. Overnight borrowings for reserved books increased by almost 20% and undergraduate use of books within the library also increased substantially.[23] Centralization, because it brings greater con-venience, undoubtedly contributed to these and other results, as did the availability of books and the improvement of the book stock by increased duplication of heavily used titles. This duplication made it possible to restrict to closed shelves, which are behind the issue desks in Lamont, fewer reserved books than ever before. Closed reserves can probably never be abolished completely, but they can be reduced in number still further when student enrolments eventually become more steady and as more of the books that are needed come back into print.

Writing on the Michigan Undergraduate Library a few years ago, Dr. Wagman reported considerable increases in library use by students and in the amount of material read in the library and borrowed for home reading since its opening at the beginning of 1958. Analysis of the circulation for home use indicated that 37·7% represented voluntary reading and 62·3% was course-related. Further analysis of the course-related reading revealed that a very large part of this also was not required but apparently stimulated by the course work. Dr. Wagman continues:

> Other less measurable effects of the new library are noteworthy. It has definitely become the hub of undergraduate activity on the campus. Its central location has made it possible for the students to spend the hours between classes reading in the library and thousands of them do so. Many students are now using the library who confess that hitherto they had preferred the movies to the study halls and had rarely or never ventured into the General Library. Obviously, also, the undergraduates are reading a great many more good books than before and under the guidance of the reference staff, short-handed as it is, are learning how to use a library catalog, indices, biblio-graphies, and other reference works. Psychologically, the effect of this library on the students has been extremely gratifying.[24]

It was feared that free access to the reserve books would result in their rapid disappearance and, in fact, 1% of the total bookstock did disappear during one spring term, but since new regulations have been brought in regarding theft and mutilation of books, there are indications that book losses have decreased.

The vast majority of the teaching staff at Michigan understood the poten-tial value of the new library before it was completed and it is now becoming apparent that their interest in using the library as an aid to their teaching has begun to exceed the library's ability to keep up. In short, as Dr. Wagman says, "Both building and staff have proved to be much too small."[25]

Another implication of the undergraduate library, stemming from the fact that it enables all student services to be centralized in one location, is the economies made possible by such special facilities. When Lamont was being planned it was claimed that costs were lower because simpler and cheaper cataloguing could be used for undergraduate books; undergraduates use an expendable type of book and by not mixing these with the less expendable type certain losses could be avoided; the library is in smaller units and expansion can be made without as much danger of over-expansion; and the type of service differs enough for staff differentiation to be a good idea. Taken as general statements these claims seem rather arbitrary and questionable, but when applied to a specific situation there appears to be a good deal of truth in them. Special undergraduate provision should also mean much easier communication with students and teaching staff and, in giving students some sense of independence and a proprietary feeling towards the library, should provide the type of personal library service which can be found where there is not the overwhelming pressure upon limited resources and staff which is likely to exist in a large university library system. Required seminars and final year dissertations for honours students undoubtedly result in more concentrated use of library materials, and any shift from the textbook method of instruction invariably puts additional demands upon the library.

Finally, the establishment of a separate undergraduate library does relieve demand upon central and departmental libraries and helps to release them for purposes of research. In his address at a Conference on the Place of the Library in the University, held in March 1949, Keyes Metcalf stated in order of importance the three premises on which the Lamont Library was planned. First, "The undergraduates will make more and better use of a library designed expressly for them", and then the practical considerations, "That this was the best way to relieve the pressure in the Widener building and make unnecessary a new central building; and that if the pressure were relieved, the Widener Library Building would become a more satisfactory research center than it has been in the past".[26]

Since the opening of Michigan's Undergraduate Library, its General Library and branch libraries have come to be used predominantly by graduate students and the teaching staff, as was anticipated. The stacks of the General Library have been opened to all and it also is now, for the most part, an open-shelf library. Graduate students are working in the General Library and the branches in much greater number than ever before, and it has become possible to adapt much of the space formerly employed for undergraduate reading rooms to special uses. The Reference Department and the branch librarians have more time to spend on service to teaching staff and graduate students and on bibliographic enterprises. It has also been possible to curtail the staff of the Circulation Department in the General Library despite the fact that circulation of books from that collection has not decreased.[27]

Little or no mention has been made so far of the existence of any opposition to the idea of the separate undergraduate library, and although the case in favour of such a library seems overwhelming and has, indeed, been argued far more frequently than the case against it, a number of valid objections have been raised from time to time and the subject has remained a lively and mildly controversial one. There are both librarians and teachers who remain unconvinced of the educational value of a separate facility for students, although almost all those who are familiar with the Lamont Library think it a successful operation. They argue, as stated earlier, that in principle there should not be a division into a scholars' library and a students' library, that the separation of students into graduate and undergraduate is purely arbitrary and a formal, institutional issue, and that the use of libraries should be independent of the status of the student. Recognition of this last point has led almost all American universities with an undergraduate library on the campus to permit and to encourage undergraduates to use the main research library for material which their own library does not possess.

It is also pointed out[28] that if good undergraduate libraries are provided, a large percentage of students may never seek to use the general library and will be the poorer for it. There are some students who will one day be university teachers and there are others whose way of life may lie in other directions but who are not content with books selected for them, who like to look into sources and test statements, who are interested in other matters than their course of study, and these should be allowed freedom to browse among the mass of the main library, the miscellaneous treasures perhaps collected over many generations and by many divers interests. There is no means of selecting such students from the general body of students and there is certainly no validity in the separation of students for the pass or the honours degree. While one may meet this point by maintaining that, in any case, the really keen students will always make the necessary effort to use the general library, the fact remains that opposition to the separate undergraduate library is largely based on the contention that students may be led to believe that its book collection represents everything that they need to read.

A further argument against the undergraduate library arises from the recognition that the characteristics of the large university library have positive as well as negative values for the undergraduate users of its collections and services. The positive values are seen in the greater abundance and variety of the book collections and the fact that the service staff usually includes a number of subject specialists who, taken together, will have both a broader range and a greater depth of bibliographical knowledge than the relatively small staff of the undergraduate library.

When attempting to arrive at policy decisions regarding undergraduate library users, librarians may have been asking the questions in relation to the capacities or abilities of the student and not in relation to his educational needs. Thus, it is suggested that the university librarian must ask, not can the student use our library facilities, but should the undergraduate students be able to use our library? If this is so, the student is still in the unsatisfactory position of experiencing difficulty in using the library, but the university librarian will be less concerned with changing his library to match undergraduate capacities and will devote himself rather to attempts to bring the students' abilities up to the level of the library and its services. In order to achieve this, it is argued, a broader and more basic method of library instruction is needed to give the student an understanding of the library as a social agency and to enable him to grasp the means by which knowledge is recorded and arranged in the library as well as practical knowledge of the working of the catalogue and the use of reference tools and bibliographies. This type of instruction would require a special series of lectures which might be made an integral part of the courses the student will take during his university career, as present methods of instruction in library use are very often too narrowly conceived and executed.[29]

Doubt has also been cast on the various devices employed by librarians in an attempt to encourage the reading habit and the love of books in students to enable them to read more widely and more profitably. It is argued that since the habit of reading and the love of books are attitudes and a preference for books and reading the exercise of a sense of values, of the establishment of which very little is known, it is safe to assume that they flow far more frequently from the home and other early influences, and from persons or groups of persons than they do from books or collections of books. Hence it is held that these qualities which librarians try so hard to instil are already in the student when he arrives at the university or that they are developed, where they are developed at all, from influences received in the lecture room, the department and the hall of residence.

To accept this position is not necessarily to say that the library should not consciously play a part in stimulating an interest in books and in reading. It does suggest, however, that the librarian as a person may be far more influential than the luxuriously furnished reading rooms and the invitingly arranged shelves. The Librarian of Princeton University may well have had this point in mind when he wrote some years ago:

> I really suspect that the range of performance between different systems of organization—unified collection, divisional plan, special undergraduate collection, or what you will—is considerably less than the difference in performance caused by a host of other factors, and further that we are talking solemn nonsense when we pretend that there is much science at work in the selection of any form of arrangement.[30]

And this in turn suggests that the chief librarian might put his money into staff rather than into special undergraduate collections. These staff would need to be competent, interested people, sufficiently numerous to have time to work with undergraduates and sufficiently learned to make the association fruitful. Librarians who take this line of argument believe it unwise to divorce undergraduate facilities physically from the university library itself. While they may concede that in some situations it may be necessary or expedient to create separate facilities and a separate collection, they feel that the student has so much to gain by being required to use a large collection that they regard a separate, selected library as a poor second choice. Even those who approve of the Lamont Library and its large collection point out that the Harvard undergraduate must still use the other Harvard libraries on occasion and wonder whether he should not be trained for such use from the very beginning of his university career.

Other librarians who agree that undergraduates merit a special type of library service and form a sufficiently homogeneous group to lend themselves to a separate service question the need to house it in a separate building and cite such universities as Yale, Chicago, Duke, Texas, Illinois and UCLA where the main library building is utilized for the undergraduate collection. In addition to cost, of course, this is largely a matter of existing accommodation and the size of the student population, factors which have in fact compelled Chicago and Illinois to start planning separate undergraduate libraries, while UCLA has built a new research library and is adapting the original library building to services for undergraduates.

The stage is being reached where even small universities are being obliged to plan ahead and allow for rapidly increasing student enrolments up to at least 1970. Writing in 1953, William Dix, Librarian of the Rice Institute in Texas, speaking from his experience of this institution with its 1500 students including some 200 graduates and a post-war library containing about 225,000 books, could see no reason for making any special provision for undergraduates in such a situation.[31] He felt that with a little care and planning there was no reason for the undergraduate to become lost in working with a unified collection numbering not more than half a million volumes, and in the circumstances his policy seems justified, though it does not take future development into account. Until recent years only the larger libraries were being caught out by rising student numbers but the pressure is now being felt among the smaller universities with smaller libraries and similar problems are having to be faced.

Arising from the fear that the student would lose much of the value that comes with the complete facilities of the main collection is the argument that he needs the intellectual stimulation of an unselected collection and that the closer one comes to establishing for undergraduates the library setting a researcher needs, the better. Dix, following this line of argument, writes:

"In principle we feel that the undergraduate should be constantly confronted by books a little beyond his grasp, that we are not concerned primarily with his finding specific books but with instructing him to learn to think, to use the library, and to grow intellectually."[32]

Thus it is argued that when the student goes to the shelves of the main collection for a particular elementary book he finds there also the major standard works on the same subject.[33] Even if some of these are written in a language which he does not read or are accounts of original research which he cannot understand, he at least becomes aware of their existence, and if he is of the material from which scholars are made, there is just a possibility that he might be led gradually to more advanced material. Such an effect, it is claimed, cannot be produced if the undergraduate works entirely with a few basic books which have been placed on reserve, or if he works entirely with a small collection supposedly within his grasp.

Furthermore, it is not only stimulating for an alert student to find books slightly beyond his grasp, but it is also good for him perhaps to see graduate students and teaching staff working at the same table and in the same part of the building on problems like his, except more advanced. This argument seems to be on less certain ground and is based on the assumption that research workers and undergraduates are not segregated within the main library. In any case, the alleged benefit for the undergraduate resulting from working in company with graduates and teaching staff seems at best elusive and remote and unlikely to apply generally.

The argument for teaching students to use a research collection of moderate size in smaller institutions may be strengthened by the fact that, with the exception of Michigan, Harvard and a few other universities with large undergraduate libraries and substantial financial resources for stocking them, limited budgets have resulted in many of the smaller universities in America providing less than satisfactory book collections for their students. Indeed, some seem little better than the small reading room and reserve book collections which were a common form of service to undergraduates long before the principle of the undergraduate library came to be generally accepted.

It seems very dubious whether undergraduate library provision on this scale is worth providing at all and it may well be preferable in such cases for all available funds to be devoted to the building up of the general collection to a level of size and comprehensiveness satisfactory for both research scholars and undergraduates. In addition to helping to maintain the quality of library service offered, centralization of facilities also serves to keep administrative problems to a minimum. The librarian may find it difficult not only to justify the setting up of such small collections for undergraduates but also to agree to suggestions, sometimes made by teaching staff, to reduce the library from 50,000 to 10,000 volumes, for example, in order to prevent the students from being confused over which books they should select.[34] This practice seems to be a complete negation of the role of librarians and teaching staff in setting up good working collections for the purpose of extensive undergraduate reading and in encouraging students to make intelligent use of these collections.

The validity of the various criticisms made will largely depend upon the nature of the individual undergraduate library and the system of which it forms a part. What is important is the size and scope of its collections, the quality of service offered to its users and the extent to which both library and teaching staff are successful in finding all the true readers and potential readers in the undergraduate population and in ensuring that these students obtain the books they want and have the opportunity to discuss these books, to broaden their reading and to grow intellectually to the limits of their natural capacity.

CONCLUSION

Thus, although a comparatively recent phenomenon in higher education in America, the undergraduate library has been in the making for many years. Indeed, it appears that as early as 1765 the Harvard College Records referred to the need for separate library facilities for undergraduates.[35] In Britain, too, as has already been mentioned, reference was made to a similar need at Oxford when Bodley was librarian, and Oxford was in fact the first university in this country to make special provision for undergraduates in the form of the Radcliffe Camera. But with the exception of Glasgow where a Reading Room for junior undergraduates was opened in 1939 with a collection of 13,000 volumes on closed reserve and seats for 530 readers,[36] special library provision for undergraduates has been of a most limited kind. This is partially explained by the fact that British universities have not been considered large enough to warrant a separate collection for undergraduates, but inadequate service has been largely due to the constant stringency of financial resources which has dogged university libraries in this country for many years and given them a poor basis for expansion.

Early awareness of the existence of a problem in relation to undergraduates and the university library was assured in the United States by the extremely rapid development of many of its university libraries after the turn of the century together with a swiftly growing student population. The increasingly unsatisfactory nature of library service and facilities led to much thought being given to the problem and the wide variety of attempted solutions culminated in the Lamont Library at Harvard, the planning of which by Keyes Metcalf and his colleagues began in the late thirties. The opening of the Lamont Library had a considerable influence on American librarianship and efforts began to be made to make the library the focal point of study, and to develop the library staff's educational role in the university. It is this concept of the university library as an educational force, a teaching instrument as the Americans call it, which has been one of the major distinctions between university librarianship in Britain and the United States. Even at the present time some British universities may not aspire to this concept of library service, feeling that it is out of their sphere of influence, and some would perhaps question whether it was an advance at all.

However, there comes a point when libraries reach a size where they are so difficult to use that only the most persevering reader can really get what he wants. It is at this point that it becomes apparent that the library must not only provide in an efficient manner the services that make books available, but must give its readers some help in searching for what they require.

As well as a greater range of instruction in library use, however, the growing influx of students to the universities may also call for a student reference service with suitable collections and fully trained staff. This has long been an accepted part of the function of the American university library, but in Britain lack of staff and a general reluctance on the part of students to approach those available has made for an almost non-existent reference service in our university libraries. A certain amount of bibliographical help is given, of course, but this appears to be mainly to research students and teaching staff.

The older and larger universities may soon have to give serious thought to the advisability of establishing separate undergraduate libraries. Some have already committed themselves in one way or another. In January 1964 Liverpool University opened a new Arts Reading Room with shelving for 60,000 volumes and seating for 460 readers. It is intended primarily for undergraduates, and houses what were previously the departmental collections of social science, geography and history. Several universities, including Manchester, Liverpool and Birmingham, have set aside capital sums for the purchase of multiple copies of standard material, and a number of other universities such as Keele and Reading contain special undergraduate collections of prescribed texts within the main library. However, one of the most interesting developments in this respect on the British university scene at present is the proposed undergraduate library at Leeds.[37]

At the moment the Brotherton Building is in need of considerable enlargement for increased reading room facilities, administrative offices and an enlarged bookstack, but as it is very much hemmed in by other departments, there is no possibility of providing any substantial enlargement without first demolishing some of the surrounding buildings. One of the proposals of the University of Leeds Development Plan is to establish a separate undergraduate library containing 30,000 to 50,000 books and seats for about 800 students. The building of such a library has the advantage of being able to start without having to wait for the demolition of active departmental buildings, as the architects point out. It would also, of course, relieve much of the pressure on the main Brotherton Library which could then become the principal research library of the university. It is hoped to complete the new library at Leeds in the late sixties.

Other universities may well follow suit, particularly under the pressures of the still more rapid expansions that are asked for in the next few years. The Robbins Report on Higher Education recommends a target of 350,000 university places by 1980–1,[38] and the pattern of service suitable for a student population of 5000 is not necessarily the best for 10,000, which is the figure now being aimed at by the 1970's by many of the larger civic universities. An important consequence of all this activity is the genuine interest which is being awakened in American experiment and experience, especially in such well-established buildings as those at Harvard and Michigan.

The present problems of undergraduate students in terms of library service and the possible solutions for the future are two of the most important questions facing any university with inadequate undergraduate provision, since their solution will help considerably in planning for other library facilities. In his description of the steps which led to the decision to build an undergraduate library at Michigan, Dr. Wagman listed some of the reasons which were present in the Harvard situation. He also wrote: "Relatively few of the larger universities are blessed with library facilities adequate to meet the demands of present student bodies, and the problem of providing meaningful service to undergraduate students is likely to yield, ten years from now, to the more pressing problem of how to provide any service at all for the entire group."[39]

REFERENCES

1. See, for example, TAUBER, M. F., *et al.*, *The Columbia University libraries; The college library and the undergraduate library problem at Columbia*, Columbia University Press, 1958, pp. 152–60.
2. WHEELER, G. W. (Ed.), *Letters of Sir Thomas Bodley to Thomas James*, Oxford, Clarendon Press, 1926, p. 183.
3. McCOLVIN, L. R. (Ed.), *A survey of libraries. Reports on a survey made by the Library Association during 1936–1937*, London, Library Association, 1938, p. 414.
4. LUNDY, F. A., The divisional plan library, *Coll. Res. Libr.* **17**, 145 (1956).
5. HURT, P., *The university library and undergraduate instruction*, Berkeley, University of California Press, 1936, pp. 24–7.
6. In the survey at Southampton University 19% of the sample admitted to finding the library intimidating at first and 48% mildly intimidating. See LINE, M. B., Student attitudes to the university library . . . *J. Docum.* **19** (1963).
7. It is disturbing to find it taken for granted in a recent discussion that the young research worker begins "by spending considerable time and energy learning library technique which he should have learnt as an undergraduate". SHARPE, L. J., *Information methods of research workers in the social sciences*, London, Library Association, 1961, p. 20.
8. JOLLEY, L., The function of the university library, *J. Docum.* **18**, 136 (1962).

9. HAVILAND, M. C., The reference function of the Lamont Library, *Harvard Libr. Bull.* **3,** 297 (1949).
10. SHEPLEY, H. R., The Lamont Library. I. Design. *Harvard Libr. Bull.* **3,** 24 (1949).
11. WOLEDGE, G., and PAGE, B. S. (Eds.), *A manual of university and college library practice,* London, Library Association, 1940, p. 54.
12. WAGMAN, F. H., The case for the separate undergraduate library, *Coll. Res. Libr.* **17,** 153 (1956).
13. LUNDY, F. A., The divisional plan library, *Coll. Res. Libr.* **17,** 145 (1956).
14. METCALF, KEYES D., The undergraduate and the Harvard Library, 1937–1947, *Harvard Lib. Bull.* **1,** 305 (1947).
15. Lamont, opened as long ago as 1949, provided seats for three of every eight undergraduates.
16. METCALF, *op. cit.,* p. 305.
17. American undergraduate library collections vary enormously in size from 12,000 volumes at Minnesota to some 150,000 volumes at Michigan. Lamont's collection numbers about 100,000 volumes but these represent only 39,000 titles.
18. WAGMAN, F. H., The undergraduate library of the University of Michigan, *Coll. Res. Libr.* **20,** 184 (1959).
19. *Ibid.,* p. 185.
20. McNIFF, P. J., and WILLIAMS, E. E., Lamont Library: the first year, *Harvard Libr. Bull.* **4,** 207 (1950).
21. ARRAGON, R. F., The relationship between the library and collegiate objectives, *Libr. Q.* **20,** 284 (1954).
22. WAGMAN, *op. cit.,* p. 185.
23. McNIFF and WILLIAMS, *op. cit.,* p. 205.
24. WAGMAN, F. H., The undergraduate library of the University of Michigan, *Coll. Res. Libr.* **20,** 186 (1959).
25. *Ibid.*
26. *The place of the library in a university: a conference held at Harvard University, 30–31 March 1949,* Cambridge, Harvard University Library, 1950, p. 42.
27. WAGMAN, *op. cit.,* p. 188.
28. SHARP, L. W., What do we look for in a university library?, London, Library Association, *Proceedings of the Annual Conference,* 1955, pp. 31–2.
29. GWYNN, S. E., The liberal arts function of the university library, *Libr. Q.* **24,** 313 (1954).
30. DIX, W. S., Undergraduates do not necessarily require a special facility, *Coll. Res. Libr.* **17,** 150 (1956).
31. DIX, W. S., Undergraduate libraries, *Coll. Res. Libr.* **14,** 271 (1953).
32. *Ibid.*
33. The larger and better undergraduate libraries are attempting to achieve this range of choice.
34. GOVAN, J. F., This is, indeed, the heart of the matter, *Coll. Res. Libr.* **23,** 470 (1962).
35. NcNIFF, P. J., Lamont Library, Harvard College, *Coll. Res. Libr.* **14,** 269 (1953).
36. *Library Association Record,* **41,** 522 (1939).
37. *University of Leeds Development Plan . . .,* prepared by Chamberlin, Powell and Bon, Architects, April 1960. The University, Leeds, 1960, pp. 26, 55–6.
38. COMMITTEE ON HIGHER EDUCATION, *Higher education: report of the committee appointed by the Prime Minister under the chairmanship of Lord Robbins 1961–63,* Cmnd. 2154, October 1963, pp. 151–2.
39. WAGMAN, F. H., The case for the separate undergraduate library, *Coll. Res. Libr.* **17,** 151 (1956).

5. SURVEY OF BORROWING FROM THE UNIVERSITY OF SHEFFIELD LIBRARY DURING ONE ACADEMIC YEAR

W. L. SAUNDERS

Postgraduate School of Librarianship, University of Sheffield

and

E. W. ROBERTS

University Library, University of Sheffield

and

LISBETH J. WICKISON

University Library, University of York

THE Nuffield pilot survey of library use in the University of Leeds[1] was the first large-scale statistical survey of borrowing from a British university library. It represented a major attempt to provide a sound factual basis for many important aspects of university library organization and administration, and in reporting the results of the survey Mr. B. S. Page and Mr. P. E. Tucker expressed the hope that it would be followed by others. They acknowledged that much of the value of such a survey is domestic, but many of the results which they reported, if tested by and compared with the findings of similar surveys elsewhere, gave promise of pointing to aspects and patterns of library use of a more general validity. For this reason, the first-named author of this paper, in planning the Sheffield survey, had in mind not only its domestic use but the possibility of comparisons with the Leeds survey. The appearance of Mr. K. W. Humphreys's "Survey of borrowing from the Main Library, the University of Birmingham"[2] has made it possible to extend comparison to a third library, and whenever it seems to be relevant and is technically possible, the Leeds, Birmingham and Sheffield findings are considered side by side.

This Sheffield survey covers borrowing by teaching staff, research workers and undergraduate students for a full year, commencing on 1 August 1960 and ending on 31 July 1961. This covers the normal academic year, and in comparing Sheffield figures with those for Leeds and Birmingham it must be borne in mind that the Leeds survey covers a calendar year (1957) and therefore straddles two academic years, and the Birmingham survey excludes the long vacation and covers only the 9 months period October 1960 to June 1961, inclusive. Furthermore, the Leeds survey covers loans from *all* libraries in the University, the Birmingham survey is confined to the Main Library, while the Sheffield survey takes account of all libraries in the University which are built up mainly from University Library funds, but excludes "class" libraries. There were a fair number of the latter, normally built up by teaching departments from their own departmental grants and other sources, but the only ones of any size were those in the Geography, Architecture and Physics Departments.

The libraries which are covered by this survey are the following:

The Main Library. This is a new building, which had been in use for a full year when the survey commenced. It houses all the arts, social science, and medical collections and all the pure science collections except geology and chemistry. At the time of the survey it seated approximately 450 readers. It opened in term time from 9.00 a.m. to 9.30 p.m. Monday to Friday, and 9.00 a.m. to 12.30 p.m. on Saturdays, but closed at 5.00 p.m. during vacations. Its stock comprised about 225,000 items and its catalogue recorded the holdings of all libraries covered by this survey. Like all other libraries in the University of Sheffield, it is classified by the Dewey decimal system.

The Applied Science Library. This is a branch of the University Library, in charge of a sub-librarian and situated at St. George's Square with the Faculties of Engineering and Metallurgy, about one-third of a mile from the Main Library. Also situated at St. George's Square is one pure science department, Geology. The Applied Science Library houses the main collections in the applied sciences and some general reference works. At the time of the survey it offered seats for only thirty readers. The library was not open in the evening, its hours being 9.00 a.m. to 5.30 p.m. on weekdays and 9.00 a.m. to 12.30 p.m. on Saturdays. Its stock numbered about 24,000 items at the time of the survey.

Chemistry Departmental Library. This is on the ground floor of the Chemistry building, opposite the Main Library. It was open from 9.00 a.m. to 5.30 p.m. Monday to Friday, and on Saturday mornings. It houses virtually all the University Library's chemistry collections and at the time of the survey offered seats for a fairly small number of readers. Its stock was about 4000 items.

Geology Departmental Library. Situated within the Geology Department at St. George's Square, this library contained about 3000 items, the greater part of the University Library's holdings in its subject. It opened for only one half-hour in the morning and one half-hour in the afternoon, Monday to Friday. (These hours have since been very considerably extended.)

Law Departmental Library. This library was housed in the Department of Law, about 250 yards from the Main Library. Its holdings of approximately

5000 items represent the University's main collections in law. It opened from 9.30 a.m. to 9.00 p.m. Monday to Friday, and offered space for a limited number of readers. Law reports and periodicals could not be borrowed but were available for reference only.

Music Departmental Library. This library contained virtually all of the University Library's collection of scores, but only a few shelves of books.

The book stock. In round figures the combined stock of all the libraries covered by this survey was 261,000, compared with 533,000 at Leeds and 400,000 at Birmingham. In considering the use made of a library's stock, however, particularly when much of the analysis is by subject, as in this survey, it is helpful to know something about the composition of the stock in addition to its gross total. It was not feasible to make a count of the number of volumes in each subject section, but it so happens that a year before the survey, in preparation for moving into the new Main Library, shelf space occupied by each subject destined for the new building was carefully measured in feet. For the Main Library then, at least, some idea of the relative size of each subject section can be gained from Table 1, which may, in addition, be of some interest in its own right as indicating the composition of a small to medium-sized collection serving Faculties of Arts, Medicine, Social and Economic Studies, and (except for Geology and Chemistry) Pure Science. It will be seen that the greater part of the book stock was on open access, and so were all the bound volumes of journals. Current

TABLE 1. *Main Library Book Stock*

| Dewey class | | Shelf room in feet | | | | Number of current journal sub- scriptions |
| | | Books | | | Total footage, books and journals | |
		Open access	Closed stack	Journals		
000	Generalities	61	49	451	561	71
100	Philosophy and Psychology	211	195	169	575	35
200	Religion	320	287	56	663	21
300	Social Sciences	527	912	367	1806	142
400	Language	234	53	9	296	16
500	Pure Science	421	480	1330	2231	247
600	Applied Science	335	173	1577*	2085	264†
700	The Arts	303	78	96	477	27
800	Literature	2415	848	656	3919	110
900	Geography and History	1560	1116	609	3285	49
		6387	4191	5320	15898	982

* 1522 ft. of which were medical journals.
† 245 of which were subscriptions to medical journals.

journals were on display in a large Periodicals Room, and the number of subscriptions in each Dewey class is indicated in the last column of the table.

Virtually all material in the library was available for loan, the principal exceptions being works of reference. Teaching staff could borrow up to 20 books, research students up to 5, undergraduate students up to 3.

Methods. The results which emerge from a survey of this type can be presented in many ways. In the present case attention is focused on the type of library user and the analysis falls into three main sections: teaching staff, postgraduate and undergraduate. Such matters as the proportion of book to journal borrowing, the amount of foreign language borrowing, the range of "off-subject" borrowing and the use of departmental libraries are considered to be of particular significance, as are differences of borrowing patterns between faculties and between departments of the same faculty. Emphasis is therefore placed on these particular aspects within each of the three categories.

A 5 × 3 inch guide card was made out for each member of the teaching staff, for every postgraduate and for every undergraduate. The charging system in use requires every item borrowed from the library to be recorded on a triplicate loan voucher, and the third copy of this voucher was filed, in each case, behind the appropriate survey guide card. At the end of the survey year particulars of all loans were therefore available, arranged according to borrower. The information on the vouchers was then transferred to specially designed foolscap forms, one for each borrower, which gave particulars of the borrower's department and also, in the case of undergraduate students, the course being followed, the subjects being studied and the year of study. The greater part of this preparatory work was done by Miss C. M. Rodgers of the Sheffield University Library, and we are very much in her debt for the painstaking care and thoroughness with which she carried out this stage of the survey. The loan particulars recorded on the form included in each case the name of the author, the title and the classification number. If the loan was not from the Main Library, the library from which it was borrowed was indicated. A special note was also made of loans in foreign languages. In the case of undergraduate students, more detailed analysis was facilitated by transferring the information recorded on the sheets to 5 × 8 inch Cope-Chat edge notched cards. One such card was made out for each student.

It is necessary to make clear the composition, at the time, of the various faculties referred to in the survey. Many departments belong to more than one faculty and in such cases, unless otherwise indicated, they have been included with the one which seems most appropriate.

The Faculty of Arts includes the Departments of Ancient History, Architecture and Building Science, Biblical History and Literature, English Language, English Literature, French, Geography, German, Greek, History,

Latin, Music, Philosophy and Spanish. For convenience Ancient History, Latin and Greek are grouped together in the survey and referred to collectively as Classics. Similarly, English Language and Literature are considered jointly and are referred to as English. The Department of Geography belongs to both the Faculty of Arts and the Faculty of Science. In the staff analysis it is considered only under Arts, but in the postgraduate and undergraduate sections it is possible to identify particular students with either the Science side or the Arts side, and Geography is accordingly to be found under both Arts and Science Faculties in the undergraduate and postgraduate sections of the survey.

The Faculty of Pure Science. This comprises the Departments of Botany, Chemistry, Genetics, Geology, Applied Mathematics, Pure Mathematics, Microbiology, Physics, Statistics and Zoology. In the undergraduate and postgraduate sections, this faculty also includes Geography.

Faculty of Engineering. This includes the Postgraduate Department of Applied Mechanics, the Departments of Civil Engineering, Electrical Engineering, Mechanical Engineering, Fuel Technology and Chemical Engineering, and Mining. The Department of Glass Technology, which belongs to this Faculty, was excluded from the survey as it was served by the library of the British Glass Industry Research Association, with which it was closely associated.

Faculty of Economic and Social Studies. This includes the Departments of Accountancy and Financial Administration, Economics, Sociological Studies and, for the staff and postgraduate sections of the survey, Psychology. Undergraduate students whose courses include Psychology are included in the Faculty of Arts.

Faculty of Metallurgy. This comprises two departments: Metallurgy and Refractories Technology.

Faculty of Medicine. This comprises the Clinical, Pre-clinical and Dentistry Departments, and though Medicine and Dentistry are sometimes referred to separately in the survey, all the departments in the Faculty of Medicine will normally be referred to collectively as *Medicine.*

Faculty of Law. This is usually considered on its own, though it comprises only one department. In the undergraduate section of the survey, however, it is sometimes included with Economic and Social Studies.

Education. This is not a faculty, but it has seemed appropriate at times to consider Education as a distinct group. It does not include the University Institute of Education.

TEACHING STAFF

This analysis has taken account of the borrowing of 338 full-time members of teaching staff. Honorary and part-time lecturers are excluded and this should be particularly borne in mind in the case of medical departments, where such appointments are relatively numerous.

I

Between them, the 338 members of staff borrowed 12,417 items, made up of 8222 books and 4195 journals. This gives an average of 24·3 books and 12·4 journals (i.e. 36·7 items) for each member of staff. The only comparable figures from the other two surveys are the Birmingham average totals of 30 for arts, 29 for commerce and 15 for science. The high proportion of journals in the Sheffield figure (33·8% of the total) is interesting and compares with 33·9% at Birmingham and 25% at Leeds. The total of 12,417 items is high, too (the Birmingham and Leeds figures were 7621 and 8951 respectively), and suggests quite intensive use of a relatively small collection.

One of the most striking features of the pattern of their borrowing is the very high proportion of staff who borrowed from the library—320 out of 338, or 94·7%. This compares with approximately 67% in the Birmingham survey. Figures for Leeds do not appear in the relevant article.

The distribution of borrowing by faculties reveals, somewhat unexpectedly, that the highest borrowing figures are not those for Arts but for Economic and Social Studies, whose 24 members of staff borrowed an average of 78 items (65 books and 13 journals) each. Arts, the second highest, are a fair way behind with an average of 58·4 items. The ranking order for average borrowings is as Table 2.

TABLE 2. *Staff Borrowing Analysed by Faculties*

Average total borrowings per member of staff		Average no. of books borrowed per member of staff		Average no. of journals borrowed per member of staff	
Economic and		Economic and		Medicine	21·2
Social Studies	78·0	Social Studies	65·0	Pure Science	18·9
Arts	58·4	Arts	54·0	Economic and	
Education	43·4	Education	39·1	Social Studies	13·0
Pure Science	40·4	Law	32·7	Metallurgy	11·4
Medicine	37·0	Pure Science	21·5	Dentistry	8·6
Law	34·4	Medicine	15·8	Engineering	5·5
Metallurgy	22·8	Engineering	13·9	Arts	5·0
Engineering	19·5	Metallurgy	11·4	Education	4·3
Dentistry	13·0	Dentistry	4·4	Law	1·7

Tables 1 and 2 confirm in striking fashion the overwhelming importance of books to Arts staff and the significance of journals in Medicine and Pure and Applied Sciences, with Economics and Social Studies borrowing both books and journals in quite considerable numbers.

An examination of the figures at departmental level reveals that the heaviest borrowing departments are as shown in Table 3. The figure in brackets after the name of the department indicates the number of members of staff:

TABLE 3. *Staff Borrowing Analysed by Departments*

Average total borrowings per member of staff		Average no. of books borrowed per member of staff		Average no. of journals borrowed per member of staff	
Economics (12)	116·8	English (10)	105·4	Botany (6)	42·2
English (10)	112	Economics (12)	97	Physiology (9)	40·6
Classics (8)	95·2	Classics (8)	85	Bacteriology (3)	40·3
Geology (9)	95	History (7)	84	Geology (9)	37
History (7)	86·3	Geology (9)	58	Pharmacology (3)	37
Botany (6)	84·8	French (9)	55	Pathology (5)	28·2
Bacteriology (3)	65·3	Sociological Studies (5)	50		

The high Geology figures undoubtedly reflect the limited times during which the Departmental Library was open for use; had the stock of this library been accessible over the whole day, much of what was borrowed might well have been consulted in the library. No such considerations influence the very high figures of borrowing by the botanists, whose use of the library is greater than that of most of the Arts departments. The heaviest borrowers of journals are the Pure Science and Medical departments. The low average borrowing figures for journals within the Faculty of Arts as a whole is also true of its constituent departments, only two of which (Geography—11 and Classics—10) reached double figures.

At the level of individual borrowing, the highest total was recorded by a member of the Faculty of Arts, with 346 items (314 books and 32 journals), closely followed by an economist with 343 (263 books and 80 journals). One other total exceeded 300, two more were between 200 and 300 and a further 20 borrowed between 100 and 200 items. Of this total of 25 members of staff who borrowed more than 100 items, 9 belonged to the Faculty of Arts, 6 to Medicine and 5 to Pure Science. Taking book and journal borrowings separately, 16 (8 from Arts) borrowed more than 100 books while one (Medical) borrowed more than 100 journals. Ten borrowed between 50 and 100 journals. Of the 11 borrowing more than 50 journals, 5 were Medical and 5 Pure Science. It is interesting to notice that with individual as with departmental totals, Botany and Geology emerge as the Science departments to which the library appears to be of greatest importance.

STAFF BORROWING: FOREIGN LANGUAGE MATERIAL

In analysing the borrowing of books and journals in foreign languages, account was not taken of material borrowed by the staff of language departments written in the languages which they teach. The object was to obtain some indication of the extent to which teachers in general used books and journals in languages other than English, and it may be taken that most of the borrowing described will be on the specialized subject of the staff members in question. It should also be noted that multi-lingual journals which include English language contributions are not counted as "foreign language" journals for the present purpose.

On the above definition of foreign language borrowing, 525 (6·4%) of the 8222 books borrowed and 210 (5%) of the 4195 journals were in languages other than English. German and French were the most-used languages, 203 of the books and 123 of the journals being in German, 249 of the books and 75 of the journals in French.

The Faculty of Arts with 369 books (average of 5·1 per member of staff) and 38 journals (average 0·5 per member of staff) accounts for the greatest part of the foreign language borrowing, with French (182 books and 4 journals) the most important language and German (122 books and 32 journals) a quite substantial second. Of individual Arts departments, Geography, Classics and History are by far the heaviest users of foreign language books, Classics (18 out of the total of 38) the heaviest user of journals.

The Faculty of Science with 98 books (average 1·2) and 103 journals (average 1·3) was the only other faculty borrowing foreign language books and journals in significant numbers. German (53 books and 58 journals) was the most-used language, with French (45 books and 45 journals) second. Of individual Science departments, Geology (28 books, 19 journals), Applied Mathematics (21 books, 14 journals), Physics (3 books, 29 journals), Chemistry (1 book, 24 journals), and Pure Mathematics (21 books, 3 journals) were the heaviest users of foreign language materials.

In all other faculties the borrowing of foreign language materials was insignificant: Medicine borrowed 17 books and 31 journals, Metallurgy 11 books and 19 journals, Economic and Social Studies 13 books and 3 journals, Engineering 10 books and 5 journals, Dentistry 3 journals, Education 3 books and 1 journal, Law none at all.

Direct comparison with the foreign language borrowing shown in the Birmingham survey is not possible, but Mr. Humphreys comments that loans of *books* in foreign languages are few. Except for the interestingly high figure for *current* journals the Birmingham figures for foreign language *journal* borrowing are also on the low side. Neither Birmingham nor Sheffield approached the extremely high total of foreign language borrowing recorded in the Leeds survey, which shows that staff borrowed from the Brotherton Library 2203 foreign books and journals, as compared with 6281 books and journals in the English language. The Leeds figures, unlike Sheffield's, do not exclude borrowing by language departments in the languages taught, but even allowing for this the difference is apparently so great that it would repay further investigation. One's subjective impression, from conversations with various university librarians, is that the Sheffield situation is probably more usual than that at Leeds.

There is perhaps a tendency to assume that academics will have a working knowledge of at least French and German, and will be prepared to read materials on their subjects in foreign languages, if the occasion demands. The high number of foreign language journals to which most university libraries subscribe, particularly in the Sciences and Medicine, certainly assumes the absence of a significant language barrier. There appears to be reason for questioning this assumption: it may well be that many university library holdings of foreign language materials reflect a pre-war situation, when the foreign language competence of university teaching staffs was probably greater than it is now. If this is the case the continuation of many expensive subscriptions to foreign journals may well be queried, particularly if they are fairly easily obtainable on loan from the NLL or elsewhere. One must stress, however, that such decisions could not be taken solely on the basis of evidence about borrowing: much more needs to be known about use of such material within the library.

Applied Science Library, St. George's Square. This branch library, which contains the University's Engineering and Metallurgical collections, is the most important collection outside the Main Library. It serves the Faculties of Engineering and Metallurgy, and the Department of Geology (which belongs to the Faculty of Pure Science) is also situated at St. George's Square. The Applied Science Library was used by 14 departments other than the Engineering, Metallurgy and Geology departments (which are those located at St. George's Square). All Medical departments are counted as one department for this purpose. The 14 departments borrowed between them 110 books and 96 journals, distributed on a faculty basis as follows: Pure Science 64 books, 74 journals; Arts 22 books, 8 journals; Medicine 11 books, 12 journals; Education 6 books, 1 journal; Dentistry 6 books, 1 journal; Economic and Social Studies 1 book.

Conversely, the 9 St. George's Square departments (6 Engineering, 2 Metallurgical, 1 Pure Science) borrowed 93 books and 78 journals from the Main Library and 44 books and 5 journals from the Department of Chemistry Library.

All of these figures should be viewed against total borrowings of 864 books and 455 journals, from all sources, by the staff of the Engineering and Metallurgy Faculties and a total borrowing use of the Applied Science Library, by all university staff, of 896 books and 541 journals.

Geology Departmental Library. This departmental library was very heavily used by its 9 members of staff who between them borrowed 494 books and

255 journals. Its use by other faculties was small: Arts 8 books, 6 journals; Pure Science 8 books, 2 journals; Engineering 6 books, 3 journals; Metallurgy 1 book, 2 journals; Dentistry 1 book. As mentioned elsewhere, the hours when this library was open for borrowing were very restricted and may account to some extent for the small amount of use by other departments.

The borrowing of the Geology Department staff themselves was by no means restricted to their own library. They accounted for 38 of the total of 180 books borrowed from the Chemistry Departmental Library, and they borrowed 19 books and 32 journals from the Main Library and 9 books and 46 journals from the Applied Science Library.

Chemistry Departmental Library. University staff borrowed 180 books and 219 journals from this library, 129 (71·7%) of the books and 190 (86·8%) of the journals being borrowed by the Chemistry Department's own staff. Borrowing by staff other than members of the Chemistry Department was as follows: Geology 38 books; Medicine 6 books, 22 journals; Metallurgy 6 books, 5 journals; Physics 1 book, 2 journals.

As chemical literature is important to several other disciplines and this departmental library contains virtually the whole of the research collections in the subject, it is perhaps surprising that more use was not made of the library by other departments, though the 28·3% of its book borrowings and the 13·2% of its journal borrowings which were accounted for by outside departments is by no means negligible. When considered together with the pattern of postgraduate use of this library, described on p. 132 below, it appears that restricting research collections in this subject to a departmental library might well have adverse implications for other departments in the university in a way which is apparently not true of some other subjects, e.g. Law.

From the point of view of the Chemistry staff themselves, it is perhaps significant that they went to the Main Library for 64 (25·2%) of the 254 journals they borrowed and for 32 (19·4%) of their 165 books. Their borrowing from elsewhere was negligible: one book from the Department of Music and 3 books from the Applied Science Library. The range of their borrowing is further described on p. 128 below.

Law Departmental Library. Periodicals may not normally be borrowed from this departmental library. Of the 177 books which were borrowed, Law Department staff borrowed 165, the other 12 being borrowed by staff from the Faculty of Economic and Social Studies. This suggests that other university departments have comparatively little need for the literature of law. On the other hand, Law Department staff had to turn to the Main Library for 54 (23·6%) of their total borrowings of 229 books.

Music Departmental Library. The borrowing from this library was negligible, totalling only 16 items.

STAFF: RANGE OF BORROWING

The Leeds and Birmingham surveys indicated that teaching staff drew on a considerable range of subjects in connection with their researches. This is such an important aspect of library use and has such fundamental implications for university library organization, particularly in relation to centralization or decentralization of the research collections, that it was decided to analyse the Sheffield figures from this particular point of view in some detail.

All books and journals borrowed by teaching staff were divided by subject into their Dewey divisions: 90 in all, comprising one for each division of classes 100–900, inclusive (with the exception of class 100, in which Sheffield used only 9 out of the 10 divisions), and one for all of class 000, Generalia. It was then possible to calculate the extent to which staff of each teaching department borrowed outside their particular subjects, e.g. the chemists from divisions other than Dewey's 540's, the German Department from divisions other than Dewey's 430's and 830's.

Table 4 shows this "off-subject" borrowing on a faculty basis, by Dewey main classes. It shows that 4073 (49·5%) of the 8222 books borrowed were "off-subject" and so were 973 (23·2%) of the 4195 journals. That Arts staff should borrow from 78 of the 90 subject divisions is impressive evidence of the range of their requirements, but perhaps even more noteworthy is the fact that Medical Faculty staff borrowed 49·2% of their books from subjects outside medicine in the narrow sense and, in fact, borrowed from 57 out of the 90 divisions. This is particularly significant in the unusual Sheffield situation, where there is no separate Medical library, medical books being merged with the Main Library's general collections. Though it is recognized that some of their "off-subject" borrowing is probably not directly connected with research and professional interests, there seems little doubt that Medical staff benefit quite considerably from access to a library covering virtually the whole field of knowledge.

The Faculty of Pure Science staff borrowed from 62 divisions out of 90, but the bulk of their "off-subject" borrowing is concentrated into classes 500 and 600; in fact only 17·5% of their book borrowing and 5·3% of their journal borrowing was from subjects outside the 500 and 600 classes. A similar pattern is to be observed in the borrowing of the Engineering and Metallurgy Faculties, and this might be taken as evidence that most of the library requirements of the Pure and Applied Science Faculties could be met by a specialized Science library. It should be remembered, though, that the Applied Science Departments are situated at some distance from the Main Library and have their own Applied Science Library at St. George's Square. Had they been nearer the Main Library, the range of their borrowing might well have been greater. Furthermore, even if the Pure and Applied Science Faculties do not borrow heavily outside classes 500 and 600, it can be seen

TABLE 4. "Off-subject" Borrowing of Teaching Staff

	No. of Dewey divisions from which items were borrowed	Total "off-subject" borrowing		"Off-subject" borrowing as a percentage of total borrowing		"Off-subject" borrowing by Dewey main classes																				
						000		100		200		300		400		500		600		700		800		900	
		Bks.	Jnls.	Bks. %	Jnls. %	Bks.	Jnls.	Bks.	Jnls.	Bks.	Jnls.	Bks.	Jnls.	Bks.	Jnls.	Bks.	Jnls.	Bks.	Jnls.	Bks.	Jnls.	Bks.	Jnls.	Bks.	Jnls.
Arts	78	1558	166	40·3	48·4	8	15	111	4	114	—	249	15	86	5	79	28	60	25	231	19	340	35	280	20
Economic and Sociological Studies	54	432	73	27·6	23·2	6	4	20	12	12	2	160	23	2	—	79	14	26	10	17	1	34	1	76	6
Law	10	31	—	13·5	—	—	—	6	—	—	3	23	3	—	—	—	—	1	—	—	—	—	—	1	1
Education	48	330	35	87	81·4	3	3	23	23	7	—	90	4	2	—	49	2	23	77	8	—	46	—	79	3
Pure Science	62	776	368	41·4	22·5	1	1	21	2	17	—	37	2	13	—	448	281	65	24	57	—	63	—	54	—
Engineering	36	317	126	46·5	46·2	—	—	—	—	3	—	9	—	23	—	232	100	33	17	4	—	2	—	10	—
Metallurgy	21	137	85	75·3	46·7	—	—	1	—	—	—	1	—	5	—	96	68	27	7	3	—	—	—	3	—
Medicine	57	466	118	49·2	9·3	3	—	49	20	18	—	74	—	4	—	145	91	31	—	31	—	67	—	44	—
Dentistry	13	26	2	45·6	1·8	1	—	5	—	—	—	1	—	1	—	12	2	4	—	1	—	—	—	1	—
Total		4073	973			23	23	236	61	172	5	644	47	136	5	1140	586	270	160	352	20	552	36	548	30

from Table 4 that these two classes are quite heavily used by other faculties who would be very much the losers if Pure and Applied Science were segregated.

When we consider the position at departmental level, Arts departments, as might be expected, show the greatest range of "off-subject" borrowing. English Language and Literature between them borrow from 65 of the 90 subject divisions, Classics and French from 41 each, History from 40 and Geography from 31. Education borrowed from 47. The Department of Sociological Studies borrowed from 34 and so did Economics. Of the Pure Science departments, Pure and Applied Mathematics together borrowed from 38 divisions, Botany from 28, Physics from 25 and Zoology from 23. Electrical Engineering and Fuel Technology each borrowed from 16 divisions, Metallurgy from 21.

Related to the range of borrowing by departments is the extent to which particular subject divisions were used by the 38 departments covered in this survey. The 500–509 division was most heavily used from this particular point of view, 26 different departments having borrowed from it. Twenty-four departments borrowed from the 530's, 21 from the 370's, 20 from each of the 330's, 610's and 940's, and 19 from the 510's and 820's. The use of the 610 (Medicine) division by 20 departments perhaps merits special comment, for it demonstrates that the benefit which Medical staff appear to derive from access to a general collection is to some extent paralleled by the advantage to non-Medical staff of easy access to the specialized literature of Medicine.

At the other end of the scale, 2 subject divisions, 460–469 and 640–649, were not used at all. In the case of the 640's the library's holdings are extremely small.

If individual Dewey classes are considered, the average number of departments using each subject division was highest in the 500's, with an average of 14·5 departments borrowing from each of its 10 subject divisions. The 300's were next with 11·4. Each of the whole range of 90 subject divisions was used by an average of 8·8 departments. It should be remembered, of course, with all of these figures, that only "off-subject" use is being considered so that, for example, use of the 460's and 860's by the Department of Spanish is excluded.

The Birmingham and Leeds surveys gave figures to indicate the range of borrowing in particular departments and subjects. In Tables 5 and 6 it is interesting to compare them with the corresponding Sheffield figures, but it must be borne in mind that Sheffield borrowing was divided into 90 subject divisions which is probably more than was the case at Leeds and Birmingham.

The Sheffield figures confirm in general the Leeds and Birmingham findings, that many teaching departments need to range over a large number of subjects. It is interesting, however, that whereas most of the Sheffield figures

TABLE 5. *Teaching Staff: Borrowing by Departments from Subject Divisions other than their own*

	Sheffield No. of sections	Leeds No. of sections	Birmingham No. of sections
History	40	34	—
German	23	18	—
Economics	34	26	—
Chemistry	10	30	—
Botany	28	13	15
Mechanical Engineering	12	16	15

TABLE 6. *Borrowing from Subject Divisions by other Departments*

	Sheffield Borrowed by staff from the following no. of departments	Leeds Borrowed by staff from the following no. of departments	Birmingham Borrowed by staff from the following no. of departments
History	26	22	24
German	11	10	—
Economics	20	13	—
Chemistry	16	17	—
Botany	7	10	3
Mechanical Engineering	—	10	5

are higher than the corresponding ones for Leeds, the Sheffield Chemistry department confined its borrowings to a much narrower range of subjects than its Leeds counterpart. The Sheffield figure of 10 is low in comparison not only with Leeds, but with other Sheffield Science departments. A possible reason for this is that having their research collections within the Chemistry department may have meant comparatively infrequent visits to the Main Library, though as recorded earlier they borrowed approximately a quarter of their books and a fifth of their journals from the Main Library.

POSTGRADUATE RESEARCH BORROWING

The greater part of this section is concerned with library borrowing by 323 postgraduate students reading for masters' or doctors' degrees. These 323 were not, of course, the only postgraduate members of the University, and if account is taken of independent research workers, research fellows and others who are neither full-time members of staff nor candidates for higher degrees, the total is increased from 323 to 415. For the sake of completeness something should be said about the borrowing of this group as a whole, before proceeding to a more detailed consideration of the borrowing of higher degree candidates.

Between them these 415 postgraduate users borrowed a total of 9639 items, 4944 of which were books and 4695 journals. This figure gives an average of 11·9 books and 11·3 journals (or 23·2 items for each postgraduate user). The corresponding total for Birmingham was 8194, made up of 5248 books and 2946 journals. The Leeds figures were 4222 books and 2052 journals, making a total of 6274. A most striking fact which emerges from the comparison is the relatively high proportion of journals borrowed at Sheffield: 48·7% of the total borrowing, compared with 35% at Birmingham and 32·9% at Leeds. This may simply reflect, of course, the high proportion of postgraduates at Sheffield who belong to the Pure and Applied Science faculties.

Of the 415 research workers, 67 (16·1%) did not borrow at all from the library. This compares with approximately 40% at Birmingham. The corresponding figures for Leeds are not given in the Nuffield survey.

In Table 7, an analysis at faculty level, the Faculties of Arts and Economic and Social Studies are considered under one heading, Arts, and the Faculties of Engineering and Metallurgy are combined. The figures in brackets show the number of research workers in each group.

TABLE 7. *Total Postgraduate Borrowing, by Faculties*

Average total borrowings by postgraduates		Average no. of books borrowed by each postgraduate		Average no. of journals borrowed by each postgraduate	
Law (4)	56·0	Law (4)	55·5	Medicine (30)	33·5
Medicine (30)	52·7	Arts (27)	25·1	Engineering and	
Arts (27)	30·4	Medicine (30)	19·1	Metallurgy (179)	11·5
Engineering and		Engineering and		Pure Science (155)	9·5
Metallurgy (179)	23·5	Metallurgy (179)	11·9	Arts (27)	5·3
Pure Science (155)	17·6	Pure Science (155)	8·0	Law (4)	0·5
Education (20)	4·4	Education (20)	4·3	Education (20)	—

The only comparable figures from the other two surveys are the Birmingham postgraduate average totals of 13 for Arts, 22 for Commerce and 10 for Science.

The number of students covered by the Law figure is too low to permit useful generalizations and it should also be mentioned that a high proportion of the Education students are not full time. With these reservations in mind the general pattern is seen to be not unlike that revealed in the similar table for the staff section, earlier in this survey.

HIGHER DEGREE STUDENTS

The rest of this section is concerned with the 323 postgraduate students who were reading for higher degrees. Of these, 95 were reading for a master's degree, 228 for a doctorate. Between them they borrowed 3383 books and 3156 journals, making a total of 6539 items. The average total borrowing for each student was 20·3 items, made up of 10·5 books and 9·8 journals. Only 39 (12·1%) of the 323 students did not borrow at all.

Table 8 shows borrowing analysed on a faculty basis, and again it is necessary to draw attention to the small number of students in Law, to a similarly small number in Medicine and to the preponderance of part-time students amongst those working for higher degrees in Education. Caution is clearly required in interpreting the figures for these three groups, at least. It should also be mentioned that the Arts Faculty journals figure is inflated by the borrowing of one Economics student who accounted for 25 of the Faculty's total of 46 journals.

TABLE 8. *Higher Degree Students Borrowing, by Faculties*

Students	Faculty	Total borrowings		Average per postgraduate student	
		Books	Journals	Books	Journals
12	Arts	262	46	21·8	3·8
20	Education	87	1	4·3	<0·1
4	Law	222	2	55·5	0·5
4	Medicine	9	41	2·3	10·0
142	Pure Science	1136	1317	8·0	9·3
79	Engineering	845	448	10·7	5·7
62	Metallurgy	822	1307	13·2	21·0
323	Total	3383	3162	10·5	9·8

A faculty analysis of *non-borrowing* reveals at least one striking result: every one of the 62 postgraduate students in the Faculty of Metallurgy borrowed from the library. *Non-borrowing* in other faculties was as follows: Arts 8%; Pure Science 8%; Engineering 16%; Education 65%.

Foreign language borrowing. The total foreign language borrowing by this group was 242 items, made up of 63 books and 179 journals. Books and journals in the languages being studied by postgraduates in Language departments have been ignored. Again, direct comparison with Birmingham and Leeds is not easy, but the general impression is of very much lighter use of foreign language materials in Sheffield than in either of the other universities, though it must always be kept in mind that compared with Leeds and Birmingham, Sheffield's postgraduate activity is very heavily biased on the side of Science and Technology.

German and French are the only foreign languages in which items were borrowed to any extent: 25 of the 63 books and 119 of the 179 journals were in German, 33 of the books and 56 of the journals in French.

A break-down by faculty shows the Faculty of Pure Science to be the principal and, indeed, the only significant user of foreign language materials. Their postgraduates borrowed 36 of the 63 foreign language books and 113 of the 179 foreign language journals, and of this faculty's total postgraduate borrowing, 4% of their books and 9% of their journals were in languages other than English.

It is worth mentioning that the general situation looks very little different if the foreign language borrowing of all 415 postgraduate students, and not just that of the 323 higher degree students, is considered: figures of 63 and 179 for books and journals respectively would be increased only to 85 and 203. The remarks about foreign language borrowing by staff, earlier in this study, are equally applicable to postgraduates, and the very low level of use of foreign language materials is one of the most interesting of all the findings of this survey.

HIGHER DEGREE STUDENTS: USE OF BRANCH AND DEPARTMENTAL
LIBRARIES

Applied Science Library, St. George's Square. Although only a tenth of the size of the Main Library, the Applied Science Library must be regarded as an important second focal point in the pattern of the University's library provision, not only because of the geographical divorce between the faculties it serves and the Main Library, but also because these two faculties—Engineering and Metallurgy—between them account for a very substantial proportion of the University's postgraduate students (141 out of 323).

The sectional nature of this library's provision can be gathered from the fact that Metallurgy borrowed 91% of its books and 95% of its journals from the Applied Science Library, Engineering 83% of its books and 89% of its journals, Geology 17% of its books and 14% of its journals, Chemistry 6% of its books and 0·7% of its journals, Pure Science (excluding Geology and Chemistry) 7% of its books and 3% of its journals. Medicine, Arts and Law did not use this library at all.

It is apparent from this that the Applied Science Library provided a high proportion of the materials borrowed by engineers and metallurgists, but a very low proportion of the materials borrowed by Pure Science postgraduates. The exception is the Department of Geology, which is, of course, located at St. George's Square. The books and journals borrowed by this department from the Applied Science Library were only in part specialized geological materials: items such as general scientific journals and books on a variety of scientific topics (including crystallography) were also borrowed.

Geology Departmental Library. The thirteen postgraduate students in this department accounted for virtually all the items borrowed by postgraduates from the Geology Departmental Library: 152 out of 156 books and all 122 journals. The Departmental Library accounted for 79% of the total book borrowing by these students and 84% of their journal borrowing. The Applied Science Library, with 16% of their books and 14% of their journals, provided most of the balance of their borrowing, leaving only approximately 5% of their books and 2% of their journals to be provided by the Main Library. No items were borrowed from the Chemistry Departmental Library by Geology postgraduates, though, as recorded earlier, Geology staff borrowed 38 books from that library.

The impression then is that this departmental library is fairly self-sufficient so far as Geology postgraduates are concerned and its resources would appear to be in very little demand by postgraduates from other departments.

Chemistry Departmental Library. The breakdown of postgraduate borrowing from this source is in sharp contrast to the situation in Geology, just described. Thirteen departments, in addition to Chemistry, had recourse to this library, and between them accounted for approximately 21% of the books and 29% of the journals borrowed from it. The Biochemistry Department alone accounted for 8% of the book issues and 5% of the journals; 7 other Pure Science departments together accounted for a further 3% of the books and 7% of the journals; while 3 of the Engineering departments and 2 Metallurgical departments at St. George's Square between them borrowed the remaining 10% of books and 16% of journals.

Turning to the Chemistry department's own postgraduates, it must be recognized that they formed a large proportion (60 out of 323) of the entire postgraduate population. Their average borrowing per head was low: 3 books and 5·8 journals compared with an average for all Pure Science postgraduates of 8 books and 9·3 journals. The sources of their borrowing were as follows: Chemistry Departmental Library: 67% of their books, 69% of their journals; Main Library: 25% of their books, 29% of their journals; Applied Science Library: 6% of their books, 1% of their journals.

The borrowing of the Chemistry department's own postgraduates, when considered in association with the borrowing from the Chemistry Departmental Library of all other postgraduates, suggests that a separate Chemistry Departmental Library, holding much of a university's research literature in chemistry, has substantial repercussions on the whole pattern of postgraduate borrowing. Borrowing by other departments from the Chemistry Departmental Library is high and widespread compared, for example, with the Law and Geology libraries; and the department's own postgraduates had to turn to other sources, predominantly the Main Library, for 30% of their borrowings.

The low average borrowings of the Chemistry postgraduates might indicate that the Departmental Library's accessibility is such that its convenience to them, for immediate consultation, more than offsets recourse to the Main Library for a substantial amount of borrowing. It seems fairly clear, however, that part of the price of this accessibility is some inconvenience to other departments who need to use the Chemistry collections.

Law Departmental Library. Of the 222 books borrowed by Law postgraduates, 142 were borrowed from the Departmental Library, the other 80 from the Main Library. This Main Library borrowing was almost entirely in the field of forensic medicine and sociology. Only one item was borrowed from the Law Departmental Library by postgraduate students from other departments.

As in the staff analysis, the impression emerges that other university departments have little need for the literature of Law. On the other hand, members of the Law Department lean quite heavily on the resources of the Main Library, in addition to making good use of their own departmental holdings.

Borrowings for the two levels of research. Of the 323 postgraduates, 95 were reading for a master's degree, 228 for a doctorate. The distribution of the two levels of research between the various disciplines is uneven: of those reading for a master's degree 30·5% were in Arts, Education and Law (29 out of 95); of doctoral students only 3·1% (7 out of 228) were in these fields, the vast majority being in Pure Science, Engineering and Metallurgy.

The average borrowing of those reading for masters' degrees was significantly higher than that for those reading for doctorates. The average borrowings per head for masters were 27·6, made up of 11·8 journals and

TABLE 9. *Borrowing by Doctoral and Masters' Degree Students*

Faculty	Masters				Doctorates			
	Students	Books	Jnls.	Total	Students	Books	Jnls.	Total
Arts	7	201	32	233	5	61	14	75
Education	18	70	—	70	2	17	1	18
Law	4	222	2	224	—	—	—	—
Medicine	—	—	—	—	4	9	41	50
Pure Science	9	148	110	258	133	988	1207	2195
Engineering	31	400	271	671	48	445	171	616
Metallurgy	26	461	701	1162	36	361	606	967
Total	95	1502	1116	2618	228	1881	2040	3921

15·8 books; the corresponding figures for doctoral candidates were 17·2 items, made up of 9·0 journals and 8·2 books.

On a faculty basis, the breakdown between these two groups was as shown in Table 9.

It is interesting to notice that only in Metallurgy did those reading for a master's degree borrow more journals than books. Doctoral students, on the other hand, borrowed more journals than books, except in Education, Arts and—interestingly—Engineering.

HIGHER DEGREE STUDENTS: RANGE OF BORROWING

As the postgraduate population is so heavily weighted on the side of Science and Technology their range of borrowing is not so illuminating as that of the teaching staff, from the point of view of library use as a whole. One Dewey "ten" division contains the bulk of many a department's borrowing of journals, with much of the remainder being borrowed from 500 to 509 (General Scientific Periodicals). Even with books, where the spread is greater, the number of subject divisions from which many of the scientific and technological departments borrowed is very limited. If we try to assess "off-subject" borrowing, in the same way as with staff borrowing, we find that one book and one journal only were borrowed from class 000, 24 books and one journal from class 100, 33 books and no journals from class 200, 51 books and 8 journals from class 300, 26 books and no journals from class 400, 906 books and 706 journals from class 500, 334 books and 375 journals from class 600, 30 books and 12 journals from class 700, 115 books and 9 journals from class 800, and 74 books and 3 journals from class 900. This gives a total "off-subject" borrowing of 1594 (47·1%) out of 3383 books and 1115 (35·3%) out of 3156 journals. These numbers, however, fall dramatically to 354 books (10·3% of total book borrowing) and 34 journals (1·1% of total borrowing of journals) if classes 500 and 600 are excluded.

It is clear that science and technology students borrowed very lightly but quite widely in the fields of philosophy and psychology, religion, fine arts, literature, geography and history. These borrowings, though small, are a reminder that the University Library's cultural role should not be overlooked.

Finally, under this heading, it is of interest to consider the range of departments borrowing from individual subject divisions. 610–619 Medical Sciences, 580–589 Botany, and 530–539 Physics are examined from this point of view in Table 10.

From Table 10 it can be seen that 12 departments borrowed from the Medical Sciences and 11 from the Physics subject divisions, 6 borrowing quite substantially in each case; while 10 departments borrowed from the Botany division, 4 of them fairly substantially.

TABLE 10. *Postgraduate Borrowing from Three Subject Divisions*

Medical Sciences (610–619)			Botany (580–589)			Physics (530–539)		
Borrowing dept.	Books	Jnls.	Borrowing dept.	Books	Jnls.	Borrowing dept.	Books	Jnls.
Law	20	—	Biochemistry	3	—	Biochemistry	4	15
Medicine	6	40	Botany	45	66	Chemistry	14	65
Biochemistry	12	97	Chemistry	4	2	Geology	3	4
Botany	1	8	Genetics	20	1	Maths.	76	9
Chemistry	2	12	Microbiology	—	2	Physics	54	220
Genetics	1	4	Physics	3	14	Civil Engng.	7	5
Microbiology	2	87	Zoology	—	1	Elect. Engng.	89	29
Physics	3	—	Fuel Tech.	1	—	Mech. Engng.	12	11
Zoology	23	97	Metallurgy	1	—	Fuel Tech.	69	15
Civil Engng.	1	—	Geology	11	—	Metallurgy	74	205
Fuel Tech.	1	—				Refractories	8	12
Metallurgy	2	1						
Total	74	346	Total	88	86	Total	410	590

BORROWING BY UNDERGRADUATES

This section is concerned with the borrowing of 2595 undergraduate students. In addition to students reading for degrees it includes candidates for the Diploma in Education, the Diploma in Architecture and the Certificate in Social Studies.

Total issues to these students, compared with the corresponding Birmingham and Leeds figures, were as follows:

	Books	Journals	Total
Sheffield	27,747	1827	29,574
Leeds	33,320	2562	35,882
Birmingham	31,058	3400	34,458

The highest number of items borrowed was 139 books, by a third-year dual honours student in the Faculty of Arts. Next was an engineer, way ahead of any other applied scientist, with 89 books and 7 journals. A second-year Geology student borrowed 59 books and 36 journals (95 items), a third-year Geology student 42 books and 48 journals (90 items). In Economic and Social Studies the highest number of items borrowed was 74, in Medicine and Dentistry 28.

K

Journals accounted for 6·2% of the total borrowing at Sheffield, compared with 7·1% at Leeds and 9·9% at Birmingham. This is in interesting contrast to the similar comparison for staff and postgraduate borrowing of journals, where on the whole Sheffield journal borrowing was heavier than that of Leeds and Birmingham.

In comparing average borrowing figures with those of Leeds and Birmingham there is need for caution. For example, Arts in Leeds includes some departments that Sheffield covers under Economic and Social Studies; Science in Birmingham includes departments that are separated out under Engineering and Metallurgy in Sheffield. With reservations of this sort in mind, the following comparisons can be made.

Average total borrowing per student in Sheffield was 11·4 items made up of 10·7 books and 0·7 journal. The corresponding figures at Leeds were 10·7, 9·9 and 0·8. The Birmingham figure does not include Law, Medicine and Dentistry so that no useful comparison can be made.

Average total borrowing by Arts students in Sheffield was 21·0 compared with 17·0 in Birmingham and 17·89 in Leeds. Average Science totals were 8·1 in Sheffield, 10·76 in Leeds and 10·0 in Birmingham. Sheffield's Economic and Social Studies average of 18·2 compares with Birmingham's Commerce average of 14; Sheffield's Engineering and Metallurgy average of 6·8 with Leeds' Technology average of 8·87; Sheffield's Medicine and Dentistry averages of 4·9 and 2·7 respectively compare with the averages of 8·39 borrowed from the Leeds Medical Library and 7·52 from the Leeds Dental Library. The latter figures must raise the question of whether the comparatively low medical and dental borrowing figures in Sheffield were in any way connected with the fact that Leeds has special libraries for Dentistry and Medicine whereas at Sheffield the medical and dental literature is part of the main collection, though they could equally well be attributed to the existence in Sheffield of a "Reference Only" collection of the important basic medical textbooks.

Table 11 shows total borrowing analysed in some detail on a faculty basis. It can be seen that gross totals and averages conceal a wide variety of differences in faculty borrowing patterns: for example, well over half of total borrowings of journals were concentrated in one faculty, Pure Science.

Non-borrowing. Table 12 shows that 607 out of 2595 students (i.e. 23·4% of the total) did not borrow from the library at all. This compares with 26% at Leeds. Again, the general average conceals wide variations by faculties. In particular, the figure is heavily weighted by the large number of Medicine (33·7%) and Dentistry (47·8%) students who did not borrow from the library.

Of Sheffield's Arts students 8·5% did not borrow, a lower figure than the 14% at Leeds and 12% at Birmingham, but still surprisingly high for such a library-centred faculty. 32·3% of Sheffield's Science students did not

TABLE 11. *Undergraduate Borrowing*

	No. of students	No. not borrowing	% not borrowing	Students borrowing no journals	% borrowing no journals	Students borrowing no books	% borrowing no books	Total books borrowed	Average no. of books borrowed	Total journals borrowed	Average no. of journals borrowed	Combined total of books and journals borrowed	Average no. of items borrowed
Arts	627	53	8·5	547	87·2	53	8·5	12,934	20·6	210	0·3	13,144	21·0
Economic and Social Studies (including Law)	204	14	6·9	178	87·3	14	6·9	3,615	17·7	95	0·5	3,710	18·2
Medicine	288	97	33·7	246	85·4	103	35·8	1,297	4·5	100	0·3	1,397	4·9
Dentistry	182	88	47·8	158	86·6	96	52·7	462	2·5	39	0·2	501	2·7
Engineering and Metallurgy	513	140	27·3	439	85·6	144	28·1	3,235	6·3	279	0·5	3,514	6·8
Pure Science	641	207	32·3	503	78·5	214	33·4	4,136	6·5	1,087	1·7	5,223	8·1
Education (Pure Science)	46	4	8·7	40	86·9	4	8·7	540	11·7	7	0·2	547	11·9
Education (Arts)	94	4	4·3	127	92·6	4	4·3	1,528	16·2	10	0·1	1,538	16·3
Total	2,595	607	23·4	2,238	86·2	632	24·4	27,747	10·7	1,827	0·7	29,574	11·4

TABLE 12. *Analysis of Undergraduate Non-borrowing and Borrowing, by Year of Study*

	Not borrowing at all			Borrowed no journals			Borrowed no books			Average no. of books borrowed			Average no. of journals borrowed			Average total items borrowed		
	Yr. 1	Yr. 2	Yr. 3	Yr. 1	Yr. 2	Yr. 3	Yr. 1	Yr. 2	Yr. 3	Yr. 1	Yr. 2	Yr. 3	Yr. 1	Yr. 2	Yr. 3	Yr. 1	Yr. 2	Yr. 3
	%	%	%	%	%	%	%	%	%									
Arts*	6·7	8·6	3·4	94·8	85·9	77·6	6·7	8·6	3·4	17·3	21·1	29·0	0·1	0·4	0·6	17·4	21·5	29·6
Economic and Social Studies (including Law)	8·3	5·9	4·1	95·0	76·5	75·5	8·3	5·9	4·1	16·0	17·2	22·2	0·2	0·77	1·0	16·2	18·0	23·2
Pure Science	45·5	26·8	20·9	96·3	77·3	54·9	46·7	27·7	22·0	3·6	6·4	10·4	0·1	1·2	4·5	3·6	7·6	15·0
Engineering and Metallurgy	38·3	26·6	10·9	97·5	94·0	54·7	40·0	27·2	10·9	4·6	5·7	10·0	0·1	0·1	1·9	4·6	5·8	11·8

* Third-year arts includes final (fifth) year students of architecture.

borrow, compared with 39% at Leeds and 11% at Birmingham (where the "Science" figures include Technology); Sheffield's 6·9% of non-borrowing by Economic and Social Studies compares with the 5% for Commerce at Birmingham, and Sheffield's 27·3% of non-borrowing by Engineering and Metallurgy compares with 39% for Technology at Leeds.

An analysis by faculty is by no means the full story, of course, and Table 12 shows the very interesting changes which take place if faculty non-borrowing is further divided by year. Except in the case of second-year Arts students there appears to be a steady fall in non-borrowing as students progress through the university, the most dramatic difference being between the 38% of non-borrowing by first-year engineers and metallurgists and the 10·9% of non-borrowing by third-year students in the same group. Similarly, 3·4% of non-borrowing by third-year Arts students is not so depressing a picture as the overall average of 8·5%. The other side of the coin, of course, is the high level of non-borrowing by first-year students and this underlines the need to make every effort to familiarize new students with the library.

In every group, too, the average number of books borrowed by each student increases as the student moves through the university, and similarly with journals. The most striking figure in this connection is the 4·5 journals per head borrowed by third-year pure scientists, which is 30% of their average borrowings of 15·0 items.

Medicine and Dentistry borrowing, if analysed by year of study, reflects the very distinctive pattern of these courses, medical non-borrowing, for instance, being 42·3% in the first year, 60% in the second, falling steeply to 18% in the third year and 3·9% in the fourth year, then rising to 27·7% in the fifth year and 48·1% in the final, sixth year.

General faculty averages, in addition to concealing differences by year, also cover wide variations between individual departments. They do not reveal, for instance, the following extremely high levels of average journal borrowings: 20·0 by third-year botanists, 35·1 by third-year geologists, and 14·8 by third-year zoologists. At a much lower level, but diverging greatly from their faculty averages, were the 4·3 for third-year Psychology, the 4·0 for third-year Spanish, and the 3·3 for third-year Economics.

Similarly, the following average borrowings of books by third-year students are very much higher than their faculty averages: English 52·6, Philosophy 47·0, Spanish 42·6, German 41·6, Economics 39·1, French 36·7, Geology 24·6, Botany 21·7, and Zoology 19·5. At the other end of the scale are Architecture with 8·5, Law with 8·5 and Geography (Arts) with 11·3.

Foreign language borrowing. It was not to be expected that undergraduate use of foreign language materials would be significant, except in the case of students following foreign language courses. If borrowing by language students is excluded, only 161 books and 2 journals in foreign languages were borrowed, distributed on a faculty basis as follows: Arts 81 books; Pure Science 38 books, 2 journals; Education 31 books; Economic and Social Studies 8 books; Engineering and Metallurgy 3 books.

The range of languages was as follows: French 69 books, 1 journal; German 54 books, 1 journal; Italian 17 books; Spanish 11 books; Latin 5 books; Greek 5 books.

Mr. Humphreys draws attention to the fact that the Birmingham survey revealed very few undergraduate loans of books in foreign languages. Sheffield's figures appear to be even lower than those for Birmingham and it is clear that, outside the language departments, borrowing of this type of material by undergraduates is on a small scale.

UNDERGRADUATE USE OF BRANCH AND DEPARTMENTAL LIBRARIES

Applied Science Library, St. George's Square. This library provided 2898 out of the 3235 books and 270 out of the 279 journals borrowed by undergraduates from the Metallurgical and Engineering faculties. Geology, the only Pure Science department situated at St. George's Square, borrowed 55 books and 169 journals from it. Undergraduates from the other Pure Science departments, which are situated near the Main Library at some distance from St. George's Square, borrowed to the extent of 100 books and 34 journals and 16 books were borrowed by Arts undergraduates. Traffic in the other directions is by no means negligible, for Engineering and Metallurgy students borrowed a total of 296 books and 14 journals from the Main Library.

430 out of the 513 Engineering and Metallurgy undergraduates borrowed from the Applied Science Library only, but it is interesting to note that 12 borrowed only from the Main Library, which is some distance away, 2 from the Chemistry Library only and 6 from the Geology Departmental Library only.

The distance by which the Main Library is separated from the Applied Science departments and the Applied Science Library from the Pure Science departments must have quite a considerable influence on the borrowing patterns of the Pure and Applied Science faculties, but their interdependence can be seen from the above figures. It is equally clear that in the present situation the Applied Science Library has very limited significance for undergraduates from any of the other faculties.

Geology Departmental Library. 429 books and 209 journals were borrowed from this library by undergraduates. Except for 13 of the books, which were issued to students of Engineering and Metallurgy, all items were borrowed by students who were taking Geology as a degree subject.

Chemistry Departmental Library. 436 books and 48 journals were issued from this library to undergraduate students, 379 of the books and 45 of the journals being borrowed by the department's own students. The Engineering and Metallurgy faculties at St. George's Square accounted for 23 of the books and 1 journal, the balance of 34 books and 2 journals being issued to students from the other Pure Science departments.

Only six students from Pure Science departments other than Chemistry used this library, and one is left wondering how many students from elsewhere are reluctant to follow through their library needs if by so doing they would need to venture into the territory of another department. As 20% of all the Chemistry department's own students confine their borrowing to the Chemistry Departmental Library and the average borrowing of $4 \cdot 1$ books and $0 \cdot 4$ journal by each student of the Chemistry department is significantly lower than the average for the Pure Science faculty as a whole, it is possible that having their own departmental library may be a restrictive influence on the reading of Chemistry undergraduates. On the other hand, it could mean that access to their own departmental library for on-the-spot reading removes some of the need to borrow books for reading outside the library.

Law Departmental Library. Borrowing from this department was predominantly by its own students, who accounted for 616 out of 654 books issued. One book was borrowed by a pure science student, one by a student working for the Certificate in Social Studies, two by education students, 33 by one student from the Faculty of Arts and one by another arts student.

Music Departmental Library. Issues from this library, which is in the main a collection of scores, totalled 121, 104 of which were to students from the Department of Music. Other Arts students borrowed 5, Engineering and Metallurgy students 3, and Education students 9 items.

UNDERGRADUATES: RANGE OF BORROWING

At undergraduate level many students are studying a number of subjects, not always closely related, which between them can require the students to read in many different subject divisions. For this and other reasons it would be very difficult and probably not very profitable to identify and analyse "off-subject" borrowing on the comprehensive scale that was attempted with staff borrowing. It has been decided, instead, to single out particular aspects of each faculty's "off-subject" reading that appear to warrant special mention.

Arts. In the Faculty of Arts, which for this purpose includes the "Arts" Education students, no attempt has been made to analyse borrowing from Dewey classes 100, 300, 800 and 900, all of which are in heavy use by Arts undergraduates. It is worth recording, however, that 102 out of 721 students borrowed 258 books and 5 journals from class 500, Pure Science. Geography, Education and General Degree students between them accounted for a high proportion of this total, and the heavy borrowing from Dewey 550, Geology (112 of the 258 books), is mainly accounted for by geographers.

In class 600, Applied Science, 87 Arts students borrowed 230 books and 7 journals, but 58 of the 87 were Architecture students, borrowing from the 590, Building Science division, and they accounted for 182 of this total so that the residue is on the small side.

In class 700, Fine Arts, if the borrowing of students of Architecture and Music is excluded, only the very low figure of 18 Arts students, borrowing 31 books and 2 journals, remains.

Economic and Social Studies. Borrowing by the 204 students of Economic and Social Studies and Law also shows small use of class 700, 8 students borrowing 9 books from this class between them. Class 800, Literature, was more popular and 28 students borrowed 58 books. The only other "off-subject" class to merit attention was 200, Religion, from which 10 students borrowed 16 books.

Medicine and Dentistry. Eighteen of the 470 medical and dental students borrowed between them 35 books from class 700, more in fact than either of the faculties already mentioned. Thirty-one medical and dental students borrowed 63 books from class 800; 14 borrowed 26 books and 2 journals from class 900; 11 borrowed 18 books and 1 journal from class 300 and 8 students borrowed 15 books from class 200. It would appear that medical and dentistry students, possibly because of their longer courses, range more widely than most.

Engineering and Metallurgy. Students from the Faculties of Engineering and Metallurgy borrowed not insignificantly, if thinly, over a number of non-curricular subjects, though the extent of their "off-subject" borrowing must have been affected in some degree by the distance which separates them from the Main Library. Nevertheless, they borrowed 24 books from class 700, 23 from class 900, 72 from class 300, and 16 from class 200.

Pure Science. The 641 students in the Faculty of Pure Science were, with the exception of the geologists, within easy reach of the Main Library and this is reflected in quite substantial "off-subject" borrowing: 35 books and 3 journals from class 700, 179 books from class 800.

It would be unwise to generalize too freely from these figures of under-graduate "off-subject" reading, particularly as many students undoubtedly turn to the public libraries and the hall of residence libraries for reading of this type. It is, however, a little surprising that so little is borrowed from the excellent collection of fine arts books which the Main Library has built up without reference to any particular curriculum requirement. It may simply be, of course, that students do not often need to go to the part of the library in which these books are located. The extent of non-curricular borrowing by students of the applied sciences gives clear encouragement for continuing the policy of building up a carefully selected "general" section in the Applied Science Library, comprising books of general cultural interest, unrelated to the professional requirements of Metallurgy and Engineering.

LIMITATIONS OF THIS TYPE OF SURVEY
AND SOME GENERAL CONCLUSIONS

A survey of borrowing is concerned with only one aspect of library use, albeit an important one. To mention only two omissions, it takes no account at all of the hundreds of users who visit the library each day to consult books on the spot or of the regular visits made by members of staff and research workers to scan recent issues of important journals. Furthermore, records of borrowing can themselves be misleading: books can be borrowed and not read; academic fathers in the Arts Faculty may be borrowing from the Pure Science section for the benefit of their scientific wives or offspring. Such potential weaknesses are inherent in a statistical exercise of this character and counsel caution against excessive generalization. On the other hand, the scale of this survey, covering all members of the university over a full year, should iron out all except the major aberrations in borrowing. Whenever possible, too, we have attempted to give reality to averages and percentages by linking them to the number of users to whom they apply, so that the prudent reader can make his own interpretations of any of our figures.

Throughout this article comparisons have been made with the Leeds and Birmingham surveys and particular attention has been paid to points of difference. But probably more informative than any of the differences are the broad similarities between the results of all three surveys. A pattern of borrowing begins to emerge which, to the extent that Birmingham, Leeds and Sheffield are typical civic universities, is at least a firm starting point for generalizing about the borrowing behaviour of academic communities. Similarities between the general scale of borrowing at different levels and in different subjects, for instance, are quite marked. So, too, is the importance of "off-subject" borrowing in all three libraries, with the clear implication of the academic benefits which derive from a unified rather than a fragmented library. The use of foreign language material in our university libraries is a matter on which all three surveys also report interesting findings, and which appears to warrant further investigation, perhaps linked with consideration of the provision and use of translation services and facilities.

During recent years there have been signs of increasing interest in attempting to measure or quantify library use. Borrowing use has proved comcomparatively easy to measure, but the objective assessment of the use made of a library by readers browsing round its shelves or using it as a base for study (or even for activities very far removed from study) will present a much more formidable problem, but a problem which should nevertheless be tackled. Though surveys of use may simply confirm what an experienced librarian knows "in his bones" they often throw light on some shadowy areas. Perhaps above all, they provide the sort of quantitative evidence that carries weight with those who are responsible for the allocation of resources, both at national and university level, and in the social and economic climate of the mid-1960's this is a consideration which any librarian neglects at his peril.

REFERENCES

1. PAGE, B. S., and TUCKER, P. E., The Nuffield pilot survey of library use in the University of Leeds, *J. Docum.* **15,** 1 (1959).
2. HUMPHREYS, K. W., Survey of borrowing from the Main Library, the University of Birmingham, *Libri* **14,** 126 (1964).

6. A CRITICAL REVIEW OF THE SURVEYS OF SCIENTISTS' USE OF LIBRARIES

A. STEPHANIE BARBER

University Library, Cambridge

ABSTRACT

The subject is the surveys made of the scientists' use of libraries for acquiring information. Surveys which deal only with the use of the various forms of literature (its age, language, etc.) are not included. The methods used in the surveys are considered briefly in order to show how they may have affected the results. The analysis of the available data has been done under the following headings: preferred ways of finding information; reading; use of review articles; abstracts; personal indexes; catalogues; library services; differences between scientist populations (by subject field and type of work). The main features of the analysis are summarized in the first part of the discussion. The rest of the discussion deals with the data which should be collected, including information on the influence of the variables subject field, type of work, availability of library stock and previous experience of library services. The use of the data obtained is considered. A list of items read and a citation index of the surveys and important articles in the field are included.

INTRODUCTION

Studies of scientists' use of scientific literature and libraries have usually been made with the ultimate aim of increasing the scientist's effective use of published scientific knowledge. The studies range from internal surveys by individual librarians of their own libraries to detailed investigations of every incident in the working days of the scientist by social research experts.

The majority of the surveys have been of a "domestic" nature, involving only one particular group of scientists using a single library. Herner said in 1958 that "librarians are notorious collectors of statistics" and the analysis and publication of their records has proved equally tempting. Their general applicability is reduced by their sampling method and their usefulness is frequently limited by the fact that they do not describe the library resources and services which are available to the scientist whose habits they are

145

reporting. Possibly Herner had this kind of survey in mind when he said in 1958 that

> . . . there has been no dearth of attempts to analyse libraries and the organization of information. What has been lacking is an understanding of the purposes for which the analyses have been done. This failure to ascribe real purposes and applications has resulted in studies which have been puzzling bits and scraps, rather than meaningful entities. . . . They have produced data and not used them.

Since this was said social scientists have been taking an increasing interest in the investigation of the scientist's habits of literature use. The sampling of the scientist population and the choice of method of investigation have been so meticulously planned that the results obtained from these surveys are firm enough to support a theory—should anyone be found willing to produce one. The main difficulty is that the steps taken have been so small and cautious that the results are as yet meagre. This difficulty will no doubt be reduced as research proceeds; when reliable information about the habits of users is available perhaps someone will be bold enough to make scientific suggestions for improvements.

Unfortunately, the efforts of social research workers to build up a complete picture of scientists' "information-gathering habits" may not provide the key to the solution of the problem. Professor Bernal pointed out again in 1958 a difficulty which was raised by a scientist answering his questionnaire in 1948. The argument is as follows:

> The essential difficulty is that, though the user may well know what he *wants* from an information service he is in no position to know what he *needs* from it, namely what variation in the system would help most to further his work. Consequently, any action based on analysis of present user habits is unlikely to produce impressive results.

Despite this warning, surveys of all sizes are still being made. In view of the importance of finding better ways of keeping the scientist well informed it is a pity that the data amassed by these varied methods do not correlate well and therefore form no sound basis to a theory for increasing the scientist's effective use of published information.

NOTE ON SAMPLES

The refined techniques of random sampling have not generally concerned the librarian conducting his own survey. The limitations of the single library survey in this respect have been recognized and are not, therefore, likely to mislead anyone, although the influence of individual library characteristics upon scientists' habits has yet to be investigated. One or two of these limited surveys are alleged to have fallen into the error of using only those scientists who "take an interest" or are sufficiently methodical and co-operative to return diaries and questionnaires. The co-operative scientists may well be those who most appreciate the usefulness of the literature. Only

100% responses, interviews and external observations can eliminate entirely this potential bias.

Recent investigations by social scientists have been extremely scientific and thorough in their sampling of much wider populations. The usefulness of the "standard scientist" who should eventually emerge from their results will be discussed in a later section.

METHODS

The methods used by investigators have been subjected to very careful scrutiny and discussion; the justification of the method used occupies considerable space in many surveys. Tornudd (1958) puts the methods into four categories:

1. Questionnaires.
2. Interviews.
3. Diaries.
4. Case studies.

(Methods adopted in studies dealing only with type of literature used have not been included.)

Many writers have pointed out the weaknesses of all the first three methods. In practice the investigator's choice of method is sometimes determined mainly by the resources available to him. Case studies are out of the question for anyone without trained personnel, who will have to be employed for a considerable time. Most of the surveys have been conducted by only one or two people, often within the framework of the day-to-day running of an information service; under these conditions even holding useful interviews must be difficult to manage. From this point of view the written questionnaire is the most convenient method and it has in fact been the most widely used.

The questionnaire. A large and scattered sample can conveniently be dealt with by using a questionnaire; also, the distribution of questionnaires to scientists and the analysis of their replies appear to be relatively simple administrative procedures. A great deal of careful thought has been given to the structure of questions, arrangement of topics and choice of response method. Despite this care there are inherent and widely recognized difficulties. One is the framing of the questions in such a way as to avoid misinterpretation, which will have a disastrous effect on the results. Tornudd (1958) comments on the effect of a difference in wording in the Finnish version of her questionnaire. Another problem is that of providing for answers sufficiently uniform to make analysis feasible but not so rigid as to exclude any of the possible responses.

Even questions with simple yes/no answers may produce difficulties unless pages of explanation are appended. The near-impossibility of anticipating every source of confusion is a major obstacle to exactness. The Bureau of Applied Social Research at Columbia University (1960) has demonstrated the point very nicely in its review of use studies by noting that questions "Do you do . . .?" may get positive replies from those who have only once performed the particular task. The importance of giving realistic time intervals in questions of the form "Have you within the last . . . done . . .?" is also emphasized.

Questions on tasks performed during a certain previous period of time have been a source of one of the two most commonly quoted objections to the questionnaire method; that is, that scientists' recollections of what they did correlate poorly with the facts obtained by observation. The other objection is to the subjectiveness of the method. Glass and Norwood's comment (1958) on the difference between the scientists' expressed opinions of the usefulness of abstracts and the actual use the scientists made of them is a good example of the dangers. (Their comment is quoted in full in the section on abstracts.)

The interview. An advantage which the interview has over both the questionnaire and the diary is that the collection of replies from the sample does not depend upon the goodwill and interest of those participating. Herner (1954) considered that Bernal's use (1948) of mailed questionnaires caused his results to be unrepresentative, because he was dependent on the recipients' interest in their completion and return. The diaries are notoriously difficult to control and have been a source of sorrow to many investigator (see Maizell's remarks (1958)).

The interview has been criticized, like the questionnaire, for its subjectiveness and susceptibility to inaccurate recollection. A further criticism is that replies may be influenced by the personality of the interviewer—the objection to the librarian's asking the staff what they think of the library service is obvious. Nevertheless, the interview's flexibility is a big point in its favour Fishenden (1958) notes it as a particular advantage and Voigt (1961) records that the interviewers had a list of questions but not all the interview covered all topics—there was no insistence on answers if the scientist seemed to have nothing to contribute.

The diary. Hogg and Smith (1958) say in their remarks on methods that interviews are good for collecting preferences and views, but that diaries are more accurate for recollection of reading. The whole case for the use of the diary method rests on its claim to be a better way of obtaining facts about scientists' habits than the questionnaire and the interview can be. Investigators are rather divided on this point; ensuring the return of reasonably complete diaries is a well-known difficulty, but trusting memory is unsatisfactory. Fishenden (1958) says in favour of the diary that it is "method of securing an accurate record of the information used by the diary keeper . . .", but he also said that it was more dependent on co-operation from diary-keepers, was unlikely to be 100% complete and that the omissions might not be random.

After a study of the question of method, Shaw (1956) concluded that the diary seemed best, but by the end of the study his opinion was that ". . . the diary method, even with better than average co-operation and supervision, is not reliable enough to justify further studies over extended periods of time".

The case study. The replacement of the diary method, for fact-finding, by the case study seems desirable and obvious. However, the detailed study of a scientist's actions during several working days is an undertaking costly enough to put it out of reach of most libraries. In spite of this, exhaustive research into what a scientist (as opposed to an "average") does with his time is under way. As a method of finding out what scientists actually do it seems eminently satisfactory, although a useful opinion could not be given except by the social scientists, who are conducting this kind of research. Certainly case study fills the gap left by the uneasiness about the diary method of acquiring factual information. It can, of course, do nothing to elucidate the role of opinion, and doubt has been expressed for some time about the usefulness of exact data on present use. Stevens said in 1956:

> Perhaps the most serious disadvantage of the questionnaire–diary–interview method . . . is that it describes the searching and use of literature as practised, with the implication that this practice is correct and that it will continue and will form the basis for efficient library management. These methods, together with their conclusions, form a circular path. An escape from this problem may lie in the use of the techniques of operational research.

Bernal (1958) is even more sceptical,

> . . . if the matter be treated as one of operational research, it follows that all enquiries as to present use of scientific information services, though necessary background, can by themselves tell us little of use for improving the service.

In the last section, case study was said to be undertaken by social scientists. They have also done considerable work on the construction of questionnaires and it seems likely that before long the usual paragraph of investigator's comments on the unsound methods of previous investigators will be obsolete. This dissatisfaction with previous samples, methods and questions has contributed to progress in the field but it has left an unfortunate legacy—no two surveys can ever be directly compared because each investigator has introduced modifications. Someone facing the task of correlating their results might almost feel that more would have been achieved if they had all used the same questionnaire.

ANALYSIS

The difficulties of correlating the available reports on scientists' habits have already been mentioned in the section on methods. An attempt to collect and correlate the results was made by the Bureau of Applied Social

Research of Columbia University in 1960. They obtained the largest possible number of results for each aspect of information flow among scientists by using data from the text as well as that presented in the tables to calculate figures which some authors had not given directly. Such calculations have not generally been made in this account.

The diversity of the forms in which the results are presented in these studies is well demonstrated by the tables which the Bureau of Applied Social Research compiled. Footnotes and modifications are numerous in all of them, despite efforts to achieve uniformity. It is very difficult to quote more than two or three results for each aspect which are directly comparable; therefore in the present analyses some of the original authors' exactness of definition has had to be abandoned in order to obtain an overall picture. In cases where the description and method of presentation were particularly varied notes have been added to give the author's original description. Only those aspects for which several figures were available have been considered in the analysis.

The differences between types of scientist are not well brought out by comparisons *between* the studies (as opposed to comparison within studies) but some differences in results are undoubtedly due to the differences in scientist populations; therefore the nature of the sample and the method used are listed below for each study quoted in the analysis, in order to reduce repetition in the text and tables.

BERNAL, J. D. (1948)
   Scientists who replied to a written request, from Cambridge University, Imperial College, Medical Research Council, Rothamsted Experimental Station, General Electric Co. and Shirley Institute.
   All graduates; some "top men" included.
   Questionnaire.
BUSH, G. C., GALLIHER, H. P., and MORSE, P. M. (1956)
   Users of Massachusetts Institute of Technology science library.
   Questionnaire. 70% response.
FISHENDEN, R. M. (1958)
   Scientists who volunteered from AERE, Harwell Divisions. All honours graduates.
   Questionnaire and diary. 80% response.
GLASS, B., and NORWOOD, S. H. (1958)
   University biologists.
   Interview.
HERNER, S. (1954)
   Johns Hopkins University science personnel from all fields; 69% applied scientists, 31% pure scientists.
   Interview.
HERNER, S. (1958)
   Medical research scientists selected specifically from establishments with good library and information facilities.
   Interview.
HOGG, I. H., and SMITH, J. R. (1958)
   Applied scientists and technologists from UKAEA.
   Interview and diary. Diary 92% response.

MAIZELL, R. (1960)
    Chemists from one industrial research laboratory.
    Questionnaire and diary.
MARTIN, M. W., and ACKOFF, R. L. (1963)
    1. Chemical engineers and chemists;
    2. Chemical engineers, chemists and physicists, from American Chemical Society and
    American Physical Society rosters.
    Observation.
MARTYN, J. (1964)
    Industrial chemists from the Royal Institute of Chemistry list; academic scientists from
    "Scientific Research in British Universities and Colleges 1961–2"; government scientists
    from the staffs of DSIR laboratories.
    Questionnaire. 83% response for 1st; 88% for 2nd.
MENZEL, M. H. (1958)
    University scientists in chemistry and biological sciences.
    Interview. 10% refused interview.
SCOTT, C. (with L. T. WILKINS) (1956)
    Technologists in British electrical and electronic industries; 17% with degrees, 61%
    with no technical qualification.
    Interview.
SHAW, R. R. (1956)
    Professional research workers at Forest Products Research Laboratory.
    Diary.
SLATER, M. (1964)
    Users of academic, industrial, government and learned society libraries.
    Questionnaire. 80% industrial response; 62% others.
TORNUDD, E. (1958)
    Finnish and Danish scientists from industrial laboratories, research institutes and
    academic institutions.
    Questionnaire. 97% response.
UNIVERSITY OF MICHIGAN, INSTITUTE FOR SOCIAL RESEARCH (1954)
    Physiologists; taken from journal readership.
    Questionnaire. 76% response.
URQUHART, D. J. (1948)
    Users of Science Museum loan service.
    Questionnaire.
VICKERY, B. C. (1961)
    Summary of previous surveys.
VOIGT, M. J. (1959)
    Chemists, biologists and physicists in Scandinavia; 50% had doctorates, considerable
    research experience.
    Interview.
WELLISCH, H. (1963)
    Technologists of "Water Planning for Israel".
    Questionnaire. About 38% response.

PREFERRED WAYS OF FINDING INFORMATION

Quite a number of surveys have included questions of the type "Where
would you search for information?" or "How did you find your last reference?" The questions and replies have been presented in so many different
ways that direct comparison is impossible. In the hope of finding general
agreement upon which methods of obtaining information are the best, the

L

tables have been drawn up to indicate only the order of preference (1, 2, 3, etc.) which the scientists expressed in the original text.

TABLE 1. *How Was the Information Found?*

Chance	Personal recom- mendation	Abstracts and indexes	Cited refer- ences	Regular perusal	Personal file	
4	3	2	1	—	—	Bernal
—	2	(3)	6	1	—	Fishenden
2	6	5	3	1	—	Glass and Norwood
2	4	3	1	—	2	Herner (1958)
3	1	5	2	—	—	Martyn
5	1	6	—	(3)	2	Shaw
—	3	1	(————2)		4	Urquhart
—	3	2	4	1	5	Vickery (average)
1	2	5	4	—	(3)	Voigt (average)

Very little can be gained from this. A particularly striking feature is the absence of agreement between Voigt's (1961) and Vickery's (1961) "averages of previous surveys". In view of the lack of uniformity in the possible methods listed in the various surveys (some did not include chance) a certain amount of confusion is to be expected, but since the methods of discovering information should be largely independent of the type of library and service the poor result is disappointing.

Personal recommendation usually appears high on the list; cited references and regular perusal also seem to be frequent sources. The figures for regular perusal may well be affected by the wording of the question—Shaw (1956) gives figures for both "all material" and "non-routed material only" (the figures quoted in the table); his results differ from each other quite considerably. The discovery of a useful item during regular journal reading may be classed as "chance" or "regular perusal", depending on the alternatives available in the question. From the results above the discovery of references by chance during regular journal reading is the most likely method.

It is interesting to try to compare the figures given above with the scientists' ratings of the various methods. Not much material is available, but two comparisons can be made (Table 2).

Following up cited references appears to be rated the best method; abstracts and recommendations from colleagues are also considered good ways. The librarian's help has a much lower ranking, a position which is confirmed by findings on scientists' delegation of searches (library services

TABLE 2

Ratings of	Use for searching		General opinion	
	Herner (1958)	Martyn	Herner (1954)	Martyn
Books	5	5	6	6
Research journals	1	—	7	—
Review publications	6	—	9	—
Library card catalogues	12	11	8	11
Personal recommendation	4	3	1=	4
Abstracts and indexes	2	4	4	3
Cited references	3	1	1=	1
Bibliographies	10=	9	5	9
Regular perusal	—	2	3	2
Personal file	7	6	—	5
Ask librarian	8	12	—	12
Correspondence	9	7	—	8

(These figures are the *order* cited in the original texts, not the figures for use; see introduction to previous table.)

section). As the DSIR survey reported, there is no clear-cut agreement on the best way of locating scientific information.

READING

Time. The number of hours per week which scientists spend in reading scientific literature has been investigated in many surveys. The results are set out in Table 3.

TABLE 3. *Hours per Week Spent in Reading*

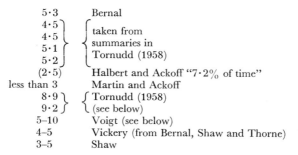

5·3	Bernal
4·5	⎫	⎧ taken from
4·5		summaries in
5·1	⎬	Tornudd (1958)
5·2	⎭	⎩
(2·5)	Halbert and Ackoff "7·2% of time"
less than 3	Martin and Ackoff
8·9	⎫ ⎰ Tornudd (1958)
9·2	⎭ ⎱ (see below)
5–10	Voigt (see below)
4–5	Vickery (from Bernal, Shaw and Thorne)
3–5	Shaw

Tornudd (1958) suggests that the high figures recorded in her survey are due to the large proportion of foreign-language literature Scandinavian scientists have to read; Voigt (1961) says that scientists tend to exaggerate the time they spend in reading and quotes Shaw (1956) to this effect.

Number of Items

TABLE 4. *Number of Items Read per Week*

9·2 seen ⎱ 3·1 read ⎰	Bernal
7·7	Hogg and Smith
6 (median)	Scott
15	Tornudd (see below)
4·3 average	Fishenden
4·8–5·8	Shaw
5–10 ⎱ 15·2 ⎬ 7 ⎰	⎧ Tornudd from ⎨ summaries of ⎩ papers (1958)

Tornudd (1958) explains her high figure, as well as those (already mentioned) in the previous section, by saying that they "... are due partly to the fact that library services have not been available or have not been utilised sufficiently". This comment suggests that there is some scope for investigations of use correlated with library facilities actually available to the scientists answering a questionnaire.

TABLE 5. *Place where Material Is Read*

Home (%)	Work (%)	Library (%)	
(28)	58	14	Hogg and Smith (see below)
24·2	63	10·1	Martin and Ackoff
60	27	3	Scott
46	5·2	4·6	Wellisch
5·4–6·4	89·5–90·3	3·9–3	Shaw

The first figure for library reading (percentage of "all reading") may be high because of the inclusion of security-classified reports which could not in fact be read elsewhere. Hogg and Smith (1958) also report that 73% of their entire sample claimed to have inadequate time for reading, although the survey does not show to what extent they solve the problem by reading at home.

The following item noted by Martin and Ackoff (1963) is interesting:

64·7% read journals in firms where there is a library.
56·3% read journals in firms where there is no library.

The difference is surprisingly small.

REVIEW ARTICLES

A lot of data have been collected on the use which scientists make of journals, monographs, textbooks, handbooks, standards, etc. These data have not been considered here, although they form an important section of our available information on scientists' literature use, for two reasons: firstly, because of the sheer bulk of the literature on scientists' use of journals and, secondly, because the relative use of the other sources of written information must depend greatly on the field in which the individual scientist is working. Variations due to differences in subject do, of course, occur in the other types of information gathering, but the effect on these is probably smaller than the effect on the relative use of, say, journals and unclassified reports.

Review articles, which discuss and evaluate work in a particular field and give lists of references, have been included because many writers have mentioned their use as a possible way of ameliorating the scientist's difficulty in keeping up with the literature of his subject. A summary of scientists' review-reading habits therefore seemed relevant and important (Table 6).

TABLE 6. *Review Reading*

Used %	"Use for reference" %	"Reference found" %	
41	—	—	Fishenden
		4	Glass and Norwood
(7% of "total vote"; pure, 10%; applied 5%)			Herner (1954)
—	25	—	Herner (1958)
63	—	—	Tornudd
77 (31% considerable use)			University of Michigan
—	7	—	Herner taken from Vickery
—	9	—	Moss

Fishenden (1958) comments on the low figure for review use and attributes it to the characteristics of the subject field, which is new.

The scientists in the DSIR survey quoted reviews as the most useful method of keeping up to date, and from the figures given above scientists seem to make quite good use of review articles. However, the percentage of references obtained from them is lower than some writers have hopefully suggested.

ABSTRACTS

The questions asked about the use of abstracts fall into three main categories:

1. Do you (ever) use abstracts?
2. How did you find/have your attention drawn to your last reference?

3. What techniques would you use to search the literature? (Including preferences and estimate of usefulness.)

The replies to the first question have produced quite high percentages of use; some of these drop considerably when the question is modified to "regular use". For example:

95% had come across references in abstracts or indexes.
53% would use to find a reference (Herner 1958).

82% use abstracts.
41% make considerable use (University of Michigan).

The figures for the use of abstracts produced by the surveys differ considerably. All that can reasonably be deduced from these figures is that the regular users of abstracts constitute between 20 and 40% of the population of scientists sampled (Table 7).

TABLE 7. *Use of Abstracts*

%	Comment	
17–25	Estimate (see below)	Fishenden
32		Hogg and Smith
13+	61% no technical qualifications	Scott (1959)
80	From figure "20% never use"	Tornudd (1958)
41		University of Michigan
25—	Average, including bibliographies and catalogues	Vickery
22·4	Comparatively isolated sample scientifically	Wellisch
11	Used for searching more than $\frac{1}{2}$ hr. per week	Voigt
4·8–6·5		Shaw (1956)

Both the first two figures were obtained from atomic energy establishment personnel, whose use of *Nuclear Science Abstracts* may affect the results, particularly those of Fishenden (1958), who states that *NSA* is used instead of a card catalogue for some classes of report literature. Fishenden's sample has been criticized by Fussler (1949) on the grounds that the use of "volunteers" may have introduced bias.

The most extreme results are those of Tornudd, of Shaw, and of Scott. Scott's low results for technologists in the electrical industry may be due to the lower qualifications and information requirements of his sample (29% could in fact not recall any "recent useful article"). It is less easy to explain Shaw's low results from two almost identical surveys, except perhaps in terms of subject fields—engineers and botanists as well as chemists. Tornudd's high result may be due to language or isolation factors. (Voigt's Scandinavian results also show fairly high use, although it is differently expressed.)

The proportion of references to which the scientists' attention was drawn by an abstracting journal is considerably lower than that of alleged use, though it is unfortunately not possible to discover from the data whether the regular users included in their "attention drawn" category references found in their regular reading of abstracting journals. Glass and Norwood (1958) allege that

> The comments made by the scientists who were interviewed contrasted considerably with the data they provided. Many of them spoke of the importance of abstracts, the use they made of them, and the need for a better coverage of the literature and prompter publication. The data show that for this group of scientists (university biologists) abstracts were not often of primary importance.

A comparison of figures obtained by "questionnaire" surveys with those obtained by "interview" surveys did not demonstrate this effect.

As is to be expected from this low use, references were not very frequently found through abstracting journals (Table 8).

TABLE 8. *References Found Through Abstracts*

Abstracting journal (%)	Reference citation (%)	Best method (%)		
5	9	Regular scanning	23	Fishenden
5·2	6·9	Regular scanning	30·4	Glass and Norwood
12·6	17·6	Personal recommendation	32·6	Martyn
4	—	Chance	41	Scott
22·4	—	Library	57·9	Wellisch
4 (with catalogue)	—	No reference	40	Hogg and Smith
4–7	—	Chance	36	Voigt (average)
3·3	—	Personal recommendation	12·3	Shaw

Wellisch's (1963) high result may be due to the isolation of his sample from other ways of communication used by European scientists. His high figure for "library" suggests this.

As a technique for searching the literature the abstracting journal is not the first choice; following up cited references, regular scanning and oral communication seem to be considered as good or better. Martyn's (1964) table of the opinion of scientists confirms this (Table 9). The industrial scientists' much higher opinion of abstracts is probably due to the fact that the industrial scientists were almost all chemists, whose greater appreciation of abstracts is confirmed by several surveys (see section on subject differences).

TABLE 9. *Opinions of Usefulness of Abstracts* v. *Other Methods*

Abstracts	Cited references	Regular scanning	Oral communication	
+54	+60	+44	+20	Industrial
+25	+59	+44	+41	Academic
+22	+69	+52	+45	Government

Rating: "high" +100; "moderate" 0; "low" −100.

Some writers have commented upon the widespread use of abstracts for current information rather than for retrospective searching. The figures obtained are given in Table 10.

TABLE 10

Mainly for news (current) (%)	Mainly for search (retrospective) (%)	Both equally (%)	
64	36		Hogg and Smith
43	21	34	Scott
25	30	45	Glass
22	30	48	Gray

The DSIR survey reported that 40% of their sample used abstracts for both purposes equally.

The use of abstracts for retrospective searches will depend on the need which the scientist has for such searches. Recent authors (notably Voigt, 1959) have pointed out that the comprehensive literature search is not needed very frequently; this explains the findings in Table 10, which show that abstracts are used less for searching than for current information.

Gray says that informative abstracts are preferred; 46% of physicists use abstracts as a guide rather than as a substitute, 48% use them in both ways. Martin and Ackoff (1963) say that "abstracts are used more as a substitute for articles than as a guide to them". It has been said that scientists are just as willing to have titles only as they are to have abstracts of the current material. Gray's physicists (1950) thought that the more information which they had about the paper the better, even for indicative purposes. Of course, this reduces the promptness of publication.

The percentage of scientists who know of abstracts is considered to be low by some investigators. Scott (1958) gives a figure of 38% and Wellisch (1963) one of 29·6%. According to Martyn (1964), about 9% did not use a library abstracting service which was available.

PERSONAL INDEXES

Among the varied results produced by surveys of scientists' information-gathering habits, one fact is unanimously agreed upon—between 50 and 80% of scientists keep personal indexes. The figures obtained in the various surveys are listed in Table 11.

TABLE 11

Keep (%)	Use for references (%)	Reference found (%)	
65			Bernal
	45	4 ⎫	
76		⎬	Fishenden
75		⎭	
81	22		Herner (1958)
66+ (10% relied on someone else's index, 5% intended to keep one)			Hogg and Smith
	47		Martyn
63 ⎫			
57 ⎬			Tornudd
54 ⎭			
		9	Urquhart
34+23+8			Voigt
		(summary) 8	Vickery
	0·4–0·1	2·8–2·3	Shaw

Voigt's total for personal index-"keeping" is made up of three categories: extensive (34%), small (23%), special (8%); 25% did not keep an index.

Fishenden (1958) says that the incidence of private indexes is probably higher than stated. Although the habit of keeping a private index is so widespread, the number of references obtained from them is not very great. Martyn (1964) found that the scientists in his sample did not regard the private index as a very useful tool in searching. His figures were:

Rating ("high" +100; "moderate" 0; "low" −100)

+3   industrial scientists
+11 academic scientists
+2   government scientists
+20 chemists   average +7
−18 physicists
+8   biologists

Compare this figure for the average rating with that of −63 for their opinion of the library card catalogue. The extensive use of personal indexes seems to show that scientists do not object to using an index or file as such, therefore other reasons must be sought for their distrust of library catalogues.

CATALOGUES

Not many surveys have asked questions about the scientist's use of the card catalogue. This may be because the catalogue generally records only a library's book holdings and inquirers have concentrated more upon journal use. The surveys which have dealt with catalogue use have put the question in very varied ways, but the general impression made is that the card catalogue is not a popular method of finding useful items of scientific information (Table 12).

TABLE 12. *Library Card Catalogue Use*

%	Wording of question	
17	Of tasks were catalogue consultations	Bush *et al.*
(0·557)	Mean number of tasks per visit	Bush *et al.*
1	"Found in library indexes"	Fishenden
8	Of "total vote", for library catalogue	Herner (1954)
69	"Came across references" in library catalogue	Herner (1958)
6	Would use to search	Herner (1958)
10	Used library card index	Martyn
less than 4	Estimates from previous work	Voigt
1·3	Of all references to material	Shaw
3·8	Of all references to non-routed material	Shaw

The first two figures are taken from a survey of the science library at MIT, and it is reasonable to suppose that the larger and more unfamiliar the collection of books the greater the use of the catalogue will be. Tucker (1961) considers the reliance of science students upon a "sense of location" and the help of the library staff to be surprisingly high, although 38% of the scientists use the author catalogue at the university library (technology students 25%) and 21% use the subject catalogue (technology students 17%).

Martyn's (1964) collection of scientists' opinions of the usefulness of the card catalogue shows that it is not very popular as a finding method, since their rating of −63 meant that they considered it less than half-way up the scale from "low" to "moderate" (i.e. "moderate" 0; "low" −100). Fishenden's (1958) figure is the lowest, but it may have been reduced (in spite of the possibly favourable bias of his "volunteers") because the library used did not catalogue large classes of report literature which must frequently have been required.

The library catalogue therefore does not appear to be a major source of references for the scientist populations studied. This result contrasts with Maizell's (1958) statement that creative chemists rated the subject catalogue of books of major importance.

LIBRARY SERVICES

Quite a lot of information on scientists' opinions of librarians' helpfulness and the services they provide has been recorded, but the factual evidence is rather fragmentary. The reliability of some of the replies obtained in face-to-face interviews with librarians or their agents, or even those from internal questionnaires, may be open to doubt. A quotation from Shaw (1940) gives a qualitative opinion:

> To meet his [the scientist's] needs the librarian should be able to handle library tools, should find obscure and incomplete references, should call to his attention articles in his field which appear in journals in related or general fields and . . . do the bibliographical and bibliothecal dirty work upon which the scientist does not wish to spend his own time.

Slater (1964) found that up to 40% of her sample of library users had tried to obtain information elsewhere before coming to a library. This result is in keeping with the high place given to "personal recommendation" in the results of many of the surveys. There are a few figures quoted for the usefulness of the librarian's help and these are shown in Table 13.

TABLE 13. *Guidance Sought from Library Staff*

Frequently (%)	Sometimes (%)	Never (%)	
	(70)	24	Hogg and Smith
	28% of "total vote"		Herner (1954)
	9% "would ask"		Herner (1958)
	divided 50–50 on desirability of conducting own search		Maizell
6	20	74	Voigt
10	50		Tornudd (1958)
	8% would ask		Martyn
	(23% of industrial, 1% academic)		
	34% librarian did search, 55% did own search		Slater (1964)

Slater found that the librarian's searches were 10% less successful, although this may perhaps have been due to a tendency to give the librarian the questions which were likely to prove difficult. Tornudd makes the point that her figures might have been higher if a librarian's services were more widely available in Scandinavia. The answers made to this question must be influenced by the service available to the scientist. An indication of this is given by the wide difference in Martyn's figures for industrial and academic scientists. University library staffs would not generally be expected to have the time and subject knowledge to do individual scientific searches. Slater's figures for complete self-use : ask librarian are:

industrial scientists   1 : 1

government scientists   1 : 0·9

academic scientists   1 : 0·5

However, the picture is further confused by Martyn's figures for his scientists' opinions of the usefulness of the method "asking the librarian for references", as given below:

Rating ("moderate" 0; "low" —100)

—40 industrial scientists
—66 academic scientists
—73 government scientists
—62 chemists
—84 physicists
—78 biologists   average —75

These figures indicate that academic scientists rated a librarian's help a more useful method of obtaining references than the government scientists did. This peculiar result (peculiar in view of the limited staff help a university library can give in this way) is possibly due to the slightly larger number of physicists (who rated the librarian's help very low) in the government sample. The only other explanations are that the academic scientists were thinking of a small departmental library, where the librarian had a good knowledge of the stock, or that they gave their answers on a hypothetical basis: "we would if we could".

It seems fairly safe to assume that up to 50% of scientists would ask for a librarian's help if it were available. Hogg and Smith (1958) asked the 70% of their sample who sometimes or always asked for help why they did so. Their answers are as follows:

42% thought librarian better qualified.
40% thought it saved time.
14% thought librarian had sources to hand.

The finding that 42% of the scientists thought that the librarian was better qualified to search is gratifying, but it is unfortunately not matched by any particular enthusiasm for increasing the librarian's qualifications by introducing subject specialists. Even Maizell's (1958) chemists held the view that "Technical information services offered by library staff were of only moderate importance . . . ". Hogg and Smith found that their sample ranked actual information from the library seventh out of eight as an information source. Ten per cent suggested that the library needed more qualified staff, but the absence of details of the current staffing made this piece of information almost useless except for internal library purposes.

Stevens (1950) says (from Shaw, 1940 and Carlson, 1946):

> Above all, he [the scientist] does *not* want the "specialist" librarian to abstract and interpret the literature, nor otherwise to assist in a subject capacity, but only in a library capacity.

Whether or not this statement is correct, it fades almost to insignificance beside the report of another writer that "more than half of those who had a library did not use it" (Scott, 1959).

DIFFERENCES BETWEEN SCIENTIST POPULATIONS

Differences due to subject fields. It is difficult to deal simply with the large number of comparisons of literature use by scientists of different disciplines, and even harder to assess to what extent these undoubted differences are caused by the differing forms of material available in the various fields.

Some variations of usage have been frequently noted. For example, the belief that applied scientists make less use of the literature but seek the librarian's help more often is confirmed by Herner (1954) and Francillon (1959). Rees (1963) suggests that this is because applied scientists do not feel that literature searching is a vital part of their professional activity. The feeling that chemists use a lot more periodical literature than other scientists is confirmed very nicely by the findings of Bush, Galliher and Morse (1956) at MIT:

	Chemists	Biologists	Physicists
Ratio of visits to enrolment	0·348	0·286	0·228
Use of books (no. of "tasks")	201	42	165
Use of journals (no. of "tasks")	806	82	122

The chemists' journal/book use ratio is clearly much higher than that of the other two disciplines and this result is confirmed by the figures the authors have given for the mean number of tasks per visit—the chemists performed fewer of all types of task except that of periodical consultation. Further evidence of the chemists' relative neglect of books is given by the following figures.

Mean no. of tasks per visit	Chemists	Biologists	Physicists
Catalogue consultation (to find books)	0·294	0·889	0·594
Books withdrawn	0·113	0·25	0·211

Shaw's (1956) results also show that chemists make more use of periodicals.

The expectation that chemists would find abstracts (i.e. *Chemical Abstracts*) more useful than other scientists find abstracts is also confirmed by Martyn (1964) and by Voigt (1961):

Martyn: Use subject or author indexes in journals (including abstracts)

Chemists	71% use to search +56 rating ("high" +100; "moderate" 0)
Physicists	47% use to search +13 rating
Biologists	61% use to search +28 rating

Chemists	18 (72%)	very little or none	7 (28%)	$\frac{1}{2}$ hr. per week or more
Physicists	24 (95·5%)	very little or none	2 (7$\frac{1}{2}$%)	$\frac{1}{2}$ hr. per week or more
Biologists	16 (94%)	very little or none	1 (6%)	$\frac{1}{2}$ hr. per week or more
Average	89%		11%	

(The percentages quoted for Voigt's results have been roughly estimated from the figures given to allow comparison with the overall percentages given by Voigt in his table.)

According to Martyn, chemists are also rather more in favour of help from the librarian in searches:

Chemists   12% would use −62 rating ("moderate" 0; "low" −100)
Physicists   8% would use −84 rating
Biologists   3% would use −78 rating

It must be remembered, however, that the majority of chemists in this sample came from industrial libraries. Voigt's figures do not confirm chemists' greater use of the librarian.

Martyn's results indicate other interesting possibilities of subject differences, notably the physicists' much lower regard for subject bibliographies:

Chemists   18% would use −15 rating ("moderate" 0; "low" +100)
Physicists   9% would use −57 rating
Biologists   23% would use −18 rating

Some of these differences are not immediately explicable in terms of variations in the pattern of literature forms of the subject.

Differences due to type of work. This side of the question has not had a great deal of attention. Francillon touches on it in her analysis of reference questions, but Mote (1962) has made a much more definite effort to link demand for library services with the difficulty of the area of work from a bibliographic viewpoint. His three groups were (1) occupation in a subject of which the underlying principles are well developed and the literature well organized, (2) wider field—"applied" research going over subject boundaries, (3) worse form of second—literature almost non-existent or organzied in an unhelpful way.

The relative use quotients were (1) 3, (2) 28, (3) 44.
Average number of inquiries per person (1) 1·4, (2) 3·6, (3) 20.

$$\text{Relative use quotient} = \frac{\text{no. of inquiries}}{\text{no. of staff in category}}.$$

It could be argued that in his selection of categories Mote begged the question, but any investigation of this relationship is of interest.

Another demonstration of the differences between groups of scientists with similar qualifications working in almost identical subject fields is given by Herner (1954). Table 14 has been constructed from data given in the text, because Herner does not consider the point in detail in his article.

TABLE 14

	School of Engineering (graduate and undergraduate teaching)		Applied Physics Laboratory (non-teaching; engineers' replies only)	
Median estimate of information obtained from literature	80%		50% "indicating that type of institution is probably a factor influencing degree of dependence on literature"	
Direct sources (in order of preference)	Advanced texts	1	Handbooks	1
	Research journals	2	Classified reports	2
	Tables	3	Advanced texts	3
	Unclassified reports	4	Research journals	4
	Theses	5	Trade publications	5
Indirect sources (in order of preference)	Cited references	1	Personal record	1
	Regular perusal	2	Cited references	2
	Abstracts and indexes	3	Regular perusal	3
	Bibliographies	4	Abstracts and indexes	4
	Personal records	5	Library card catalogue	5
	Book reviews	6	Book reviews	6
	Library card catalogue	7	Bibliographies	7
Reference services (in order of preference)	Translating	1	Accession and reading list	1
	Guidance by library staff	2	Bibliographies	2
	Accession and reading list	3	Guidance by library staff	3
	Bibliographies	4	Translating	4
	(Use services less)			

These results have been quoted at some length because the marked differences between the habits and preferences of these two sets of engineers are very interesting. If there can be so much difference between university engineers with roughly similar library resources Martyn's division into Industrial, Academic and Government scientists, while useful, does not go far enough.

The introduction of yet another variable into considerations of library use will undoubtedly confuse the picture even more, but on this evidence the question of the exact nature of a scientist's work will have to take its place with his subject field as an influence upon his information-gathering habits.

DISCUSSION

Summary of results. The results collected in the previous sections can be summarized as follows: scientists seem to have no clear-cut opinion on the best methods of acquiring information. If they needed information they would probably consult their colleagues first, then follow up references in journals and possibly use abstracts. They will try to get the information without coming to the library and are quite likely to ignore the librarian's help if they do come. The amount of reading which they do is not in itself of great significance, unless one takes that amount as the maximum the scientist is prepared to get through and plans some complicated way of spending the same time in more fruitful reading. Four to five hours per week seems to be the usual time spent. Review articles are read and appreciated, but the rate of use of abstracting journals is definitely unsatisfactory. More scientists should be using them. Although their use for "keeping up" is not really what librarians expect it does enable the scientist to spread his net wider and it will bring to his attention items of interest which are published in journals he would not think of searching, let alone regularly reading. The more widespread use of abstracts would help to convince scientists that, when they need information on a subject, they should not limit themselves to what their familiar journals, professional colleagues and private indexes can supply.

The only danger in keeping a private index is that the scientist may feel that everything he needs to know on a subject is covered by his entries there. It is surprising that not more librarians have attempted to extend and supplement their catalogue empire by providing ready-made entries and abstracts for personal filing.

The library staff are not usually called upon to give much help except in finding specific documents. This is probably due to a distrust of the librarian's capacity to deal usefully with a subject he does not understand.

The obvious influence of subject field and type of work upon a scientist's information-gathering habits introduces two more variables into this complex subject without as yet doing anything to illuminate it.

Data which should be collected. The failure of the library surveys to achieve any very useful results could charitably be ascribed to the involved nature of the subject. The main variables influencing the behaviour of scientists are:

1. Subject field.
2. Type of work.
3. Availability of library stock and services.
4. Previous experience of library use.

(Individual disposition is omitted. The recently discovered factor "type of employer" can probably be considered as a mixture of 2 and 3.)

Theoretically there should be no difficulty in observing and questioning large samples of scientists from populations which only differ substantially in one of the above variables. Ultimately it would from this be possible to assess the separate effect of each variable upon scientists' information-gathering habits. Should such numerous investigations be impossible to organize, the alternative is to obtain from one extremely large random sample of the entire scientist population a set of figures for the "normal" scientist's habits. Samples (from individual libraries if necessary) could then be compared with the standard and the points of difference correlated with the known values of the variables in that particular sample.

This could have been done by now, despite the limited resources of money and manpower. However, the knowledge of how these variables affect scientists' library use is in itself not particularly valuable. The knowledge must be applied in such a way as to increase scientists' effective use of published information. The surveys' failures to relate their results to the factors likely to have influenced those results are in a way less important than their failure to start with any definite aim other than that of adding to the subject's already ample collection of undigested facts. This has been said before. There are honourable exceptions of surveys which set out to provide the data needed to solve a specific library problem and have in fact formed a basis for successful action.

Use of data. Although the collection of data has been made to appear extremely involved, with all sorts of subjective influences and unreliable methods, the actual use of data will undoubtably be made very complicated by more concrete difficulties.

The basic choice of attacks is very straightforward—if the user–system interaction is inefficient (which we assume it to be) either the library system or the user must be deliberately altered. In theory it is very inadvisable to try to alter both at once, because the disentanglement of the cause of an adverse change would be a horrible task, but there is a pressing need for rapid changes.

Altering the system. It is not really necessary to wait until the social scientists have provided the librarians with exact figures for library use before making any alterations. For example, the knowledge that only 25–30% of scientists use abstracts is sufficient indication that a lot of scientists are probably missing a useful tool. The possible courses of action include: provision of abstracting journals if they are not available; the wide circulation of copies of abstracting journals; if the library service permits, the provision of abstracts bulletins tailored to the needs of individual scientists. Similarly, the knowledge that between 50 and 80% of scientists keep and use private indexes is striking enough to suggest that some way of supplying references in a form suitable for inclusion in private files might encourage use of the library's stock.

M

These examples of the sort of action which could be taken without waiting for more exact data are extremely simple. Most librarians make such adjustments to their services without waiting for elaborate surveys to demonstrate the needs.

Changes in library services can produce very large increases in use—see Johnson's mention of the results of indexing reports (1963)—and changes in library practice do not generally present insuperable difficulties. It is, however, doubtful if changes such as those mentioned above will prove sufficient to deal with the present information problems. The question which now arises is whether it is reasonable to try to produce any alteration in the users' habits, particularly those of the scientists who make very little use of libraries.

Altering the user. Alteration of scientists' habits has been declared by Scott (1958) to be impossible. He considers the difficulty of modifying the user–library system as follows:

> The problem therefore becomes that of the optimum allocation of the load between two very different types of system, one mechanical, the other biological. [The human brain, which has smaller storage capacity but much greater rapid-retrieval ability.] In solving it, the former system may be regarded as variable, but almost everything about the latter system is virtually fixed, including the nature of its lines of communication with the former system . . . any practical plans for changing the mechanical storage system must not pre-suppose a *radical* change in the habits of the user of scientific information. No doubt over a period of generations he can and will be modified; but if we are interested in the next decade or two we had better take the scientist broadly as we find him and build our system of information storage around him.

Nevertheless, many information systems are being set up with at least one implicit modification—that the scientist will allow librarians or information specialists to take over his searches. This is definitely not always true now. At the present state of knowledge librarians would probably be most unwilling to attempt any great modification of the scientist; they would even think it was unlikely to produce the desired improvement. There is a large industrial library where, although delegation and mechanization of the search tasks is complete for the company's internal reports, the scientists must search the published literature themselves because it is felt that they may gain from conducting their own searches. (Private information.) This is the point at which it would be useful to know how the scientist acquires his habits and how he came to adopt his methods of literature use.

Aspects which have not been investigated

   (a)   Why the scientists use the literature in the way they do.

   (b)   What the effect of the library service is on current use.

   (c)   What the effect of the scientist's previous experience of library services is.

(a) Most of the surveys have not asked the scientist to explain himself. Progress has been made recently by asking scientists why they wanted the information for which they were searching; their replies will be useful in anticipating library demand. A certain amount of information can be obtained from the many tables listing preferred methods of searching, but the answers to a direct question "why?" would be even more useful. At best they might indicate some easily corrected defect in the library system and in any case they would make the scientist think temporarily about his information-gathering habits. The data would, of course, not rank as "facts" but the replies would tell us a great deal about scientists' attitudes to information, and this will have to be known before we can either change the system to fit the scientists' preferences completely or try to persuade the scientists to modify their methods. The main difficulty in conducting an inquiry upon these lines is that the results would be very dependent upon local library conditions and individual research fields; it could probably not be conducted on a wide sample because of the likely diversity of the replies, which would make analysis meaningless.

(b) Investigation of the variation in users' habits due to differing library facilities has been strangely neglected. Many of the single-library surveys might have been rescued from Herner's (1958) condemnation "puzzling bits and scraps" by a consideration of how local conditions could have influenced the results. A description of scientists' habits is almost useless to an outsider if the stock and facilities available are not described. To take a rather obvious example, chemists' recorded use of abstracts will depend very much upon whether the library subscribes to *Chemical Abstracts*, yet this may not be mentioned at all. Sometimes, but by no means always, the conditions influencing an author's findings can be deduced from hints given elsewhere in the text. For example, M. H. Smith said in 1958: ". . . a pattern of use which has been fairly constant since 1951: that is, a heavy use of books compared with the use of journals by research personnel. . . ." Fortunately he stated that this was taken from unclassified loan records (books are more likely to be needed for an extended period); also his stock was stated elsewhere to be 2000 books and 1600 volumes of periodicals (about 80 titles, which meant an average 20-year run. No information on addition of new titles.) Taking usual science periodical figures, it is unlikely that more than 400–600 of his volumes of periodicals were potentially useful; this is much lower than the number of books and these factors probably explain his "pattern of use".

Such detective work should really not be left to readers wishing to make use of a survey's findings.

(c) Almost nothing is known about the user–system interaction at present. Cause and effect in library use are often inextricably confused. For instance, some investigators say that academic scientists ask for help less frequently because they feel that the library staff are not able to assist. Others maintain that the academic scientist is by nature and type of work more disposed to do his own searching and would not welcome more assistance.

The extent to which a scientist will ask for help and make use of library facilities depends not only on his subject field, his type of work and his present library services, but also on his previous experience of library services. As one chemist politely put it (1958 Washington Conference on Scientific Information, p. 556) : "Many libraries at present do supply information and in effect do some library research for me, but they vary in the time and effort one can reasonably ask of them, if any, and the present situation is rather haphazard."

Standardization of library and information services would do much to help the scientist to adopt sensible and efficient methods of keeping himself informed without spending an ever-increasing amount of time on reading. It must be nearly impossible to adopt a systematic approach when each employer (or even division) for whom he works will have different facilities. There is a strong argument for making the first library which the scientist is required to use—usually a university library—a model of the service he should be able to expect from all libraries. Otherwise he is almost bound to under-use the extensive services of the best industrial libraries. The difficulties of grafting such an ideal service on to the usual undergraduate scramble for set texts are unfortunately enormous and it seems unlikely that this change can be made within the next few years. Even a partial fulfilment of the aim of making all scientists accustomed to really good library services as a matter of course would raise the standard of many libraries considerably and go some way towards producing uniformity in library services to scientists.

CONCLUSION

It is customary to conclude accounts of surveys with suggestions for further surveys. The likelihood of an author's proposals being carried out by later workers depends not only upon their merit or originality. (It was suggested at the 1958 Washington Conference on Scientific Information that a study of the use of the literature in similar institutions with different library services might be made (p. 307).) Action on the proposals depends also on the availability of individuals or corporate bodies willing to provide funds and manpower for investigations, and it is this factor which determines the type of investigation made and the particular aspect which is studied.

In many of the previous surveys conducted by a single librarian there has been the mistake of trying to produce generally useful figures from a sample which was doomed to be unrepresentative from the start. Their findings are of use only to other librarians who know that their own circumstances are very similar. The most profitable line of investigation which can be pursued by a librarian who cannot go beyond his own library is that of studying the local influences on the habits of the users. He could compare figures obtained in one of the much wider surveys with those obtained by asking the same questions of his own organization's scientists. From this a valuable correlation of observed differences with the differences in the library service, subject field and type of work can be made. The librarian is also in a position to measure the effects upon use of any modifications made in the library services. Such detailed study is needed because any results of research, however widely based, will eventually have to be applied in detail in libraries.

The interest of the university social science faculties in methods of using and disseminating scientific information has received financial encouragement. Because they have comparatively large resources they are in an excellent position to establish the general outlines of scientists' habits as matters of fact. Their knowledge of sampling, questionnaire composition and statistical treatment of sociological data puts the survey business on a respectable scientific footing. In addition to their production of data on scientists' habits, they have made interesting suggestions for studies of the "diffusion" of scientific information, a task which will require considerable resources of money and skill. The conversion of their findings into usable library policies will be a difficult step and it is to be hoped that progress will not be halted permanently at that point.

In addition to individual librarians and faculties of social scientists, associations of librarians, of information officers and government departments most concerned are also working in this field. They are in a good position to fill the gap between the two previous types of investigator. This is because such bodies are large enough to be able to organize samples on a national basis and yet sufficiently in touch with the professions involved to ensure that investigations are related to the practical possibilities of the action which must follow.

The question of using the results of surveys has not yet become pressing because the data have been considered untrustworthy or inadequate so far. However, there is already sufficient evidence to show that the use of the data in practical alterations will require very careful thought. This should begin now, because the accumulation of information about the facts of, and reasons for, the scientists' habits of use is only the first half of the problem of how to increase the efficient use of published scientific knowledge.

REFERENCES

The following references are those which were read in the preparation of this account. A recent bibliography of the subject is one by Davis and Bailey (see below).

ACKOFF, R. (1957), *in* SHERA, J. H., KENT, A., and PERRY, J. W., *Documentation in action*, Reinhold, New York.

ADOLPHE, E. F. (1947), Scientists in the library, *Rochester Univ. Libr. Bull.* **2** (Feb.), 25–6.

BACH, H. (1957), Scientific literature use: a survey, *Spec. Libr.* **48**, 466.

BERNAL, J. D. (1948), Preliminary analysis of pilot questionnaire on use of scientific literature, *Roy. Soc. Sci. Inf. Conf. 1948, Rep.* 101–2, 589–637.

BERNAL, J. D. (1958), The transmission of scientific information: a user's analysis, *Proc. Int. Conf. Sci. Inf. 1958*, **1**, Nat. Acad. Sci., Washington, 77–95 (1959).

BERNIER, C. L. (1958), Documentation in the field of science, *Spec. Libr.* **49**, 415–20.

BRANNEN, G. B. (1963), A literature survey of technical information services, *Spec. Libr.* **54**, 94–101.

BRODMAN, E. (1944), Choosing physiology journals, *Bull. Med. Libr. Ass.*, **32**, 479–83.

BROWNSON, H. L. (1960), Research on handling scientific information, *Science, NY.* **132**, 1922–31.

BUREAU OF SOCIAL SCIENCE RESEARCH INC. (1962), *A survey of users of American Society for Metals—Western Reserve University searching service*, Washington, BSSR 352. Abstr. in *J. Docum.* **19**, 78 (1963).

BUSH, G. C., GALLIHER, H. P., and MORSE, P. M. (1956), Attendance and use of the science library at MIT, *Am. Docum.* **7**, 87–109.

CALDER, N. (1959), *What they read and why*, HMSO, London.

CARLSON, W. H. (1946), The research worker and the library, *Coll. Res. Libr.* **8**, 291–300.

CASE INSTITUTE OF TECHNOLOGY: OPERATIONS RESEARCH GROUP (1958), *An operations research study of the scientific activity of chemists*, Cleveland.

CASE INSTITUTE OF TECHNOLOGY: OPERATIONS RESEARCH GROUP (1961), *Measurement of value of recorded information*.

CASEY, R. J. (1958), *Oral communication of technical information*, Reinhold, New York; Chapman & Hall, London.

COLE, P. F. (1958), The analysis of reference question records as a guide to the information requirements of scientists, *J. Docum.* **14**, 197–207.

COLUMBIA UNIVERSITY: BUREAU OF APPLIED SOCIAL RESEARCH (1960), *Review of studies in the flow of information among scientists*, Columbia Univ. Also as PB 156941, Office of Technical Services (1960). Abstr. in *J. Docum.* **17**, 40 (1961).

CONNOLLY, A. G. (1943), Laboratory *vs.* library research, *J. Chem. Educ.* **20**, 531–3.

DAVIS, R. A., and BAILEY, C. A. (1964), *Bibliography of use studies*, Drexel Inst. Tech. Grad. Sch. Libr. Sci., Philadelphia.

DEPARTMENT OF SCIENTIFIC AND INDUSTRIAL RESEARCH (1964), *Annual report of the Advisory Council on Scientific Policy 1963–1964*, Cmnd. 2538, HMSO, London, 35–8.

EGAN, M., and HENKLE, H. H. (1957), in SHERA, J. H., KENT, A., and PERRY, J. W., *Documentation in action*, Reinhold, New York.

ESTERQUEST, R. T. (1963), in MULLER, R. H., Research approach to university library problems, *Coll. Res. Libr.* **24**, 199–203.

FISHENDEN, R. M. (1958), Methods by which research workers find information, *Proc. Int. Conf. Sci. Inf. 1958*, **1**, Nat. Acad. Sci., Washington, 163–79 (1959).

FOSKETT, D. J. (1957), Readers' needs in industrial libraries, *Libr. Ass. Rec.* **15**, 353–9.

FRANCILLON, M. (1959), Information retrieval: a view from the reference desk, *J. Docum.* **15**, 187–98.

FUSSLER, H. H. (1949), Characteristics of the research literature used by chemists and physicists in the U.S., *Libr. Q.* **19**, 19–35, 119–43.

GILMAN, H. (1947), What the scientist expects of the librarian, *Coll. Res. Libr.* **8**, 329–32.

GLASS, B. (1955), A survey of biological abstracting, *AIBS Bull.* **5**, (Jan.) 20–4 (Apr.) 18–21.

GLASS, B., and NORWOOD, S. H. (1958), How scientists actually learn of work important to them, *Proc. Int. Conf. Sci. Inf. 1958*, **1**, Nat. Acad. Sci., Washington, 195–7 (1959).

GOODWIN, H. B. (1959), Some thoughts on improved technical information services, *Spec. Libr.* **50**, 443–6.

GRAY, D. E. (1950), Physics abstracting, *Am. J. Phys.* **18**, 417–24.

HALBERT, M. H., and ACKOFF, R. L. (1958), An operations research study of the dissemination of scientific information, *Proc. Int. Conf. Sci. Inf. 1958*, **1**, Nat. Acad. Sci., Washington, 97–130 (1959). See also Case Institute of Technology: Operations Research Group (1958).

HANSON, C. W. (1963), Subject inquiries and literature searching, *Aslib Proc.* **15**, 315.

HARDIE, B. G., and VOIGT, M. J. (1950), Use of periodicals in petroleum research, *Oil Gas J.* **49** (May), 121–6.

HARRIS, W. E., and WALLACE, W. J. (1961), A bibliographic punched card in analytical inorganic chemistry designed for the individual research chemist, *J. Chem. Docum.* **1** (3), 36–43.

HAVARD-WILLIAMS, P. (1958), The student and the university library, *Libr. Ass. Rec.* **60**, 269–72.

HERNER, S. (1952), *The information-gathering habits of workers in pure and applied science. 1. A survey of a single research organization.* Also *Ind. Engng. Chem.* **46**, 228–36 (1954).

HERNER, S. (1958), The information-gathering habits of American medical scientists, *Proc. Int. Conf. Sci. Inf. 1958*, **1**, Nat. Acad. Sci., Washington, 277–85 (1959).

HERNER, S., and MEYER, R. S. (1957), *The use of Soviet medical information by American scientists.*

HERTZ, D. B., and RUBENSTEIN, A. H. (1953), *Team research*, Eastern Technical Publications, New York. Abstr. *in* TORNUDD, E. (1958).

HINES, T. C. (1961), Circulation systems: a critical review of three recent reports—Swedish, British and American—comparing and evaluating, *Libr. J.* **88**, 4240–3.

HOGG, I. H., and SMITH, J. R. (1958), Information and literature use in a research and development organization, *Proc. Int. Conf. Sci. Inf. Conf. 1958*, **1**, Nat. Acad. Sci., Washington, 131–62 (1959).

HOPP, R. H. (1956), A study of the problem of complete documentation in science and technology, *Diss. Abstr.* **16**, 1689.

HUSSEY, R. D. (1942), A "research man" looks at the library, *Calif. Libr. Ass. Bull.* **3** (June), 193–7.

HYSLOP, M. R. (1963), Case histories in information searching, *Metals Rev.* **36**, no. 6.

JAHODA, G. (1964), Information-gathering and use habits of chemists, *J. Chem. Educ.* **4**, 153–6.

JOHNSON, A. (1963), Practical applications of "feature card" systems. III, *Aslib Proc.* **15**, 186–8.

KEE, W. A. (1960), Must library surveys be classics in statistics?, *Spec. Libr.* **51**, 433–6.

KENT, A. (1962), Resolution of the literature crisis in the decade 1961–1970, *Res. Mgmt.* **5** (Jan.), 49–58.

KNAPP, P. B. (1957), Role of the library in a given college in implementing the course and non-course objectives of that college, PhD Thesis, Univ. Chicago. Also ACRL Monograph 23, *College Teaching and the College Library* (1959).

MACWATT, J. A. (1961), Improving scientific communication—reprints directly available from the publisher at a reasonable fee could supplement today's journals, *Science, NY*, **134**, 313–16.

MAIZELL, R. E. (1958), Information gathering patterns and creativity; a study of research chemists in an industrial research laboratory, Columbia Univ. (thesis) Abstr. in *Diss. Abstr.* **18**, 1802–3 (1958). Also as *Am. Docum.* **11**, 9–17 (1960).

MARTIN, M. W., and ACKOFF, R. L. (1963), The dissemination and use of recorded scientific information, *Mgmt. Sci.* **9**, 322–36.

MARTYN, J. (1964), *Report of an investigation on literature searching by research scientists*, Aslib, London.

MEIER, R. L. (1963), Information input overload; features of growth in communications-oriented institutions, *Libri* **13**, 1–44.

MENZEL, M. H. (1957), Flow of information on current developments in three scientific disciplines, *Fedn Proc. VI*, 706–11.

MENZEL, M. H. (1958), Planned and unplanned scientific communication, *Proc. Int. Conf. Sci. Inf. 1958*, **1**, Nat. Acad. Sci., Washington, 199–243 (1959).

MENZEL, M. H. (1959), Scientists and information. (Reply to review by R. Shaw of the Bureau of Applied Social Research's 1958 report "The flow of information among scientists; problems, opportunities and research questions") *Coll. Res. Libr.* **20**, 419–20.

MENZEL, M. H., et al. (1960), *Review of studies in the flow of information among scientists*, see Columbia Univ.: Bureau of Applied Social Research.

MOTE, L. J. B. (1962), Reasons for variations in the information needs of scientists, *J. Docum.* **18,** 169–75.

MOTE, L. J. B., and ANGEL, N. L. (1962), Survey of technical enquiry records at Thornton Research Centre, "Shell" Research Ltd., *J. Docum.* **18,** 6–19.

OFFENBACHER, E. (1958), Surveying scientific research; a new technique, *UNESCO Bull. Libr.* **12** (Feb.–Mar.), 32–6.

OPPENHEIM, A. N. (1962), Reading habits of students; a survey of students at LSE, *J. Docum.* **18,** 42–57.

ORR, R. H. (1961), The metabolism of new scientific information, *Am. Docum.* **12,** 15–19.

PHELPS, R. H., and HERLIN, J. P. (1960), Alternatives to the scientific periodical; a report and bibliography, *UNESCO Bull. Libr.* **14** (Mar.–Apr.), 61–75.

REES, A. M. (1963), *in* Western Reserve University, Center for Documentation and Communication Research. *Information research in action*, Western Reserve Univ., Cleveland.

RESNICK, A. (1961), Relative effectiveness of document titles and abstracts for determining relevance of documents, *Science, NY,* **134,** 1004–5.

RITCHIE, J., and BYRNE, B. R. (1961–2), The collection and assessment of technical information, including the language problem (with discussion), *J. Instn Loco. Engrs.* **51,** 141–71.

SABEL, C. S., TERRY, J. E., and MOSS, J. H. (1962), Edge punched card examination of retrieval patterns in information offices and related investigations, *J. Docum.* **18,** 111–32.

SCOTT, C. (with L. T. WILKINS) (1956), *The use of technical literature by industrial technologists,* DSIR Information Division, London.

SCOTT, C. (1958), The use of technical literature by industrial technologists, *Proc. Int. Conf. Sci. Inf. 1958,* **1,** Nat. Acad. Sci., Washington, 245–66 (1959).

SCOTT, C. (1959), Technical information in industry—how it is used, *Aslib Proc.* **11,** 318–26.

SHANK, R. (1959), Library services to research laboratories of a large university, *Am. Docum.* **10,** 221–3.

SHAW, R. R. (1940), *in* RANDALL, W. M. (Ed.), *The acquisition and cataloguing of books,* Univ. Chicago Press, Chicago, 284–309.

SHAW, R. R. (1956), *Pilot study on the use of scientific literature by scientists,* Nat. Sci. Foundn, Washington.

SHAW, R. R. (1959), Flow of scientific information. (Review—see MENZEL, M. H. (1959)), *Coll. Res. Libr.* **20,** 163–4.

SHERA, J. H., KENT, A., and PERRY, J. W. (1957), *Documentation in action,* Reinhold, New York.

SINGER, T. E. R. (Ed.) (1958), *Information and communication practice in industry,* Reinhold, New York.

SLATER, M. (1963), Types of use and user in industrial libraries—some impressions, *J. Docum.* **19,** 12–18.

SLATER, M. (1964), *Technical libraries: users and their demands. A classification of user groups and user demands in technical libraries,* Aslib, London.

SMITH, M. H. (1958), An evaluation of abstracting journals and indexes, *Proc. Int. Conf. Sci. Inf. 1958,* **1,** Nat. Acad. Sci., Washington, 321–50 (1959).

STEVENS, R. E. (1950), A summary of the literature on the use made by the research worker of the university catalog, *Univ. Ill. Libr. Sch.,* Occ. Pap. no. 13.

STEVENS, R. E. (1953), *Characteristics of the subject literature,* ACRL Monograph no. 6.

STEVENS, R. E. (1956), The study of the research use of libraries, *Libr. Q.* **26,** 41–51.

TAUBE, M. (1958), *An evaluation of "use studies" of scientific information,* AD 206987.

TAUBER, M. F. (1961), A survey of library surveys, *Libr. J.* **86,** 1351–7.

TAUBER, M. F., *et al.* (1954), *Technical services in libraries,* Columbia Univ. Press, New York.

THORNE, R. G. (1954), *A survey of the reading habits of scientific and technical staff at the Royal Aircraft Establishment,* RAE, Farnborough.

TORNUDD, E. (1953), Professional reading habits of scientists engaged in research as revealed by an analysis of 130 questionnaires, Carnegie Int. Tech., Pittsburgh (MS thesis). Abstr. *in* TORNUDD, E. (1958).

TORNUDD, E. (1958), Study on the use of scientific literature and reference services by Scandinavian scientists and engineers engaged in research and development, *Proc. Int. Conf. Sci. Inf. 1958,* **1,** Nat. Acad. Sci., Washington, 19–75 (1959).

TUCKER, P. E. (1961), The sources of books for undergraduates—a survey of Leeds University Library, *J. Docum.* **17,** 77–95.

TURNER, W. A. (1960), Information requirements of electronic research, *Aslib Proc.* **12,** 186–90.

UNIVERSITY OF MICHIGAN, INSTITUTE FOR SOCIAL RESEARCH, SURVEY RESEARCH CENTER (1954), *The attitudes and activities of physiologists: a nation-wide study,* Univ. Michigan. Abstr. *in* TORNUDD, E. (1958).

URQUHART, D. J. (1948), The distribution and use of scientific and technical information, *Roy. Soc. Sci. Inf. Conf. 1948, Rep.* 468–72.

VICKERY, B. C. (1961), The use of scientific literature, *Libr. Ass. Rec.* **63,** 263–9.

VOIGT, M. J. (1959), The researcher and his sources of scientific information, *Libri* **9,** 177–93.

VOIGT, M. J. (1961), *Scientists' approach to information,* ACRL Monograph no. 24.

VOLLANS, R. F. (1958), The research student and the public library, *Univ. Lond. Sch. Librnshp Archs,* Occ. Publn. no. 8.

WELLISCH, H. (1963), What they read and why—Israeli version, *Aslib Proc.* **15,** 323–32.

WILSON, C. W. J. (1958), Report literature used by aerodynamicists, *Aslib Proc.* **9,** 194–7.

APPENDIX I

Writers' references to previous surveys are usually polite but unenthusiastic; their work can rarely be regarded as the continuation of any previous effort. Nevertheless, the records of some of the work have been frequently mentioned by later writers and the citation index below indicates the items to which later workers most frequently referred.

AUTHOR	YEAR	JOURNAL	YEAR	VOL.	PAGE
Bernal, J. D.	48	*Roy. Soc. Inf. Conf.*			589
Bach, H.		*Spec. Libs.*	57	48	466
Bernal, J. D.		*Proc. I. Conf. Sci. Inf.*	58		77
Cole, P. F.		*J. Docum.*	58	14	197
Columbia Univ.		PB 156941	60		
Egan, M.		*in* Shera, Kent and Perry	57		137
Fishenden, R. M.		*Proc. I. Conf. Sci. Inf.*	58		163
Herner, S.		*Ind. & Engng. Chem.*	54	46	228
Hogg, J. H.		*Proc. I. Conf. Sci. Inf.*	58		131
Jahoda, G.		*J. Chem. Docum.*	64	4	153
Phelps, R. H.		*UNESCO Bull. Libr.* (no. 2)	60	14	61
Scott, C.			56		
Shaw, R. R.			56		
Slater, M.			64		
Stevens, R.		*Libr. Q.*	56	26	41
Tornudd, E.		*Proc. I. Conf. Sci. Inf.*	58		
Vickery, B. C.		*Libr. Ass. Rec.*	61	63	263
Voigt, M. J.		*Libri*	59	9	177
Bernal, J. D.	58	*Proc. I. Conf. Sci. Inf.*			77
Columbia Univ.		PB 156941	60		
Jahoda, G.		*J. Chem. Docum.*	64	4	153
Phelps, R. H.		*UNESCO Bull. Libr.* (no. 2)	60	14	61
Vickery, B. C.		*Libr. Ass. Rec.*	61	63	263
Brodman, E.	44	*Med. Libr. Ass. Bull.*		32	479
Egan, M.		*in* Shera, Kent and Perry	57		137
Fussler, H. H.		*Libr. Q.*	49	19	119
Shaw, R. R.			56		
Stevens, R.		*Libr. Q.*	56	26	41
Tornudd, E.		*Proc. I. Conf. Sci. Inf.*	58		17
Vickery, B. C.		*Libr. Ass. Rec.*	61	63	263

Author	Year	Journal	Year	Vol.	Page
Bush, G. C.	56	*Amer. Docum.*		7	87
Singer, T. E. R.			58		
Tornudd, E.		*Proc. I. Conf. Sci. Inf.*	58		19
Calder, N.	59				
Slater, M.			64		
Wellisch, H.		*Aslib Proc.*	63	15	323
Case Inst. Technol.	58				
Brownson, H. L.		*Science*	60	132	1922
Mote, L. J. B.		*J. Docum.*	62	18	6
Phelps, R. H.		*UNESCO Bull. Libr.* (no. 2)	60	14	61
Cole, P. F.	58	*J. Docum.*		14	197
Columbia Univ.		PB 156941	60		
Hanson, C. W.		*Aslib. Proc.*	63	15	313
Jahoda, G.		*J. Chem. Docum.*	64	4	153
Mote, L. J. B.		*J. Docum.*	62	18	6
Sabel, C. S.		*J. Docum.*	62	18	111
Vickery, B. C.		*Libr. Ass. Rec.*	61	63	263
Columbia Univ.	60	*Bur. Appl. Soc. Res.*			
Brownson, H. L.		*Science*	60	132	1922
Jahoda, G.		*J. Chem. Docum.*	64	4	153
Mote, L. J. B.		*J. Docum.*	62	18	6
Egan, M.	57	*in* Shera, Kent and Perry			137
Columbia Univ.		PB 156941	60		
Francillon, M.		*J. Docum.*	59	15	187
Singer, T. E. R.			58		
Tornudd, E.		*Proc. I. Conf. Sci. Inf.*	58		17
Vickery, B. C.		*Libr. Ass. Rec.*	61	63	263
Voigt, M. J.		*Libri*	59	9	177
Fishenden, R. M.	58	*Proc. I. Conf. Sci. Inf.*			163
Columbia Univ.		PB 156941	60		
Jahoda, G.		*J. Chem. Docum.*	64	4	153
Sabel, C. S.		*J. Docum.*	63	18	111
Slater, M.			64		
Vickery, B. C.		*Libr. Ass. Rec.*	61	63	263
Voigt, M. J.		*Libri*	59	9	177
Fussler, H. H.	49	*Libr. Q.*		19	119
Cole, P. F.		*J. Docum.*	58	14	197
Egan, M.		*in* Shera, Kent and Perry	57		137
Herner, S.		*Ind. & Engng. Chem.*	54	46	228
Shaw, R. R.			56		
Stevens, R.		*Libr. Q.*	56	26	41
Tornudd, E.		*Proc. I. Conf. Sci. Inf.*	58		17
Wilson, C. W. J.		*Aslib Proc.*	58	10	194
Gilman, H.	47	*Coll. Res. Libr.*		8	417
Fussler, H. H.		*Libr. Q.*	49	19	119
Stevens, R.		*Univ Ill. Lib. Sch.*	50		
Glass, B.	55	*AIBS Bull.*		5	20
Columbia Univ.		PB 156941	60		
Egan, M. C.		*in* Shera, Kent and Perry	57		137
Tornudd, E.		*Proc. I. Conf. Sci. Inf.*	58		17
Voigt, M. J.		*Libri*	59	9	177

AUTHOR	YEAR	JOURNAL	YEAR	VOL.	PAGE
Glass, B.	58	*Proc. I. Conf. Sci. Inf.*			195
Columbia Univ.		PB 156941	60		
Jahoda, G.		*J. Chem. Docum.*	64	4	153
Vickery, B. C.		*Libr. Ass. Rec.*	61	63	263
Voigt, M. J.		*Libri*	59	9	177
Gray, D. E.	50	*Amer. J. Phys.*		18	417
Columbia Univ.		PB 156941	60		
Egan, M.		*in* Shera, Kent and Perry	57		137
Herner, S.		*Ind. & Engng. Chem.*	54	46	228
Shaw, R. R.			56		
Tornudd, E.		*Proc. I. Conf. Sci. Inf.*	58		17
Halbert, M. H.	58	*Proc. I. Conf. Sci. Inf.*			97
Columbia Univ.		PB 156941	60		
Francillon, M.		*J. Docum.*	59	15	187
Vickery, B. C.		*Libr. Ass. Rec.*	61	63	263
Voigt, M. J.		*Libri*	59	9	177
Herner, S.	54	*Ind. & Engng. Chem.*		46	228
Bach, H.		*Spec. Libs.*	57	48	466
Cole, P. F.		*J. Docum.*	58	14	197
Columbia Univ.		PB 156941	60		
Egan, M.		*in* Shera, Kent and Perry	57		137
Francillon, M.		*J. Docum.*	59	15	187
Hogg, I. H.		*Proc. I. Conf. Sci. Inf.*	58		131
Scott, C.			56		
Slater, M.			64		
Smith, M. H.		*Proc. I. Conf. Sci. Inf.*	58		321
Stevens, R.		*Libr. Q.*	56	26	41
Tornudd, E.		*Proc. I. Conf. Sci. Inf.*	58		17
Vickery, B. C.		*Libr. Ass. Rec.*	61	63	263
Herner, S.	58	*Proc. I. Conf. Sci. Inf.*			277
Columbia Univ.		PB 156941	60		
Slater, M.			64		
Vickery, B. C.		*Libr. Ass. Rec.*	61	63	263
Hertz, D. B.	53				
Columbia Univ.		PB 156941	60		
Egan, M.		*in* Shera, Kent and Perry	57		137
Shaw, R. R.			56		
Tornudd, E.		*Proc. I. Conf. Sci. Inf.*	58		17
Vickery, B. C.		*Libr. Ass. Rec.*	61	63	263
Voigt, M. J.		*Libri*	59	9	177
Hogg, I. H.	58	*Proc. I. Conf. Sci. Inf.*			131
Columbia Univ.		PB 156941	60		
Francillon, M.		*J. Docum.*	59	15	187
Jahoda, G.		*J. Chem. Docum.*	64	4	153
Slater, M.			64		
Vickery, B. C.		*Libr. Ass. Rec.*	61	63	263
Voigt, M. J.		*Libri*	59	9	177
Johns Hopkins Univ.	50				
Egan, M.		*in* Shera, Kent and Perry	57		137
Shaw, R. R.			56		
Tornudd, E.		*Proc. I. Conf. Sci. Inf.*	58		17

Author	Year	Journal	Year	Vol.	Page
Maizell, R. E.	60	*Amer. Docum.*		11	9
Columbia Univ.		PB 156941	60		
Slater, M.			64		
Vickery, B. C.		*Libr. Ass. Rec.*	61	63	263
Menzel, M. H.	58	*Proc. I. Conf. Sci. Inf.*			199
Columbia Univ.		PB 156941	60		
Jahoda, G.		*J. Chem. Docum.*	64	4	153
Vickery, B. C.		*Libr. Ass. Rec.*	61	63	263
Mote, L. J. B.	62	*J. Docum.*		18	6
Hanson, C. W.		*Aslib Proc.*	63	15	315
Jahoda, G.		*J. Chem. Docum.*	64	4	153
Sabel, C. S.		*J. Docum.*	62	18	111
Scott, C.	56				
Columbia Univ.		PB 156941	60		
Mote, L. J. B.		*J. Docum.*	62	18	6
Slater, M.			64		
Wellisch, H.		*Aslib Proc.*	63	15	323
Scott, C.	58	*Proc. I. Conf. Sci. Inf.*			245
Columbia Univ.		PB 156941	60		
Francillon, M.		*J. Docum.*	59	15	187
Vickery, B. C.		*Libr. Ass. Rec.*	61	63	263
Voigt, M. J.		*Libri*	59	9	177
Shaw, R. R.	40	*in* Randall, W. M.			284
Stevens, R.		*Univ. Ill. Lib. Sch.*	50		
Tauber, M.			54		
Shaw, R. R.	56				
Bernal, J. D.		*Proc. I. Conf. Sci. Inf.*	58		77
Columbia Univ.		PB 156941	60		
Hogg, I. H.		*Proc. I. Conf. Sci. Inf.*	58		131
Jahoda, G.		*J. Chem. Docum.*	64	4	153
Scott, C.			56		
Slater, M.			64		
Smith, M. H.		*Proc. I. Conf. Sci. Inf.*	58		321
Tornudd, E.		*Proc. I. Conf. Sci. Inf.*	58		17
Vickery, B. C.		*Libr. Ass. Rec.*	61	63	263
Voigt, M. J.		*Libri*	59	9	177
Wilson, C. W.		*Aslib Proc.*	58	10	194
Slater, M.	63	*J. Docum.*		19	13
Hanson, C. W.		*Aslib Proc.*	63	15	315
Wellisch, H.		*Aslib Proc.*	63	15	323
Stevens, R.	53	ACRL Monograph			
Egan, M.		*in* Shera, Kent and Perry	57		137
Herner, S.		*Ind. & Engng. Chem.*	54	46	228
Singer, T. E. R.			58		
Stevens, R.		*Libr. Q.*	56	26	41
Tornudd, E.		*Proc. I. Conf. Sci. Inf.*	58		17
Vickery, B. C.		*Libr. Ass. Rec.*	61	63	263
Wilson, C. W.		*Aslib Proc.*	58	10	194
Stevens, R.	56	*Libr. Q.*		26	41
Shaw, R. R.			56		
Wilson, C. W.		*Aslib Proc.*	58	10	194

Author	Year	Journal	Year	Vol.	Page
Thorne, R. G.	54	*RAE Farnborough Lib. Mem.*			
Hogg, I. H.		*Proc. I. Conf. Sci. Inf.*	58		131
Tornudd, E.		*Proc. I. Conf. Sci. Inf.*	58		17
Vickery, B. C.		*Libr. Ass. Rec.*	61	63	263
Tornudd, E.	53				
Columbia Univ.		PB 156941	60		
Herner, S.		*Ind. & Engng. Chem.*	54	46	228
Stevens, R.		*Libr. Q.*	56	26	41
Tornudd, E.		*Proc. I. Conf. Sci. Inf.*	58		17
Tornudd, E.	58	*Proc. I. Conf. Sci. Inf.*			17
Francillon, M.		*J. Docum.*	59	15	187
Jahoda, G.		*J. Chem. Docum.*	64	4	153
Phelps, R. H.		*UNESCO Bull. Libr.* (no. 2)	16	14	61
Vickery, B. C.		*Libr. Ass. Rec.*	61	63	263
Voigt, M.		*Libri*	59	9	177
Urquhart, D. J.	48	*Roy. Soc. Inf. Conf.*			408
Bach, H.		*Spec. Libr.*	57	48	466
Cole, P. F.		*J. Docum.*	58	14	197
Columbia Univ.		PB 156941	60		
Egan, M.		*in* Shera, Kent and Perry	57		137
Francillon, M.		*J. Docum.*	59	15	187
Herner, S.		*Ind. & Engng. Chem.*	54	46	228
Shaw, R. R.			56		
Stevens, R.		*Libr. Q.*	56	26	41
Tornudd, E.		*Proc. I. Conf. Sci. Inf.*	58		17
Vickery, B. C.		*Libr. Ass. Rec.*	61	63	263
Voigt, M. J.		*Libri*	59	9	177
Voigt, M. J.	59	*Libri*		9	177
Columbia Univ.		PB 156941	60		
Slater, M.			64		

7. DOCUMENTATION AND INFORMATION SCIENCE ABSTRACTS: THE *REFERATIVNYI ZHURNAL:* *NAUCHNAYA I TEKHNICHESKAYA INFORMATSIYA*

HERBERT SCHUR

Postgraduate School of Librarianship, University of Sheffield

THE appearance of a major abstracting periodical covering the field of scientific and technical information is of interest especially at a time of increasing activity in and support of research and development in this field. The *Referativnyi zhurnal: nauchnaya i tekhnicheskaya informatsiya*, or *R.Zh.* in brief, began publication in 1963 at a time when no major abstracting or indexing periodical devoted exclusively, or even mainly, to covering this field was being published in the USSR, the USA, or the UK.

There are three major factors which need to be taken into account when evaluating an abstracting periodical: (1) the coverage, (2) its usefulness for current awareness, and (3) usefulness for retrospective searches.

The *R.Zh.* draws on the results of scanning of some 20,000 periodicals and serials,* as well as books, patents and other publications, but because at the time this study was carried out (July 1965) the *R.Zh.* had been in existence for only $2\frac{1}{2}$ years, no test was carried out by the bibliography method of its comprehensiveness. The coverage of a sample of abstracts was analysed by (1) subject, (2) country of origin, (3) language, and (4) type of publication, and, in addition, in order to discover the ease of access in English to items noted in the *R.Zh.*, the items in the sample were also searched for in three widely used English language abstracting and indexing publications in library science and documentation.

The *Referativnyi zhurnal: nauchnaya i tekhnicheskaya informatsiya* is published bi-monthly (i.e. six issues p.a.) in an edition of 3180 copies (March 1965), each issue containing some 800 abstracts and references arranged under ten group headings in thirty-one sections (see Appendix I). The individual abstracts and references, which are classified by UDC, include the number of the item with a type of publication suffix (Appendix II), the title in Russian (or edited translation into Russian), the authors' surnames and other names or

* A. I. Mikhailov, A. I. Chernyi, and R. S. Gilyarevskii, *Osnovy nauchnoi informatsii,* Moscow, Nauka, 1965, p. 507.

initials in the original Cyrillic or Latin characters, followed by the title in the original language (unless it is Russian), the bibliographical reference in standard form and finally a note, in brackets, stating the language of the paper or publication and of any lengthy summaries in other languages. Abstracts of and references to Japanese literature published originally in Japanese include the title in English although the authors' names are given in Cyrillic only. No language of the original is stated for patents, it being assumed that this must be in the official language of the country. The abstracts are signed or initialed.

INDEXES

There is an annual subject index and author index, published, on time, as part of issue no. 6. The subject index is of a decimally numbered alphabetico-classed type with 250 main headings, not all of which had been used so far, and up to about twenty-five sub-headings each. For instance, under the main heading "Formalized descriptive languages" we find the sub-headings and "see" references "Associative indexing, see Co-ordinate indexing", "Descriptors, see Co-ordinate indexing", "Information retrieval language of Perry, Kent, Berry, see Formalized language of Perry, Kent, Berry", "Key words, see Co-ordinate indexing", "Semantic code, see Formalized language of Perry, Kent, Berry". Edited-title entries are arranged in item number order under these headings and sub-headings. There are numerous "see" and "see also" references from the headings to other headings, and sub-headings to other sub-headings. For instance, starting with "Reprography", we are referred to "Document copying" and here we find not only numerous entries but also a "see also" reference to Diazo, magnetic, silver-halide, thermal, microform, and electrical (electrostatic, electronic, electrolytic) methods.

The author index is in two parts, Cyrillic and Latin, and it includes apart from the author's name the item number reference and the subject heading and sub-heading number reference; there is one entry for each author of a paper, book or patent and also for each reviewer of a book.

SUBJECT COVERAGE

The editorial policy of a periodical largely reflects the views of the editor and the editorial board, and it is therefore of interest to note the qualifications of the twelve members of the editorial board of this section of the *R.Zh.* These include, apart from Professor A. I. Mikhailov, the Chief Editor, two D. Tech. Sci., five Cand. Tech. Sci., two Cand. Phys.-Math. Sci., one Cand. Chem. Sci., and one Cand. Geog. Sci. who, incidentally, is the Deputy Chief Editor. Of the twelve members of the board three are women. At least two of the members are doing active research work in the field of translating and linguistics, others work on mechanization, IR system theory, classification, and other scientific and technical information problems.

The actual editorial work is carried out by nine editors, three of whom are members of the editorial board. Abstracting is carried out by the panel of external abstractors of the *R.Zh.* although a few of the abstracts are contributed by the editors themselves. The subject coverage reflects not only the needs of research and development but also of the "field". The coverage therefore includes such items as pattern recognition both in the experimental psychology and the computer input aspects, storing techniques, linguistic studies (potentially relevant to machine translation, automatic abstracting, etc.) and other subjects of actual or potential value, as well as reports on scientific libraries and information units, cataloguing, and professional education, to take a few topics at random.

An analysis of a 20% sample of the January 1965 issue gave the results shown in Table 1.

TABLE 1

Group	Subject group	Proportion of sample (%)
A	General topics and papers	4·5
B	Information analysis	9·5
C	Translating of scientific–technical texts	7·5
D	Information retrieval	36
E	Documentary sources of information	5
F	Document copying methods and equipment	7
G	Printing in information practice	5
H	Equipment (typewriters, tape-recorders, punched-card equipment, etc.)	5·5
I	Use of information material	1
J	Organization of information work	19

A further breakdown of subject groups B, D and J gave the results shown in Table 2.

There are two figures in this list which need explaining. Firstly, there is the high figure of 16·5% for "Technical means of information retrieval". Analysis of this section shows that it includes a high proportion of potential or actual computer-input devices, such as punched-card or tape readers, magnetic, electroluminescent, and other mark-sensing devices, reports on devices for recognition of connected handwritten words, speech analysis and recognition, computer store systems, read-out devices, data processing, etc.

N

TABLE 2

Group	Section	Title	Proportion of sample (%)
B	2	Classification and systematization	6
	3	Processing of primary documentary information	3
D	6	General and theoretical problems	4
	7	Information languages	3
	8	Document information-retrieval systems	7
	9	Fact-retrieval systems	1
	10	Technical means for information retrieval	16·5
	11	Programmed teaching	4·5
J	28	International information organizations	2·5
	29	Organization of information work in the USSR	1
	30	Organization of information work abroad	13
	31	Professional education	2·5

The other figure is the low one (1%) for section 29 "Organization of information work in the USSR". This represents 11 abstracts in the January 1965 issue, compared with 35 for the corresponding topic referring to Poland, Czechoslovakia, Bulgaria, Hungary and East Germany, 29 for the rest of Europe, 11 for Asia and Africa, 23 for America and 12 more general papers. A check on a much larger sample (the complete 1964 volume) showed, however, that the abstracts on the organization of information work in the "countries of the socialist camp" were roughly equal in number to those referring to all other countries.

COUNTRY OF ORIGIN OF ITEMS NOTED

It is of interest (particularly for an acquisitions section) to note the origin of the literature noted. In the present sample the figures were as shown in Table 3.

TABLE 3

Country	Proportion of sample (%)
USA	28
United Kingdom	12
Germany (East and West)	11
France	10
USSR	9
Czechoslovakia	6
International organizations	11
Other (each less than 2·5%)	13

These figures show little change from the distributions found by analysing the issues 1963 **1** (4) and (5); above-average increases in publishing during this period were noted for "International organizations", Czechoslovakia, France, and "Other countries".

LANGUAGE OF ITEMS NOTED

An analysis of the sample gave the following result:

Language	Proportion of sample (%)
English	48
German	12
French	11
Russian	10
Czech and Slovak	6
Other (each less than 2·5%)	13

These figures show that whilst, on the one hand, English is still by far the most important language in this field, on the other hand, just over one-half of literature considered to be worth noting is in languages other than English. A comparison with the 1963 sample shows that relatively more literature is now being published in "Other languages", French and Czech.

TYPE OF PUBLICATION

The definition of "published literature" varies and it is therefore of interest to see what has and has not been included. Of the 160 items in the sample 24 were of conference proceedings, 7 of patents, 4 of books and the remainder of periodical articles. There were no "unpublished" reports and none were found in recent issues of the journal. The inclusion of patents is noteworthy as this source of information is not easily covered through other publications. Of the 7 patent abstracts in the sample there were 3 USA, 2 French, 1 Czechoslovak, and 1 West German.

TIME LAG

Of the items in the sample over 54% had been published in the preceding year, 94% within 2 years, and 99% within 3 years. The date of publication of 1% of the items could not be determined.

DUPLICATION BY *Literature Notes (American Documentation)*,
Library Science Abstracts, AND *Library Literature*

Of the items in the sample nearly 80% had not been noted in these
English language publications. Analysis by *subject* groups showed that only in
subject group B (Information Analysis) had more than one-half of the *R.Zh*
items also been noted in these publications. The most significant lack of
duplication was of items referring to mechanization and to translating, of
95% and 85%, respectively. Analysis by *country of origin* showed that whilst
60% of the *R.Zh.* items referring to USA publications had not been noted,
this figure rose to 65% for publications of international organizations, 74%
for UK publications, 88% for those from France, 93% USSR, and 96%
other countries. The pattern for *language* was similar: English 64%, French
82%, Russian 94%, other languages 96%.

CONCLUSIONS

(1) The coverage by the *R.Zh.* of literature in the scientific and technical
information field is duplicated to only a small extent by the combined three
English language publications investigated.

(2) The omission by the *R.Zh.* of abstracts of report-type literature may be
serious, particularly for work carried out in the USA. However, this literature
is being comprehensively covered by the Clearinghouse for Scientific and
Technical Information publications.

(3) The absence of author and subject indexes in the individual issues of
the *R.Zh.* is a fault, especially in an abstracting journal concerned with
information, and this is particularly serious for retrospective searches for
material less than 2 years old.

(4) The time-lag between receipt of publication for abstracting and the
appearance of the abstract is such (more than 2 months, on average) that
the *R.Zh.* is not suitable for most current awareness needs.

(5) A study should be carried out on the comprehensiveness of coverage by
the *R.Zh.* of significant publications, by comparison with subject bibliographic
and literature citations in survey papers published in various countries.

Appendix I

Contents

Group	Section	Title
A	1	General
B		Information analysis
	2	Classification and systematization (General and theoretical problems: hierarchical classification systems; non-hierarchical classification systems; indexes and catalogues)
	3	Processing of primary documentary information (cataloguing, abstracting, etc.)
C		Translating of scientific–technical texts
	4	Non-machine translating
	5	Machine translating
D		Information retrieval
	6	General and theoretical problems
	7	Information languages
	8	Document information-retrieval systems
	9	Fact-retrieval systems
	10	Technical means for information retrieval
	11	Programmed teaching
E		Documentary sources of information
	12	General and theoretical problems
	13	Primary scientific–technical documents
	14	Secondary scientific–technical documents
F		Document copying methods and equipment
	15	General and theoretical problems
	16	Diazography
	17	Reflex copying
	18	Reduced-size photocopying (microfilm, microfiche, etc.)
	19	Thermography
	20	Electrography
	21	Other methods and equipment
G		Printing in information practice
	22	General and theoretical problems (incl. computerized type-setting)
	23	Preparation of documents for printing
	24	Preparation of printing masters (incl. filmsetting)
	25	Printing equipment (incl. duplicators)
H	26	General technical means for information work (incl. typewriters, punched-card equipment, dictation machines, furniture, etc.)
I	27	Use of information material (incl. films)

Group	Section	Title
J		Organization of information work
	28	International information organizations
	29	Organization of information work in the USSR
	30	Organization of information work abroad (Europe Asia and Africa; America and other)
	31	Professional education (incl. special courses, curricula etc.)

Appendix II

Item Number Suffix Letters

Letter	Type of publication
D	Dissertation, thesis
K	Book
P	Patent
R	Review

INDEX

Abstracting services 48, 53, 145, 155–8, 163, 164, 165, 166, 167, 169
  criteria for testing 181
  Referativnyi Zhurnal ix, 181–8
Abstracts, *see* Abstracting services
Academic libraries and trade literature 42
Ackoff, R. L. 151, 153, 154, 158
Agard Evans, B. 30
Allegheny Ludlum Steel Corp. 48
Allen, Edgar, & Co. Ltd. 17, 38
Aluminium Development Association 49
Aluminium—facts and figures 31
Aluminium Federation 39
American Documentation (Literature Notes), compared with *Referativnyi Zhurnal* 186
American Magnesium Corp. 48, 49
American Steel & Wire Co. 32, 49
Anatomy of prison 77
Anthony, L. J. 35
Applied Science Corporation, Princeton 43, 46, 50
Architects' File 41, 46
ASLIB vii, 16, 36
Association of Special Libraries and Information Bureaux, *see* ASLIB
Audio-visual materials 103
Avery, A. J. 5, 27
Avery, W. and T., Ltd. 49

Barber, A. S. ix, x
Bay Area Air Pollution Control District 50
B.B.C. 15, 20, 22
Bebbington, J. vii, 25
Bedford College Library 89
Behan, Brendan 74
Bendix Aviation Corp. 32, 49
Bernal, J. D. 146, 148, 149, 150, 152, 153, 154, 159, 175
Bibliographies of trade literature 47–48
Billingsley, S. V. 31, 36, 43
Birmingham Engineering and Building Centre 39–40, 41
Birmingham Public Libraries 4, 5
  trade literature collection 41
Birmingham University Library 111
  book stock 117

Birmingham University Library, Borrowing Survey
  foreign language borrowing 122, 130–1, 139, 142
  non-borrowing 120, 129
  postgraduate research borrowing compared with Sheffield and Leeds 129
  range of borrowing 125, 127, 128, 142
  scope 115–16
  similarities to Leeds and Sheffield 142
  teaching staff total borrowing compared with Sheffield and Leeds 120
  undergraduate borrowing 135, 136
  undergraduate borrowing compared with Sheffield and Leeds 135–6, 138
Blaw–Knox Co. 50
Board of Trade Statistics . . . Library 33, 40
Bodleian Library 87, 95
  undergraduate reading room 87, 88, 89, 110
Bodley, Sir Thomas 88
Boeing Airplane Co. 31
Book stock, undergraduate libraries 100
Books in Hand 25
Borrowing from University libraries 115–43
Borrowing surveys 115–43
  limitations 142–3
Borstal Boy 74
British Aluminium Co., Ltd. 31, 49
British Communications and Electronics 47
British Council 25
British Metal Sinterings Association 49
British Museum Library 43
British Nylon Spinners 37–38
British Scientific Instrument Research Association, *see* B.S.I.R.A.
Brodman, E. 175
Brotherton Library, *see* Leeds University Library
Brown–Firth Research Laboratories 37
"Browsing" 102, 142
B.S. 1311, 1955 (trade literature) 34, 53
B.S.I.R.A. 38, 44, 47
Builders' File 41, 46
Bureau of Applied Social Research, *see* Columbia University, Bureau of Applied Social Research

Burke, Edmund 22, 23
Bush, G. C. 150, 160, 163, 175

Caistor, H. C. 27
Calder, N. 176
California, University of, Los Angeles, *see* U.C.L.A.
Cambridge A.C. instruments for high frequencies 32
Cambridge Instrument Company 32
Campbell, D. J. 36
Capitation grant, Prison libraries, *see* Prison libraries, capitation grant
Carlson, W. H. 162
Carnegie Library, Pittsburgh 43, 50
Carnegie United Kingdom Trust 56
Case Institute of Technology 176
Case study method 147, 149
Cashmore, H. M. 5, 27
Catalogues, scientists' use of 145, 159, 160, 163
Catalogues, undergraduate use of 94
Cement and Concrete Association 39
Censorship in prison libraries 61, 66, 69, 75
Chandler, G. vii
Chemical Abstracts 163, 169
Chicago Historical Society Library 49
Chicago University Library, undergraduate collection 108
Chicago, University of, undergraduate library 85
C.I.B.A. 41
Citation index of surveys of scientists' use of libraries 175
Classification of trade literature 34, 39, 41, 44, 45–46, 50–52
Clearinghouse for Scientific and Technical Information 186
Cole, P. F. 176
Collison, R. L. 35
Columbia University, Bureau of Applied Social Research 148, 149, 150, 176
Columbia University, Egleston Library 43, 50
Columbia University Undergraduate Library 102
Commercial and Technical Libraries 23–24
Commercial and Technical Libraries vii, 8, 11, 12, 16, 17, 24, 41
Control 47
Convair 50
Copeland, T. W. 22
Copyright Committee 23
Corbett, E. V. 82
Cotgreave Indicator 25
Cranshaw, J. 12

Crumpton, R. H. 82
Czechoslovakia, trade literature 29, 44

Departmental libraries, *see* University libraries, Departmental libraries
Design Centre, London 40, 44
Design index 40
Designing with magnesium 48
Development association and trade literature 38–39
D.H.H.: *Prisoners need books* 74
"Diary" method 147, 148
Dix, William 108
Documentation, abstracting services for 181–8
Documentation, literature of, analysis by language 185
D.S.I.R. 153, 155, 158
Duke University Library, undergraduate collection 108
Dundee Public Library 24
Durham County Library 57
Durham Prison 57

East Suffolk County Library 56
Edgar Allen & Co., Ltd. 17, 38
Egan, M. 176
Elliott, B. A. 82
Ellis, Sir William 20
Engineer 53
Engineering 53
Engineering and Building Centre, Birmingham 39–40, 41
English Prison and Borstal System 57, 73, 75, 76
Evans, B. Agard 30

Fairbank Collection 22
Ferodo Ltd. 32, 49
Field, X. 61, 62
Filing, trade literature, *see* Trade literature, filing
Film, *Books in Hand* 25
Finance, prison libraries, *see* Prison libraries, finance
Firth–Brown Ltd. 49
Fishenden, R. M. 148, 150, 152, 154, 155, 156, 157, 159, 160, 176
Fitzwilliam Collection 22
Fondren Library, Rice Institute, Texas 87
Food Machinery & Chemical Corp. 50
Foreign language materials, borrowing of, *see* Sheffield University Library Borrowing Survey: foreign language borrowing, *and* similar entries for Leeds and Birmingham

Foreign language reading, scientists' 153
Foreign sources of trade literature, *see* Trade literature, foreign
Fox, Sir L. 57, 73, 75, 76
Francillon, M. 163, 164
Fry, Elizabeth 56
Fussler, H. H. 156, 176

Gallenkampf 42
Galliher, H. P. 150, 160
G.E.C. 35
Gilman, H. 176
Gladstone Committee on Prisons 56, 77
Glasgow, Mitchell Library 24
Glasgow University, undergraduate reading room 87, 89, 110
Glass, B. 148, 150, 152, 155, 157, 176, 177
Gordon, R. J. 5, 6, 7, 8, 9, 10, 11, 12, 13, 25, 27
Government libraries and trade literature 40–41
Graves, J. G. 14
Gray, D. E. 158, 177
Gregory, Sir Henry 23
Grindle, Harry 5

Halbert, M. H. 153, 177
Hammersmith Public Libraries 70, 71, 72, 82
Hand, T. W. 8
Hanson, C. W. 36
Harvard College Records 110
Harvard, Lamont Library, *see* Lamont Library
Harvard, Widener Library, *see* Widener Library
Henry Wiggin & Co. Ltd. 49
Herner, S. 145, 146, 148, 150, 152, 153, 155, 156, 159, 160, 161, 163, 164, 169, 177
Hertz, D. B. 177
History of the City Libraries 24
Hogg, I. H. 148, 150, 154, 156, 157, 159, 161, 162, 177
Hollesley Bay Borstal Institution 56
Holloway Prison Library 55, 57, 58–62, 74, 75, 76, 82
    accommodation 59
    book stock 59–60
    branch of Islington Public Libraries 59
    care of books 60
    charging system 60
    hours of opening 58
    issues 59, 60
    library officer 59, 60
    routines 60
Holloway Prison, population 58, 72, 73

Houston, University of, M. D. Anderson Library 43, 50
Humphreys, K. W. 115, 122, 139
Hungary, trade literature 44

I.C.I. 42
Illinois University Library, undergraduate collection 108
Illinois, University of, undergraduate library 85
Illiterates and prison libraries 61, 65, 66, 74
Indexes, personal 145, 159, 166, 167
Indexing, trade literature, *see* Trade literature, indexing
Indiana University, undergraduate library 85
Indicator, Cotgreave 25
Indanthren (Frankfurt) 41
Industrial libraries and trade literature 36–40
Information-gathering habits, scientists, *see* Scientists' use of libraries.
Information in the building industry, Conference 30
Information Science, abstracting services for 181–8
Information Science, literature of, analysis by language 185
Instrument Review 53
Interstate Electronics Corp. 50
Interview Method 147, 148, 157
Iowa State College Engineering Library 45, 51–52
Islington Public Libraries 58, 59, 60, 62, 63, 66, 67, 76, 78, 79, 80, 82

James, Thomas 87
Johns Hopkins University 177
Johns Hopkins University Library 89
Johnson, A. 168
Jolley, L. 94

Keele University Library 111
Kingsmill, Joseph 76
Klare, H. J. 77

Lamb, J. P. vii, 1–28
    and Fitzwilliam Collection 22
    and graduates in public librarianship 2, 21
    and Library Association 19
    and library classification 3–4
    and library instruction for children 22
    and open access 3, 6, 7
    and publicity 11, 15

Lamb, J. P. (*cont.*)
  and R. J. Gordon   5
  and Sheffield Information Committee   19
  and Sheffield press   11, 15
  and Sheffield Repertory Company   25, 26
  and SINTO   16, 17
  and Wentworth Woodhouse muniments
    22
  applies for post of Chief Librarian, Liverpool   17
  appointed Chief Librarian at Sheffield   13
  appointed Deputy Librarian   7
  at Sheffield   5–6, 7, 8–28
  awarded Fellowship of Library Association   18
  B.B.C. "Eyewitness" talk   22
  B.B.C. Liaison Officer, *1941*   20
  Birmingham Public Libraries   4, 5, 6
  book selection policy   13–14, 17
  boyhood   1
  children's libraries policy   2, 12, 19
  Commercial and Technical Libraries   23–24
  deputy at Sheffield   7
  designated City Librarian of Sheffield   18
  education   1, 2
  friend Tom   3
  History of the City Libraries   24
  interest in politics and current affairs   3
  interest in theatre   25, 26
  international reputation   26
  invited to A.L.A. Montreal Conference   18
  M.A. of Sheffield University   21
  musical tastes   4, 26
  on Copyright Committee   23
  opens Newcastle-upon-Tyne Commercial
    and Technical Library   17
  reading tastes   2, 3
  retirement   24, 25, 26
  Rochdale Public Libraries   5–7
  rotarian   26
  St. Helen's Public Libraries   2–3, 4, 5, 25
  service in World War I   6
  studies for Library Association examinations   3, 4, 5, 6, 18–19
  U.S.A. visit criticized   15
  visit to U.S.A.   15, 26
  World War II library activities   19
  writes for boys' magazines   5
  writings   23–24, 27
  see also Sheffield Public Libraries
Lamont Library   86, 89, 95, 97, 98, 99, 101,
  102, 110, 112
  building   99
  effect on undergraduate reading   104
  simplified catalogues   94, 105
  simplified classification   99
Lead Abstracts   39, 48

Lead Development Association   39, 45
Leeds Public Libraries   8, 9, 13
Leeds University, Brotherton Library, *see*
  Leeds University Library
Leeds University Library Book Stock   117
Leeds University Library, Borrowing Survey
  foreign language borrowing   122–3,
    130–1, 142
  non-borrowing   120, 129
  postgraduate research borrowing compared with Sheffield and Birmingham   129
  range of borrowing   125, 127, 128, 142
  scope   115–16
  similarities to Sheffield and Birmingham   142
  teaching staff total borrowing compared with Sheffield and Birmingham   120
  undergraduate borrowing   135, 136
  undergraduate borrowing compared with Sheffield and Birmingham   135–6, 138
Leeds University Undergraduate Library   viii, 111–12
Libraries, scientists' use of, *see* Scientists' use of libraries
Libraries, use of, *see* Surveys of library use;
  see also Scientists' use of libraries
Library Association   1, 19, 57, 81
Library Literature, compared with *Referativnyi Zhurnal*   186
Library of Congress   49
Library of Congress, trade literature collection   43
Library Science Abstracts, compared with *Referativnyi Zhurnal*   186
Library services, standardization of   170
Lines, Miss F. W.   82
Literature Notes (American Documentation), compared with *Referativnyi Zhurnal*   186
Liverpool University Library   85, 111
Liverpool University, undergraduate reading room   87, 111
Loans, University Library, Surveys of   115–43
London, prison libraries   55–83
London University, Bedford College Library   89
Los Angeles, University of California, *see* U.C.L.A.

Machines Françaises   53
Magnetic properties of the nickel–iron alloys   48
Maizell, R. D.   148, 151, 160, 161, 162, 178
Manchester Public Libraries   16
Manchester Public Libraries, *Report, 1962–3*   77, 78

Manchester Public Libraries, trade literature collection 41–42
Manchester University Library 111
Manual of spring engineering 32
Martin, M. W. 151, 153, 154, 158
Martyn, J. 151, 152, 153, 157, 158, 159, 160, 161, 162, 163, 164, 165
Massachusetts Institute of Technology, *see* M.I.T.
Materials Data Ltd. 46–47
Melrose, E. A. vii, x
Menzel, M. H. 151, 178
Merck, Sharp and Co., Inc. 50
Metallurgia 35, 53
Metcalf, K. 97, 98, 105, 110
Michigan University Institute for Social Research 151, 155, 156
Michigan, University of, undergraduate library 87, 89, 96, 100, 102, 104, 112
Michigan, University of, undergraduate library, effect on undergraduate reading 104
Midwest Interlibrary Center 43
Mikhailov, A. I. 182–3
Ministry of Public Building and Works Library 40, 45, 52
Minnesota University Library 99
Mitchell Library, Glasgow 24
M.I.T. Science Library 160
Mond Nickel Co. Ltd. 48, 49
Morse, P. M. 150, 160
Moscow University Library 43
Moss, M. W. viii, x
Mote, L. J. B. 164, 178
Motor Control and Power Distribution Centres 35

National Central Library 15
National Lending Library for Science and Technology 32, 123
National libraries and trade literature 29
National Reference Library of Science and Invention 40
New Mexico University Library 99
New Products Centre 46
New Products International 46–47
Newcastle-upon-Tyne, Commercial and Technical Library 17
Northwestern University Library 95
Norwood, S. H. 148, 150, 152, 155, 157
Nottingham University Science Library 42
Nuclear Science Abstracts 156
Nuffield Pilot Survey, *see* Leeds University Library, Borrowing Survey

O.E.C.D. 33
Oerlikon (Zurich) 41

Open access 3, 6, 7, 10, 11, 74
Organization for the Exchange of Technical Publications in Sheffield and District 16; *see also* SINTO
Osborn, S. 16
Osborn, T. E. 9
Oxford University Library, *see* Bodleian Library

Page, B. S. viii, 115
Parker, G. C. J. 82
Parkhurst Prison 61
Patent abstracts, in *Referativnyi Zhurnal* 185
Patent Office Library 40
"Peek-a-Boo" techniques 46, 50
Pentonville Prison 55, 57, 72
Pentonville Prison Library 62–67, 74, 75, 76, 81, 82
  accommodation 62, 72
  book stock 62, 63, 65, 66
  branch of Islington Public Libraries 62
  care of books 63
  charging system 64
  hours of opening 64
  issues 63
  library officer 63–64
  routines 64
Pentonville Prison, population 58, 73
P.E.R.A. 31, 35, 38, 45, 52
Perrine, C. J. 79, 80
Personal indexes, *see* Indexes, personal
Pickup, C 38
Playhouse Theatre, Sheffield 25, 26
Prague, Central Technical Library 33, 44
Princeton, Applied Science Corporation 43, 46, 50
Princeton University 107
Prison Act, 1877 56
Prison Commissioners 57, 67
Prison Department 81
Prison libraries viii, 55–83
  capitation grant 56, 57, 67, 79, 81, 82
  care of books 60, 63, 68, 73
  censorship 61, 66, 69, 75
  finance 55, 56, 57, 67, 72, 76, 79, 81, 82
  high percentage of borrowers 72
  illiterates 61, 65, 66, 74
  issues 72
  Readers' Advice Service 75–76
  staff 55, 58, 60, 63–64, 67, 68, 70, 71, 75, 76, 81
Prison reform 56
Prisoners
  educational courses 61, 66, 69, 71, 77
  reading tastes 60, 61–62, 63, 65, 66, 68, 69, 71, 75, 78, 79

Prisons
  Gladstone Committee   56, 77
  history   56
Prisons and Borstals   57, 77
Production Engineering Research Association, *see* P.E.R.A.
Public libraries
  and trade literature   41–42
  service to prisons   55–83
Public Service   78

Questionnaire method   147–8, 157

Radcliffe Camera, *see* Bodleian Library, Undergraduate Reading Room
R & D: Research and Development for Industry 53
Readers' Advice Service, prison libraries, *see* Prison libraries, Readers' Advice Service
Reading habits of scientists, *see* Scientists, reading habits of
Reading tastes, prisoners', *see* Prisoners, reading tastes
Reading University Library   111
Rees, A. M.   163
Referativnyi Zhurnal   ix, 181–8
  compared with *Library Science Abstracts*, *Literature Notes* (*American Documentation*) and *Library Literature*   186
  editorial board   182–3
  geographical coverage   184–5
  indexes   182, 186
  language coverage   185
  subject coverage   181, 182–4, 186, 187–8
  time lag of abstracts   185, 186
  weaknesses   186
Reference Catalogue of Current Literature   24
Reference service in university libraries, *see* University libraries, reference service
Regional prisons   58
Research associations and trade literature 38
Research collections, university libraries, *see* University libraries, research collections
"Reserve" book collections   91, 95, 99
Review articles   145, 154, 166
Rice Institute, Texas, Fondren Library   87
Rice Institute, Texas, Library   108
Robbins Report   112
Roberts, E. W.   ix, x
Rochdale Public Libraries   5–7
Rodgers, Miss C. M.   118

Rowlinson, Mrs. P. A.   viii, x
Rust Engineering Co.   50

St. Helen's Public Libraries   2–3, 4, 5, 25
Schur, H.   ix
Schweizer Archiv für angewandte Wissenschaft und Technik   53
Science and information (SIRA Symposium)   38
Scientists, reading habits of   145–79
Scientists' use of libraries   ix, 145–79
  academic scientists   158, 161, 162, 165, 169
  atomic physicists   156
  biologists   163, 164
  botanists   156
  chemists   156, 157, 162, 163, 164, 169, 170
  citation index of surveys   175–9
  electrical engineers   156
  engineers   165
  government scientists   158, 161, 162, 165
  industrial scientists   157, 158, 161, 162, 164, 165
  methods   152, 153
  physicists   158, 162, 163, 164
  see also Surveys of library use; Catalogues, scientists' use of
Scott, C.   151, 154, 156, 157, 158, 162, 168, 178
SfB system   34, 37, 39, 45, 50–51
Shaw, R. R.   149, 151, 152, 153, 154, 156, 157, 159, 160, 161, 162, 163, 178
Sheffield, England   24
Sheffield Central Day Commercial College 22
Sheffield Chamber of Commerce   12
Sheffield Civic Information Service   20
Sheffield Daily Telegraph   24
Sheffield Independent   15
Sheffield Information Committee   19
Sheffield Interchange Organization, *see* SINTO
Sheffield Public Libraries   vii, 1, 6, 7, 8–27
  adult education activities   15
  archivist appointed   22
  Attercliffe branch   9, 12, 20
  book fund   14
  branches reorganized   12
  Burngreave branch   12
  centenary   24–25
  Central Cataloguing Department   10
  Central Lending Library   11, 12, 14
  Central Library building   14, 15, 16, 18
  Children's library services   12, 19, 20, 21, 22
  Civic Information Service   20, 24

Sheffield Public Libraries (*cont.*)
closing of delivery stations by Gordon 10
Commercial and Technical Library 8, 11, 12, 16, 17, 41
co-operation with B.B.C. 15
co-operation with university 15
co-operation with W.E.A. 15
Crosspool Library Centre 19
cuts in grant, 1932 18
deficiencies in 1920 8, 9
depression years 18
Ecclesall branch 20
Fairbank Collection 22
Film, *Books in hand* 25
Fitzwilliam Collection 22
Highfield Branch 12
Hillsborough Branch 14, 15
History of the city libraries 24
hospital service 15
information service 19
issues, *1920, 1921–2, 1925–6* 11
library helpers scheme 21
Local History Department 22, 27
Manor branch 20–21, 22
manuscripts collection 9
organization for the Exchange of Technical Publications in Sheffield and District 16
Park branch 14
Patents Collection 17
post World-War II developments 20–21
recommended improvements by T. W. Hand 9
Reference Library 12, 27
reforms under Gordon and Lamb 10–12
Repository for Atomic Energy Reports 17–18
Science and Commerce Library, *see* Sheffield Public Libraries, Commercial and Technical Library
SINTO 16, 17
Southey branch 20
Tinsley branch 14, 20
trade literature collection 41
Upperthorpe branch 12
visit from A.L.A. President 16
Walkley branch 12, 15
Wentworth Woodhouse Muniments 22
Woodseats branch 24
World War II 19, 20
see also Lamb, J. P.
Sheffield Repertory Company 25, 26
Sheffield University 15, 21
Sheffield University Library 85
Applied Science Library 42, 116, 123, 124, 125, 131, 132, 139, 142
book stock, by subjects 117

Sheffield University Library (*cont.*)
Chemistry Departmental Library 116, 123, 124, 132–3, 139–40
Geology Departmental Library 116, 121, 123, 132, 139
Law Departmental Library 116, 124, 133, 140
loans 115–43
Music Departmental Library 117, 124, 140
Sheffield University Library, Borrowing Survey viii–ix, 115–43
Architecture Department 138, 141
Arts Faculty 118, 120, 121, 122, 123, 124, 125, 129, 130, 131, 133, 134, 135, 136, 137, 138, 139, 140, 142
Bacteriology Department 121
Botany Department 121, 127, 128, 134, 135, 138
Biochemistry Department 132, 135
Chemistry Department 122, 124, 128, 131, 135, 140
Civil Engineering Department 135
Classics Departments 121, 122, 127
Dentistry Departments 122, 123, 124, 136, 137, 138, 141
Departmental libraries 123–4, 131–3, 139–40
Doctoral students' borrowing 133–4
Economic and Social Studies Faculty 119, 120, 122, 123, 124, 135, 136, 137, 138, 139, 141
Economics Department 121, 127, 128, 130, 138
Education Department 119, 120, 122, 123, 127, 129, 130, 133, 134, 137, 139, 140
Electrical Engineering Department 127, 135, 138
Engineering Faculty 119, 120, 122, 123, 124, 125, 129, 130, 131, 132, 133, 134, 135, 136, 137, 138, 139, 140, 141
English Department 121, 127
faculties defined 118–19
foreign language borrowing 121–3, 130–1, 138–9, 142
French Department 121, 127, 138
Fuel Technology Department 127, 135
Genetics Department 135
Geography Department 122, 127, 138, 140, 141
Geology Department 121, 122, 123, 124, 131, 135, 138, 139, 141
German Department 128, 138
higher degree students borrowing 130–5
higher degree students borrowing, by Faculty 130

Sheffield University Library, Borrowing Survey (*cont.*)

higher degree students' total borrowing 130

History Department 121, 122, 127, 128

Law Department 124, 135, 138

Law Faculty 119, 120, 122, 129, 130, 131, 133

Masters' degree students borrowing 133–4

Mathematics Departments 122, 127, 135

Mechanical Engineering Department 128, 135

Medicine, Faculty of 119, 120, 121, 122, 123, 125, 127, 129, 130, 131, 133, 134, 135, 136, 137, 138, 141

Metallurgy Department 123, 127, 135

Metallurgy Faculty 119, 120, 122, 123, 124, 125, 129, 130, 131, 132, 133, 136, 137, 138, 139, 140, 141

methods 118

Microbiology Department 135

Music Department 141

non-borrowing 120, 129, 130, 136–8

"off-subject" borrowing 125, 126, 127, 128, 134, 140–2

Pathology Department 121

Pharmacology Department 121

Philosophy Department 138

Physics Department 122, 124, 127, 134, 135

Physiology Department 121

postgraduate research borrowing 128–35

postgraduate research borrowing, by Faculties 129

postgraduate research borrowing totals 129

postgraduate research borrowing totals compared with Leeds and Birmingham 129

Psychology Department 138

Pure Science Faculty 119, 120, 121, 122, 123, 124, 125, 129, 130, 131, 132, 133, 136, 137, 138, 139, 140, 141, 142

range of borrowing 125–8, 134–5, 140–2

Refractories Department 135

scope 115–17

similarities to Leeds and Birmingham 142

Sociological Studies Department 121, 127, 140

Spanish Department 138

teaching staff borrowing 119–28

teaching staff borrowing, by departments 121

teaching staff borrowing, by Faculties 120

teaching staff borrowing totals compared with Leeds and Birmingham 120

Sheffield University Library, Borrowing Survey (*cont.*)

teaching staff borrowing, highest totals 121

undergraduate borrowing 135–42

undergraduate borrowing, by Faculties, 136–7

undergraduate borrowing, by year of study 137, 138

undergraduate borrowing compared with Leeds and Birmingham 135–6, 138

undergraduate borrowing, highest totals 135

undergraduate borrowing totals 135

Zoology Department 127, 135, 138

Sheffield University Postgraduate School of Librarianship, Special Studies vii

Simons, E. N. 17

Simpson, C. 13

Simpson, E. 20

SINTO 16, 17

Slater, M. 151, 161, 178

Smith, Elizabeth B. vii, x

Smith, J. R. 148, 150, 154, 156, 157, 159, 161, 162

Smith, M. H. 169

Smith, S. 6

Social background of undergraduates 92

Staff, prison libraries 55, 58, 60, 63–64, 67, 68, 70, 71, 75, 76, 81

Stamp, Lord 21

Standardized library services 170

Steel: trade literature 37, 41

Stevens, R. E. 149, 162, 178

Survey of libraries . . . 1936–1937 90

Surveys of library use viii, ix, 115–79

  see also Borrowing surveys; Scientists' use of libraries

Surveys of library use: methods 146, 147–9, 170–1

Sweet's Catalogues 41

Sykes, P. 27

Taylor, C. W. 26, 27

Taylor, W. A. 27

Teaching methods, universities, *see* University teaching methods

Technical brochures 30, 31, 48–49

Technical Libraries, *see* Commercial and Technical Libraries

Technická krihovna 33

Texas University Library Undergraduate Collection 108

Textile Machine Institute, Karl Marx Stadt 44

Thorne, R. G. 153, 179

Tolson, J. E. ix
Tornudd, E. 147, 151, 153, 154, 155, 156, 159, 161, 179
Trade Association libraries and trade literature 39–40
Trade catalogues, *see* Trade literature
Trade literature vii, 29–54
  abstracts 48, 53
  and research 29
  bibliographies 47–48
  classification 34, 39, 41, 44, 45–46, 50–52
  Central Technical Library, Prague 33
  exploitation 44
  filing 34–35, 37, 38, 39, 41, 42
  foreign 32–33, 40, 41–42, 43–44, 46–47, 53
  guides 46–48
  historical uses 34
  in academic libraries 42–43
  in Czechoslovakia 29, 33, 44
  in development association libraries 38–39
  in Government department libraries 40–41
  in Hungary 44
  in industrial libraries 36–40
  in national libraries 29
  in public libraries 41
  in research association libraries 38
  in trade association libraries 39–40
  in U.K. 36–43
  in U.S.A. 29, 43, 49–50
  in U.S.S.R. 29, 43
  in university libraries 29, 42
  indexing 35, 38, 39, 41, 42, 43, 44–45, 47, 48, 50
  organization 34–35
  sizes 34
  standards 34
  value to students 32, 42
Transom, E. C. 82
Tucker, P. E. viii, 115, 160

U.C.L.A. Library, undergraduate collection 108
U.D.C. 39, 44
Under lock and key: a study of women in prison 61, 62
Undergraduate libraries viii, 85–113
  arguments against 87, 106–8, 109
  book stock 100
  planning the building 98
  site 97–98
Undergraduate reading rooms 87, 88, 89, 90, 92, 110, 111

Undergraduates, library services for viii, 85–113
Undergraduates, social background 92
Undergraduates' use of catalogues 94
Unilever Research Laboratories 37
Union Carbide and Carbon Corp. 50
United Steel Cos. 37, 41, 44
Uniterm system 43, 46, 50
University libraries
  and trade literature 29, 42
  as a teaching instrument 91–92, 95, 96, 97, 99, 105, 109, 111
  closed stacks 94, 95
  departmental libraries 96, 103, 116–17, 123–4, 131–3, 139–40
  large book stocks 92
  reference service 94, 100–1, 111
  research collections 90, 91, 92, 93
  size as obstacle to undergraduates 92
  teaching use of 93, 101, 107, 170
  U.K., deficiencies 88
University teaching methods, and the library 101–2, 105
Urquhart, D. J. 151, 152, 159, 179
U.S.A. trade literature 29, 43, 49–50
U.S.A. university libraries 85–113
U.S.S.R. Documentation and information science abstracts 181–8
U.S.S.R. trade literature 29, 43
"Use" surveys, *see* Surveys of library use

Vickery, B. J. 151, 152, 153, 155, 156, 159
Visual aids 103
Voigt, M. J. 148, 151, 152, 153, 154, 156, 157, 158, 159, 160, 161, 163, 164, 179

Wagman, F. H. 104, 112
Wakefield Central Educational Library for Prisoners 56, 57, 58, 61, 64, 70, 81
Wall, T. W. 9
Walton, Mary 27
Walton Jail 74
Wandsworth Borough Library 67, 74, 82
Wandsworth Prison 55, 57
Wandsworth Prison Library 67–70, 73, 74, 75
  accommodation 67
  book stock 67, 68, 69
  care of books 68
  issues 67
  Library Officers 68
  routines 67, 68
Wandsworth Prison population 58, 73
W. and T. Avery Ltd. 49
Watts, V. C. 35

Webster, P.   78
Wellisch, H.   151, 154, 156, 157, 158
Wentworth Woodhouse Muniments   22
Wickison, L. J.   ix, x
Widener Library   86, 89, 94, 98, 101, 105
Wiggin, Henry, & Co. Ltd.   49
Wilkins, L. T.   151
Wilson, Harold   23
Women prisoners   57–62
Women's magazines   61
Wormwood Scrubs Borstal Institution
    Library   70
Wormwood Scrubs Prison   55, 57
Wormwood Scrubs Prison Library   70–72,
    74, 75
  book stock   70, 71

Wormwood Scrubs Prison Library (*cont.*)
  branch of Hammersmith Public Libraries
    70
  Library Officer   71
  routines   70, 71
Wormwood Scrubs prison population   58,
    73

Yale, undergraduate collection   108
York, Duchess of   18
Young Radiator Co.   50

Zinc Abstracts   39, 48
Zinc Development Association   39, 45

DATE DUE

GAYLORD   PRINTED IN U.S.A.